Penguin
Random House
Grupo Editorial

A Year with God: 365 Devotionals for Women

First edition: August 2025

© 2025, Penguin Random House Grupo Editorial USA, LLC
8950 SW 74th Court, Suite 2010
Miami, FL 33156

Cover image: Wacomka/Shutterstock
Translation: PRHGE, based on a translation by Kathleen Naab

Published by ORIGIN®, a registered trademark of
Penguin Random House Grupo Editorial USA, LLC
8950 SW 74th Court, Suite 2010
Miami, FL 33156

All Scripture quotations, unless otherwise indicated, are taken from The Holy Bible, New International Version®, NIV®. Copyright © 1973, 1978, 1984, 2011 by Biblica, Inc.® Used by permission. All rights reserved worldwide. Scripture quotations marked NKJV are taken from the New King James Version®. Copyright © 1982 by Thomas Nelson. Used by permission. All rights reserved. Scripture quotations marked NLT are taken from the Holy Bible, New Living Translation, copyright © 1996, 2004, 2015 by Tyndale House Foundation. Used by permission of Tyndale House Publishers, Inc., Carol Stream, Illinois 60188. All rights reserved. Scripture quotations marked NABRE are taken from the New American Bible, revised edition © 2010, 1991, 1986, 1970 Confraternity of Christian Doctrine, Inc., Washington, DC All Rights Reserved. Scripture quotations marked ESV are taken from the Holy Bible, English Standard Version. ESV® Text Edition: 2016. Copyright © 2001 by Crossway Bibles, a publishing ministry of Good News Publishers. Scripture quotations marked NRSVUE are taken from theNew Revised Standard Version, Updated Edition. Copyright © 2021 National Council of Churches of Christ in the United States of America. Used by permission. All rights reserved worldwide.

Penguin Random House Grupo Editorial supports the protection of intellectual property and copyright. Copyright stimulates creativity, defends diversity in the realm of ideas and knowledge, promotes free expression, and fosters a vibrant culture. Thank you for purchasing an authorized edition of this book and for respecting copyright laws by not reproducing, scanning, or distributing any part of this work by any means without prior express permission. By doing so, you are supporting the authors and enabling PRHGE to continue publishing books for all readers. Please note that no part of this book may be used or reproduced, in any manner, for the purpose of training technologies or artificial intelligence systems, or for text and data mining.
If needed, please contact: seguridadproductos@penguinrandomhouse.com
The authorized representative in the EEA is Penguin Random House Grupo Editorial, S. A. U., Travessera de Gràcia, 47-49, 08021 Barcelona, Spain.

Printed in Colombia

Cataloging information for publications available at the
Library of Congress of the United States.

ISBN: 979-8-890-98437-1

25 26 27 28 29   10 9 8 7 6 5 4 3 2 1

A Year
with God

365
Devotionals
for
Women

A Year with God

365 Devotionals for Women

ORIGIN

January 1

Fear of the Lord is the foundation of true knowledge, but fools despise wisdom and discipline.

Proverbs 1:7 (NLT)

There's a saying that goes, "Books and years make a man wise." While it's true that education and life experience matter, this proverb points out something even more crucial at the core of wisdom: the fear of the Lord.

I love a story my mother-in-law shares. One of her sons-in-law, a committed Marxist with several advanced degrees, was involved in the student movement back in the '70s in Mexico. He once said he admired his mother-in-law's wisdom, even though she came from a small indigenous village and had no formal education. How could someone with so many credentials respect a woman with none? The answer lies in her secret: her faith in Jesus. It's no surprise that my mother-in-law is wise; anyone who truly knows God and studies His Word is connected to the purest wisdom there is.

So, what does it mean to fear the Lord? It's more than just having deep respect and reverence for God; it involves something deeper. In Romans 3, there's a detailed description of how we act when we sin and drift away from God. One key trait of those who reject Him is that "They have no fear of God at all" (v. 18 NLT). This shows that if someone isn't a child of God, they can't really fear Him, and they miss out on the foundation of true wisdom.

You might not have advanced degrees, but that doesn't mean you can't be wise. Even as a young person, you can make wise choices. The key is knowing Jesus as your Savior and receiving wisdom from Him. Do you believe in Jesus?

Lord, I want to grow in my reverence for You.

MH

JANUARY 2

Wise choices will watch over you. Understanding will keep you safe.
Proverbs 2:11 (NLT)

Have you heard the saying, "Better skill than strength"? While we admire bodybuilders for their impressive feats, it's the wise and insightful people who truly stand out, as the effects of their choices can last a lot longer.

Think about a woman who made some poor choices and then ended up in a profession that lacked respectability. Eventually she ends up living in a situation that reflects the poorness of her choices. We might not know what led her there—maybe she felt she had no other options to support her family. But despite her difficult circumstances, her life changed when she made a wise decision that saved her and her entire family from disaster.

I'm talking about Rahab, the harlot. This verse talks about "wise choices" that keep us safe, and Rahab's story is a perfect example. She recognized that the God of the Israelites was the true God and then hid the Hebrew spies. When they left, they told her to hang a red sash from her window to mark her home so she would be safe when the Israelites attacked (Joshua 2:18). She followed their instructions, and when Jericho fell, she and her family were saved!

This red sash can be seen as a symbol of the blood of Christ, which represents salvation. The wisest decision we can make—the one that guarantees our safety for eternity—is to believe that Jesus is the Son of God, the Savior we all need. Have you made that choice? It's entirely up to you.

Lord, help me to make wise decisions and keep me safe under Your protection.

MH

January 3

My child, never forget the things I have taught you. Store my commands in your heart. If you do this, you will live many years...

Proverbs 3:1-2 (NLT)

Have you ever heard of "the dance of the elders"? It's a cherished tradition from the pre-Hispanic Purépecha culture in Michoacán, Mexico. Four dancers wear wooden masks that represent smiling, toothless elders. With a humorous flair, they mimic the movements of older folks, leaning on their canes and shuffling about, yet they still manage to dance energetically to the music. UNESCO recognized this dance as an intangible cultural heritage in 2010.

We all hope for "many days, and years of life, and peace" (v. 2 NABRE), just like those joyful elders. We want to be healthy and able to enjoy life, maybe even dance a little! Many women use creams and makeup to hide the signs of aging, trying to mask their struggles and sadness.

Today's verse reminds us that the key to living a long and fulfilling life lies in keeping God's teachings close and obeying His commands. As the Psalmist puts it: "Joyful are people of integrity, who follow the instructions of the Lord" (Psalm 119:1 NLT).

Whether you're just starting out in life or have years of experience behind you, remember that wrinkles don't define satisfaction. True satisfaction comes from living in obedience to God, reflecting on His Word daily, which protects, blesses, and fills us with life—all for free!

God, I want to obey You and live for Your glory every day of my life.

MG

January 4

For I, too, was once my father's son, tenderly loved as my mother's only child.

Proverbs 4:3 (NLT)

Today's proverb encourages us to listen to our parents. But let's be honest—what do you think about that? We often hear silly advice like, "The answer to life's problems isn't at the bottom of a bottle; it's on TV!" Or how about, "Kids, you tried your best and failed miserably. The lesson is, never try"? Those lines are from Homer Simpson, the dad from the animated TV show The Simpsons, who is funny but not exactly a role model.

I can't say my parents were perfect. My dad was distant and tough, not the hugging type and not the type of guy with the regular word of encouragement. My mom was a teacher, always busy cooking and working at my dad's *tortillería*. They didn't know Christ, so my father's discipline was often harsh and unfair.

When I found God, it was hard for me to accept His corrections because I didn't respect my dad's discipline. I felt rebellious and even hesitated to call God "Father." But God worked in my heart, and now I can say that "God's discipline is always good for us, so that we might share in His holiness" (Hebrews 12:10, NLT).

I don't know what your childhood was like, but if your experience with an imperfect father has affected you negatively, remember there's a perfect Father out there. He's wise and loving and can help rebuild our lives. He can restore the past, so that when we hear His guidance, we gain wisdom.

Dear Father, shape my heart so that I'm always ready to receive Your righteous discipline.

YF

January 5

Let your fountain be blessed and rejoice in the wife of your youth.
Proverbs 5:18 (NRSVUE)

A spring can be blocked little by little, one stone at a time. If you keep putting rocks at the source of the water, eventually the flow will slow down or disappear altogether.

In this proverb, the fountain symbolizes marriage and the intimacy between a couple. Wisdom encourages every couple to be blessed and enjoy each other. Unfortunately, we often add stones—like unresolved issues, unrealistic expectations, or excuses to avoid spending time together—that block the flow of our relationships.

Solomon, who wrote many of these proverbs, wasn't always the best example in this area. Still, he left us some beautiful poems for one of his first wives, where he advises, "Catch all the foxes, those little foxes, before they ruin the vineyard of love" (Song of Solomon 2:15 NLT).

If you're married, don't let your fountain run dry. Address issues promptly, even the small ones. Share your feelings and desires with kindness. Apologize, even for petty things. Clear up expectations and communicate openly with your spouse. And if you're not married, the same advice applies to your relationships with your kids, friends, or colleagues. Let's take care of our healthy relationships—they can slip away one small stone at a time.

Lord, may my fountain be blessed, and may I find joy in it.

KO

January 6

Take a lesson from the ants, you lazybones. Learn from their ways and become wise!

Proverbs 6:6 (NLT)

There's a TV show that looks into the lives of people who hoard things. They often don't organize their stuff out of laziness and end up living in cluttered homes.

When I first got married, and especially when I had young kids, I realized that housework seemed never-ending. If I took a break to watch TV or read, time would fly, and I'd still have a long to-do list waiting for me. I tried to discipline myself to finish my chores before indulging in any relaxation. I won't lie; I didn't always succeed!

Nature teaches us a lot, and in this proverb, ants are our role models. They know their responsibilities, work hard, and stick to God's plan for them. They never lose focus or become lazy. The Apostle Paul also reminds us about the importance of making clever use of our time: "Those unwilling to work will not get to eat" (2 Thessalonians 3:10 NLT).

Are we using our time wisely, as our Creator intended? In today's world, the internet and social media can distract us for hours if we're not careful. Even if we don't think of it as laziness, we might be putting off important priorities, including spending time with our families. Let's learn from the ants!

Lord, I want to overcome my tendency to be lazy. Help me focus on what truly matters, out of love for You, for others, and for myself.

MH

January 7

Obey my commands and live! Guard my instructions as you guard your own eyes.

Proverbs 7:2 (NLT)

The word "pupil" comes from Latin and means girl or doll. It got this name because if you look closely, you can see a reflection of the person you're looking at in the center of your eye. In German, there's a phrase about the "apple of my eye," which carries a similar meaning: something precious.

Lisa Reed from New Zealand went blind when she was 11 due to a brain tumor pressing on her optic nerve. After years of adapting to life in darkness, one night she bent down to say goodnight to her guide dog and bumped her head on the table. A bit dazed, she went to sleep, only to wake up the next morning with her sight restored!

The Bible speaks about our pupils, the "apple of our eyes," to emphasize the value of something precious. David asks God to "guard me as you would guard your own eyes" (Psalm 17:8 NLT). Just as we treasure our sight, we should value God's guidance in His Word.

It's no coincidence that this advice appears in a chapter about sexual immorality. Warnings against immorality are as vital as our vision. Let's submit our thoughts to Christ and always seek purity. Those who engage in sexual sin act as if they're blind, missing out on a colorful and joyful life. Let's choose to see the light!

Lord, help me value my sexual purity as much as I value my sight.

MG

January 8

Listen as Wisdom calls out! Hear as understanding raises her voice!
Proverbs 8:1 (NLT)

Is wisdom a person? Ancient cultures thought so. The Greeks revered Athena, the goddess of wisdom, while the Norse credited Odin with this gift. The Aztecs had Quetzalcóatl, a feathered serpent representing life and wisdom. In other words, wisdom was seen as more than just a trait; it was personified.

From an early age, I heard about the Hagia Sophia, one of the world's most visited historical sites in Istanbul, Turkey. Today is the Hagia Sophia Grand Mosque but formerly was the Church of the Holy Wisdom of God. The church was dedicated on Christmas day to the Wisdom of God, the Logos, the second person of the Trinity. One of the most photographed frescoes in the Hagia Sophia is the face of Jesus, who embodies wisdom.

In the Bible, wisdom isn't just an abstract idea; it's a person—Jesus, the Logos of the New Testament. As it says in 1 Corinthians 1:24, "But to those called by God to salvation, both Jews and Gentiles, Christ is the power of God and the wisdom of God" (NLT).

Wisdom isn't just a concept; it's embodied in Jesus. He's the heart of the Bible and should also be at the center of our decisions. We can be wise when we trust in Christ. Let's allow Jesus, the wisdom of God, to lead our lives.

Lord, thank You for being wisdom itself in the person of Jesus.

KO

January 9

Instruct the wise, and they will be even wiser. Teach the righteous, and they will learn even more.

Proverbs 9:9 (NLT)

It can be frustrating when my computer malfunctions. But each time I must troubleshoot an issue, I become a little "wiser" and can even help others when they face similar problems.

As much as we hate to admit it, life's problems often make us wiser. Now, we tend to view the word "problem" in a negative way. But think about a math problem—it's a tool of sorts that helps us understand a complex thing in a practical way. Daily problems inspire inventors to create everything from nail clippers to washing machines.

In contrast—unlike the wise—the foolish complain or do nothing when faced with difficulties. They find themselves falling into the same patterns of mistakes over and over again. Peter uses a proverb to illustrate this, comparing the foolish to a pig that's been cleaned up but returns to the mud (2 Peter 2:22). The wise learn and grow from the challenges they encounter.

If you're reading this before your day starts, take a deep breath when you face your first challenge and decide to learn from it. Ask God for help and approach the situation with humility. If you're reading this at night, reflect on a problem you faced today. Did you learn anything? How can this experience make you wiser? Don't let the "computer crashes" in life frustrate you; use them as steppingstones to wisdom.

Father, I may not like problems, but I see their value. Help me have the right attitude toward them.

KO

JANUARY 10

Hatred stirs up quarrels, but love makes up for all offenses.
Proverbs 10:12 (NLT)

I remember saving up for my first computer. After a long time, I was almost there, but then my husband made a decision that impacted our finances, and I had to use my savings for something else. I was upset and cried, but God reminded me that I needed to use a "concealer"—not for my face or clothes, but to cover my husband's mistakes with forgiveness.

That wasn't the first time I had to forgive him, nor would it be the last. In almost 37 years of marriage, my husband and I had plenty of opportunities to practice love and forgiveness. Now that he's in heaven, I'm grateful for the chance to both give and receive forgiveness.

God teaches us that "love covers a multitude of sins" (1 Peter 4:8 NLT). When we genuinely love, we don't keep bringing up past offenses to use against others. We all make mistakes, intentionally or not. Genuine love forgives and seeks reconciliation. The ultimate example is Jesus, who gave His life to atone for our wrongs.

When you've been with someone for a long time, disagreements are bound to happen, but we shouldn't let them escalate into quarrels. The enemy wants to destroy our marriages and families. The one who saved us through His incredible love wants us to practice that same love in our daily interactions.

Father, renew Your love in me today so I can overlook offenses and defeat the enemy.

MH

January 11

Give freely and become more wealthy; be stingy and lose everything.
Proverbs 11:24 (NLT)

Many agricultural workers harvest their crops and then travel to cities to sell them. They carry their goods in heavy crates or palm baskets. When I was a girl, vendors selling avocados or dragon fruits would often knock on our door. They looked tired, with dusty feet from all their walking. My mom would invite them in, offer them cool water, and share food and clothing. She took the time to chat, learn their names, hear their stories, and even talk about God's love. Often, they left our home feeling lighter, having shared their burdens.

As I raised my daughters, I thought about my mom and how she found time to show kindness to those people. She prioritized these moments because her heart was full. My mother knew that it's better to give than to receive, and I believe God always provided for our family.

Generosity is at the heart of God's message. He says, "Give generously to the poor, not grudgingly, for the Lord your God will bless you in everything you do" (Deuteronomy 15:10 NLT).

In our busy lives, we often face interruptions. It's important to pause and pay attention to those who need our generosity. Look around—do you see someone who could use your help? God promises blessings to those who are generous.

Lord, I want to be a cheerful giver. Today, I commit to being generous. Help me share Your blessings and love.

MG

January 12

To learn, you must love discipline; it is stupid to hate correction.

Proverbs 12:1 (NLT)

Have you ever tried to learn a new language? Nowadays, there are apps that promise you can become fluent in just three months with only 15 minutes of practice a day. But we all know that truly mastering a language takes time and effort.

Willem, a Dutch friend, spoke Spanish quite well. When I asked him how he learned, he told me he fell in love with a Spanish girl and was motivated to impress her. Love drove his desire to learn. In contrast, I've seen students who settle for passing grades with no real motivation or discipline to learn. They might even resent the effort it takes.

Living the Christian life requires discipline. When we meet Jesus, we often come with habits of laziness. But when we fall in love with Him, we want to know Him better and talk to Him constantly. Like Paul said, "Everything else is worthless when compared with the infinite value of knowing Christ Jesus my Lord" (Philippians 3:8 NLT).

How motivated are you to get to know God through reading the Bible? How much time do you spend in conversation with Him? Today's proverb encourages us to embrace discipline. Let's not be foolish; let's aim to learn a new language—the language of God's love.

Lord Jesus, help me be disciplined in getting to know You. Help me make time for reading and prayer.

YF

January 13

The life of the godly is full of light and joy, but the light of the wicked will be snuffed out.

Proverbs 13:9 (NLT)

No one wants to post photos on social media showing them crying or struggling. Scroll through Instagram, and you'll see only smiles and happy moments. Is that what today's proverb is getting at? Leonard Cohen wrote in a song, "Ring the bells that still can ring. Forget your perfect offering / There is a crack, a crack in everything. That's how the light gets in."

You might read today's proverb and think, "But my life isn't full of light and joy!" Maybe your adult child is dealing with depression, your little girl is battling leukemia, or you've faced a job loss. It's tough to shine light for others when you're just trying to get through each day.

Perfect lives don't exist. We all have cracks from suffering—betrayals, losses, failures. But remember, "God is light, and there is no darkness in Him at all" (1 John 1:5 NLT). Even in the darkest moments, the light of Jesus can shine into those cracks and bring hope. When we face tough times, it's His love that sustains us, giving us more than just superficial happiness—He offers us the joy of His presence.

If you feel overwhelmed by your cracks today, remember that even in suffering, you can shine and share with others that there's a light that will never go out: Jesus.

Father, let Your light shine into my cracks today and help others see You through me.

KO

JANUARY 14

A wise woman builds her home, but a foolish woman tears it down with her own hands.

Proverbs 14:1 (NLT)

In 2014, the Council of Architects in Europe found that about 39% of active architects are women. In the U.S., while nearly half of architecture graduates are women, only 18% are registered as active professionals. This shows that many women have trained to be architects, but not all of them work in the field, possibly due to limited opportunities or life changes.

However, today's proverb tells us that all women can be "architects" of their homes. Wise women construct strong homes filled with values, love, and other lasting materials. Unfortunately, the opposite is also true. Some women may unintentionally destroy their homes by criticizing instead of encouraging, complaining instead of trusting God, or neglecting their roles as wives, mothers, and daughters. They may think they know a lot, but wisdom involves much more than just knowledge.

So how do you build a home? It takes learning from the ultimate Architect and dedicating time and effort. Any architect will tell you that it's not just about the design; it involves budgeting, constantly checking plans, and making adjustments when things don't go as expected. God has given us the tools we need—let's be wise and use them!

Lord, I want to be a positive influence for my loved ones.

MH

January 15

A glad heart makes a happy face; a broken heart crushes the spirit.

Proverbs 15:13 (NLT)

Did you know that brides can spend anywhere from $70 to $1,000 on hair and makeup for their weddings? In the U.S., couples typically spend around $300 on a stylist for their big day. This reflects just how important it is for brides to look beautiful.

I love looking back at photos from my daughter's wedding. She was absolutely radiant! For many women, their wedding day is one of the happiest moments in life, filled with dreams coming true and surrounded by beautiful flowers. This proves the proverb right: "A glad heart makes a happy face."

But sometimes, that joy doesn't last. When our hearts are hurting, it can feel like our spirits are crushed. Happiness can be fleeting when it's based on external things, but the Bible tells us that true joy is a fruit of the Holy Spirit. Unlike happiness, joy comes from within and doesn't depend on our circumstances; it flows from the fullness of God in us.

If you've been feeling down, remember that it's possible to smile again. Is something keeping your heart from joy? Surrender it to the Lord and stay connected to Him. God hears our prayers and fills us with love, joy, peace, patience, goodness, faith, and gentleness. When that happens, you radiate beauty!

Lord, turn my sadness into joy and let my smile reflect Your love.

MG

January 16

How much better to get wisdom than gold! To get understanding is preferable to silver.

Proverbs 16:16 (NABRE)

Throughout history, gold has driven people to conquer, fight, and even kill. Maybe that's because it's not easy to get. To find gold, you have to sift through crushed rock and wait patiently as the heavy minerals sink to the bottom. It takes a lot of effort, but for those who love gold, it's worth it.

The book of Proverbs encourages us to seek wisdom above all else. Imagine if gold diggers realized that pursuing God's wisdom is far more valuable than gold itself. If only they were willing to risk everything to gain wisdom, the world would be a different place, free from much of the evil we see today.

Wisdom is at the heart of God. He wants us to look within His heart and act according to what we find there. How can we do that? The Bible tells us that Jesus is the heart of God: "He is the image of the invisible God" (Colossians 1:15 NABRE).

We may not be able to change the world, but we can make a difference in our own lives and the lives of those around us. Let's seek God's wisdom daily, just like we would seek gold.

Lord, I want to know Your heart through Jesus. Open my eyes to Your wisdom.

YF

January 17

Parents are the pride of their children.

Proverbs 17:6 (NLT)

If you're ever struggling to jumpstart a conversation with someone and they happen to be a mother, just ask her about her kids. Parents usually beam with pride when talking about their children's accomplishments and unique traits. But today's proverb shifts our focus upward, asking us to consider how we, as children, view our parents.

Many of us have been blessed with parents who have passed on their faith or are good examples of responsible living. Others might not know their parents well or have experienced hurt from them. But let's take it a step further. Are you a mother? Are your children proud of you? The key to being a good mother is looking to our perfect Father.

When we put our faith in Jesus, we gain a perfect Father who we can be proud of. He's eternal, full of mercy, and overflowing with compassion. Our Father will never fail us.

When we're proud of something we talk about it a lot. One of the ways we can evaluate if we are proud of our heavenly Father is by asking the questions: Do I mention Him often? Is He a common topic of my conversations? Do I get excited to share His love with others?

Father, I have the best Father in You, and I'm thrilled to be Your daughter.

KO

January 18

Whoever isolates himself pursues selfish ends; he resists all sound advice.

Proverbs 18:1 (ISV)

Have you ever given someone advice only for them to ignore it completely? It can be frustrating! Why do people ask for advice if they aren't planning to follow it? It's a common behavior, isn't it?

After finishing college, I wasn't sure how to start looking for a job. Since my parents lived in a small town, I had to move to a city. I had only recently come to know God and, feeling nervous, I asked my dad for advice. He was surprised since I'd always been so independent. He offered some suggestions, but then added, "In the end, you've always done what you want." It was his way of saying, "Why ask for my advice if you're not going to listen?"

This proverb teaches us that selfish people resist "sound" advice. Why do we do that? Why would we shut our ears to wise counsel? James 3:15 tells us that "jealousy and selfishness are not God's kind of wisdom." When making decisions, it's crucial to listen to the advice of those who have more experience and spiritual maturity.

It's easy to look out for our own interests, but that doesn't guarantee true or lasting benefit. Let's recognize the value of receiving guidance from those who have walked the path before us.

Father, help me to be open to sound advice.

MH

January 19

A quarrelsome wife is as annoying as constant dripping.

Proverbs 19:13 (NLT)

"Just for today" is the motto that has helped millions of people worldwide quit drinking. The idea is to focus on avoiding temptation for just one day. It's a practical approach that can motivate us to leave bad habits behind.

Some women develop the habit of constant complaining, and that can wear down those around them. Living with someone who is regularly critical can feel as bothersome as a constant drip of water. Maybe we could aim to cut-out this practice from our lives using that same motto, "just for today."

The Bible gives us a splendid example in Hannah, a woman known for her persevering faith. She faced a tough situation— she was barren, and her husband had another wife who mocked her. Yet, Hannah chose to remain silent and took her troubles to God in prayer. Although her voice was barely a whisper, God heard her and blessed her with a child.

There are things that only God can change. Complaining won't help; prayer will. When you feel as troubled as Hannah, follow her lead. Keep quiet and enter the presence of the Almighty with your prayers. He will listen and respond.

Father, help me not complain, "just for today."

MG

January 20

It is honorable to refrain from strife, but every fool is quick to quarrel.
Proverbs 20:3 (NRSVUE)

Avoiding conflict often requires divine wisdom. There's a fine line between getting drawn into a quarrel and letting it go. Our old nature can easily feel offended and react to the slightest provocation.

I once worked with three other women on a service project. At first, everything went smoothly, but soon enough, tensions began to rise. Our pride and lack of consideration led to frustration, and we had to come together to sort things out. Anger bubbled to the surface, and we realized we were feeling resentment toward each other. We had to set aside our pride, apologize, and learn to understand and tolerate one another. Once we did that, the atmosphere changed, and we felt a strong bond in the Lord.

The Apostle John reminds us that if we don't love our fellow believers, we can't claim to love God. The love that should define us as believers shines brightest when someone disappoints or hurts us. If we can't let go of our pride and choose to avoid conflict, we're acting foolishly in God's eyes.

We need wise people willing to set aside their pride to guard against conflicts. It's not an easy choice, but if you choose love over strife, you may gain an amazing friend and honor Jesus in the process.

Lord, help me to be wise and avoid quarrels, choosing instead to love others.

YF

JANUARY 21

The king's heart is a stream of water in the hand of the Lord; he turns it wherever he will.

Proverbs 21:1 (NRSVUE)

Movies have a way of influencing how we see life. We often joke about living in a movie. The trouble arises when we try to be the screenwriter and director, forgetting that we're just players in a story. Some stars are in the limelight for a while, then suddenly fade away. Why? People say it's tough to work with them because they demand too much and challenge the script. Sadly, we can sometimes act the same way.

Today's proverb speaks about streams that have a defined path. When they overflow, they can cause chaos, but God's design is so amazing that, eventually, the river finds its way back. In life, we often resist the path laid out for us, acting like powerful rivers that refuse to flow in the right direction.

In the grand story of humanity, you and I are secondary characters, even if we wish to be the stars. The real lead is Jesus, who offers us salvation. God is the screenwriter, director, and producer of this incredible film, and we're lucky to be part of it! Our role is to place ourselves in the Lord's hands.

Today, let's choose not to rebel against the part God has given us in His story. We can achieve great things when our goals align with His will. Allow God to guide the course of your life, and everything will be alright.

Lord, guide my life according to Your will.

KO

JANUARY 22

The rich and poor have this in common: The Lord made them both.
Proverbs 22:2 (NLT)

"Nobody leaves here rich; you're not taking anything with you" is a well-known saying. While we often contrast rich and poor, this proverb reminds us that no matter our economic status, we can't take anything with us when we die!

Consider this saying: "To find contentment, even in poverty, is to be rich. Being poor doesn't mean having little; it means desiring much." We often label people based on their wealth, but many of us aren't truly rich or poor in the technical sense. Finding contentment with little is true abundance! Inner poverty comes from wanting more than we need.

In God's eyes, we're all equal. Having more doesn't make someone worth more, and we shouldn't look down on those with less. The Bible warns us about materialism: "Don't love money; be satisfied with what you have. For God has said, 'I will never fail you. I will never abandon you'" (Hebrews 13:5 NLT).

Our true wealth isn't measured by material possessions but by our blessings. "Better is a little that the righteous person has than the abundance of many wicked" (Psalm 37:16 NRSVUE). Today, let's count our blessings. Whether rich or poor, God has given us family, friends, the beauty of creation, new opportunities every day, and most importantly, His gift of salvation!

Lord, thank You for the many blessings You've given me. As a daughter of the King, I receive them with open hands.

MH

January 23

O my son, give me your heart. May your eyes take delight in following my ways.
Proverbs 23:26 (NLT)

Most of us love receiving gifts, especially women. We get excited about the wrapping paper, the diverse types of bows, the cards, and the feeling of surprise. The best gift is often the one we wanted the most—like a book or a perfume we've been dreaming about. Even when we receive things we don't like, we try to smile and show gratitude.

If we had to pick a gift for God, we'd want to give Him something He truly wants. Today's proverb tells us what that is: God wants our hearts. Sometimes we think we can please Him with other offerings—like volunteering at church or repeating prayers—but what He really desires is our love.

In Isaiah 29:13, God speaks about how some people honor Him with their lips while their hearts are far away: "Because these people draw near with their mouths and honor me with their lips, while their hearts are far from me" (NRSVU). He wants our walk with Him to be a genuine delight.

When we truly give our hearts to someone, we want to spend time with them, please them, listen to them, and show our love through our choices and our actions. Your heart is your life itself. Have you given it to God?

God, I love You and want to express my love with every beat of my heart.

MG

January 24

A house is built by wisdom and becomes strong through good sense.
Proverbs 24:3 (NLT)

My parents left me a small house built by my grandfather. To remodel it, I had to scrape off about seven or eight layers of paint, fill in holes, remove nails, repaint, and then choose tile for the kitchen and bathroom. Now that I'm living in this little house, I really enjoy it! But I have one challenge: humidity. My grandfather didn't know how to prevent it. But do you know? A good foundation would have made all the difference!

In ancient times, people looked for large stones to build their houses. They needed a stable spot to withstand the wear and tear of nature. Today, we conduct soil studies to determine the best foundation. The key to a solid house is its foundation!

The Bible often speaks about foundations because God refers to Himself as the Everlasting Rock, Stone of Help, Cornerstone, Precious Stone, Living Stone, and Stumbling Stone. When we choose to rest in Him, we show wisdom.

Your life and soul won't be stable without a solid foundation in Jesus. No storm can shake you if you've chosen the true Rock. Your emotional, financial, family, intellectual, and spiritual life will be strong and secure when you build your life on Jesus Christ.

Lord, I choose You as the foundation of my life. In You, I build my existence.

YF

January 25

Telling lies about others is as harmful as hitting them with an ax.
                                            Proverbs 25:18 (NLT)

There was quite a stir at school when a boy was hit by his classmates! The kid's parents demanded that the other boys be expelled. The parents of those boys felt ashamed, and they promised to keep a closer eye on their sons. The school suspended them for a week. But then a few days later, a girl was slandered by others on social media. Her parents wanted the online offenders expelled, but the other parents shrugged it off, saying it wasn't a big deal. In the end, the kids got a verbal warning that was quickly forgotten.

According to today's proverb both situations deserved grave consequences. Hurting someone physically with fists or emotionally with lies is equally violent and should not be overlooked. Lying has a terrible origin story. In John 8:44, we read that the devil "was a murderer from the beginning. He has always hated the truth because there is no truth in him" (John 8:44 NLT).

The next time you're tempted to tell a lie—whether it seems small or large—remember that your words can be weapons. And whether it's a knife or a gun, lying can truly "kill" someone emotionally.

Father, You hate lies. Help me to stay away from them, as they harm not only others but myself as well.

KO

January 26

Honor is no more associated with fools than snow with summer or rain with harvest.

Proverbs 26:1 (NLT)

The summer of 1816 was something else—it is remembered as the year without summer for many in Europe and the U.S. There were reports of snow in June and freezing temperatures in July, which ruined crops and led to hunger. Scientists later discovered that this bizarre weather was due to the massive eruption of Mount Tambora in Indonesia, which sent tons of dust and ash into the atmosphere, altering the climate worldwide.

Today's proverb tells us that just as it's unusual to have snow in summer, it's equally strange to honor fools. Unfortunately, we sometimes see the foolish and the rude praised—think of some athletes, artists, or politicians you may know. Yet, those who truly deserve recognition are the wise, honest, and kind people who uplift others.

So, who should we honor? We're encouraged to honor our elders and those who preach and teach about God (1 Timothy 5:17). And so, to avoid bringing snow in summer, let us be mindful about who we praise.

In our conversations with each other let us focus on honoring exemplary people who inspire us. Let us, in the spirit of this proverb, not bring the cold of winter into our summer conversations.

Lord, help me choose role models who deserve honor and strive to be someone worthy of it myself.

MH

January 27

A person who is full tramples on a honeycomb, but to a hungry person, any bitter thing is sweet.

Proverbs 27:7 (CSB)

In recent times, there's been a new trend called "tradwife," which refers to women who choose to dedicate themselves to their families and homes instead of pursuing careers. One such woman, Alena Kate Pettitt, blogs about this lifestyle, emphasizing traditional roles and responsibilities. In her blog, The Darling Academy, she describes this "tradwife" movement as "submitting to your husband and treating him like it's 1959." It paints the picture of women baking, cleaning, and tending to chickens.

While this movement has its controversies, I think there's something valuable in the idea of spoiling your husband. A wife, as her husband's suitable helper, can meet her husband's needs, giving him recognition, respect, sexual satisfaction, and emotional support, creating a loving home.

In Proverbs 7, we read about an immoral woman who entices men with her words, leading them astray. Perhaps the man she lured was a "hungry" husband, feeling neglected and unappreciated at home.

Today's women, whether working outside the home or not, are busy and active. As married women, we face the challenge of loving our families well, ensuring they feel loved, respected, and fulfilled when they leave our homes. Martin Luther once said, "Let the wife make her husband glad to come home and let him make her sorry to see him leave." If you're married, do you think your husband feels fulfilled?

Lord, please help me to support my husband and be a wise wife.

MG

January 28

The wicked run away when no one is chasing them.

Proverbs 28:1 (NLT)

Who was Herod the Great? When he became the governor of Galilee the Jewish people rejected him because of his cruelty, though he maintained the support of Rome. To protect his power, he banished his first wife and son and remarried. He became paranoid, seeing betrayal everywhere—even among his own family. He had his second wife and children killed, as well as his brother-in-law, for suspected treachery. The Bible tells us he even ordered the massacre of all the male children under the age of 2 in and around Bethlehem because he couldn't stand the thought of another king of the Jews.

Even in death, he was ruthless. Suffering from severe health issues, he realized that people despised him and would not mourn his passing. So, he rounded up 300 important people to kill when he died, hoping to create an atmosphere of grief.

Because of his immoral and cruel actions, we see him as a wicked man who "runs when no one is chasing." Isaiah reminds us, "There is no peace for the wicked" (57:21). The lack of peace in wicked hearts makes them see danger everywhere.

Our inner peace relies on placing our trust completely in God. Another proverb tells us, "When the ways of people please the Lord, he causes even their enemies to be at peace with them" (Proverbs 16:7 NRSVUE). If you feel like everyone is against you or that you're being criticized, take those thoughts to the Lord. Ask for His peace in your life and appreciate all the wonderful things He has surrounded you with.

Father, grant me Your perfect peace.

YF

January 29

The godly care about the rights of the poor; the wicked don't care at all.
Proverbs 29:7 (NLT)

Today, many organizations work to protect human rights, but sadly, the most vulnerable still face injustice. Can you imagine being part of that sector of society that feels invisible or unimportant?

Mary McLeod Bethune was born in a time when her skin color wasn't valued. Growing up in North Carolina at the end of the 19th century, she excelled in her studies and later dedicated herself to fighting for the rights of the poor. She founded a school for African American girls, teaching them not only academics but also about God's love.

Mary taught her students that God loves everyone, regardless of color or wealth. "Do you know who that 'whoever' is?" she would ask. "It's white people, rich people, people of color—everyone. Our dignity comes from the same Creator."

She committed her life to helping girls of color succeed, reminding them that their basic rights were part of God's plan.

Are we concerned about the rights of the vulnerable? Let's not be like the wicked, who disregard the rights of the poor.

Powerful God, creator of all people, help me see others through Your eyes, including those who are "invisible" to society.

KO

January 30

Every word of God proves true.

Proverbs 30:5 (NLT)

In 2017, a study found that only 24% of North Americans believe the Bible is the Word of God, though 71% still consider it a holy book.

Frank Morison was an investigative reporter and a skeptic about Christianity. He set out to disprove the resurrection of Christ, thinking it was a hoax. However, as he researched, he became convinced of its truth and dedicated himself to sharing his findings, writing the book Who Moved the Stone? His work later influenced journalist Lee Strobel who wrote The Case for Christ, and other apologetic texts.

The Word of God is reliable and trustworthy. Many historical events mentioned in the Bible have been confirmed and numerous prophecies have come true. Jesus Himself said, "Your Word is truth" (John 17:17 NRSVU).

How do you view the Bible? Is it just an old book that means nothing to you, or do you see it as the truth? Your perspective is crucial for your life. May the truth of the Bible resonate in your heart and give you confidence.

Lord, help me to trust in You—Your Word is truth!

MH

January 31

She makes linen garments and sells them; she supplies the merchant with sashes.
Proverbs 31:24 (NRSVU)

Sara Breedlove, born to slaves and later orphaned and widowed, started her career as a laundry worker. One day, while working, she wondered what would happen to her when she grew old and couldn't wash clothes anymore.

Struggling with hair loss, she found a product that worked wonders and decided to sell it. She developed her own formula and launched her own line of hair care products. After marrying publicist C. J Walker, she became known as Madam C. J. Walker. Her business thrived, employing 40,000 salespeople, mostly women. She even lived near Rockefeller and donated part of her fortune to educational institutions.

Like Madam C.J. Walker, the woman described in Proverbs 31 is entrepreneurial. She created fine linens and sashes to sell, providing herself with extra income while dressing beautifully and with dignity.

Acts 16:14-15 tells us about another businesswoman named Lydia, who sold "purple cloth." Her financial independence allowed her to host Paul, Silas, and Timothy, and she became the first believer in Europe, opening her home for the first church in Philippi.

The determination and energy of these women can inspire us to be productive and hardworking. They used their talents and influence for the benefit of others and the work of God. We can embark on personal, social, or business projects that utilize our gifts and creativity. Bringing us fulfillment and security.

Lord, bless my projects. I want to use them for Your glory.

MG

February 1

Their purpose is to teach people wisdom and discipline, to help them understand the insights of the wise.

Proverbs 1:2 (NLT)

In the movie *Christopher Robin: An Unforgettable Reunion,* Winnie the Pooh asks Christopher Robin for a balloon. Christopher hesitates and wonders why he needs one. Winnie replies, "I know I don't need one, but I'd like one very, very much, please." In the end, Christopher buys him a balloon, and Winnie is thrilled.

In life, we often want many things that we don't actually need. Every time we visit a store, the number of things we'd like far exceeds what we actually need to survive. Today's proverb highlights three essential things: wisdom, discipline, and understanding.

The people of first-century Palestine "wanted" a Messiah to free them from the Romans. They were looking for a liberator with a sword who would defeat their enemies. Instead, they received Jesus riding on a donkey. Although they initially welcomed him with cheers, just days later, they shouted, "Crucify him!" Many missed the greatest opportunity of their lives because they didn't recognize their need for Jesus, even though he wasn't what they were expecting.

God's wisdom, as recorded in the Bible, often gives us advice we might not like. Sometimes, we want to reject Wisdom itself—represented by Jesus—because he doesn't meet our expectations. Just as Winnie the Pooh's red balloon disappears by the end of the movie, superficial desires fade away eventually. However, the friendship between Winnie the Pooh and Christopher Robin continues, even without the balloon. Let's learn this lesson: what we don't truly need will eventually vanish. Our relationship with Jesus is the only thing that lasts.

Father, there are many things I want, but what I really need is You

KO

February 2

Tune your ears to wisdom and concentrate on understanding.
Proverbs 2:2 (NLT)

Once, some opera singers struggled to hit certain notes accurately, so they hired a voice coach. After some tests, the coach found that the singers weren't hitting the notes because they couldn't hear them! The issue wasn't their voices; it was their ears. Doesn't this happen to us too?

Maybe our difficulty in singing the divine tune comes from not hearing God's voice. We might be "tone deaf," stuck in sinful habits and negative cycles because we aren't in tune with what God is saying. So how can we hear his voice?

God speaks through creation, the people around us, and our conscience, but nothing compares to the Bible. Scripture speaks to our souls like nothing else when we take the time to read and meditate on it. Opening the Holy Bible is like God opening his mouth "to teach us what is true and to make us realize what is wrong in our lives. It corrects us when we are wrong and teaches us to do what is right. God uses [the Bible] to prepare and equip his people to do every good work" (2 Timothy 3:16-17, NLT).

Do you read the Bible every day? Do you take time to think about what you've read? Do you try to follow what you find there? Are you training your ear to hear God's voice? Just as our proverb says: "tune your ears." Loving God with all your mind starts with hearing his word and then following it.

"Holy Bible, you are a treasure to me." Thank you, Lord, for your Word.

KO

February 3

Do not withhold good from those to whom it is due, when it is in your power to do it.

Proverbs 3:27 (NRSVUE)

In Mexico, while waiting at a red light, you might be entertained by a juggler or a dancer in feathers. Others might offer to clean your windshield or sell you gum, juice, small toys, or even electric swatters for mosquitoes—all for just a few coins.

One time, I saw a driver give two bottles of sunscreen to a woman selling gum at an intersection. She had a baby on her back wrapped in a rebozo and spent long hours in the sun. Thankfully, someone found a way to help her. In our family, we've decided to keep cans of tuna in the car to give away instead of giving out money.

Like Proverbs, Galatians 6:10 also encourages us: "whenever we have an opportunity, let us work for the good of all and especially for those of the family of faith" (NRSVUE).

During the Covid-19 pandemic, something beautiful awakened in humanity: people's generosity. We became more aware of others' needs, and those of us who lost family and friends can now be more empathetic.

There's wisdom in the saying, "Do good without asking who gets it." Have you thought about all the different ways we can do good? We all have something to give, food, clothes, time, encouraging words, our prayers, or at the very least, a smile.

God, help me remember that faith without works is dead.

MG

FEBRUARY 4

Let your heart hold fast my words; keep my commandments and live.
Proverbs 4:4 (NRSVUE)

In many countries, teaching the Bible is prohibited. Believers face persecution and imprisonment, and Bibles are confiscated and burned. Once, an American preacher traveled to one of these countries to train church leaders. Twenty-two participants took a three-hour train ride to a hotel where they sat on the floor without air conditioning or Bibles. The preacher had only 15 Bibles to distribute, leaving seven people without one. What do you think happened next?

The preacher noticed that one woman gave her Bible to someone who didn't have one because she had memorized the chapter they were reading. When he asked her where she had learned to memorize the Scriptures, she replied, "In prison." He learned that in prison, they smuggled in the Word on slips of paper, which were often confiscated. "That's why we memorized as quickly as we could," she said, "because even if they take the paper away, they can't take away what's in your heart."

I really like the English expression for memorizing things: "learn by heart." It shows that when you memorize something, you learn it in your heart. Our verse invites us to hold God's words close to our hearts. When we genuinely love the Bible, we cherish it for all its worth.

Our brothers and sisters in Christ who are persecuted for their faith have chosen to carry the Word of God in their hearts during their imprisonment. Their passion has been to memorize it. How much time do you spend memorizing your Father's words?

Lord, give me the desire, will, and wisdom to memorize your Word.

YF

February 5

Let her affection (caresses) fill you at all times.
Proverbs 5:19 (RSV, with translator's note)

There is a famous song sung by Celine Dion and Barbra Streisand, "How do you keep the music playing?" That comes to my mind when reading this proverb. This verse reminds us that keeping the flame of marital love alive requires action, especially through touch.

Everyone appreciates an intentional caress. A hug, a gentle touch, a squeeze, or a pat on the back can communicate a lot and lift our spirits during tough times. This physical connection should be especially present in the closest relationship we can have: marriage.

Believe it or not, your husband craves your caresses. Your hands can convey the message he longs to hear. In the Song of Songs, the husband serenades his wife with sweet words we all want to hear. But how did she win his heart? Through subtle invitations to the garden where her touch spoke louder than her words.

We've all thought about the possibility of love fading. With divorce being so common today, we might not see it as a tragedy anymore. But God views it differently. We can make the music last if we're willing to be affectionate.

May it be so.

Lord, may my caresses show my love.

KO

February 6

What are worthless and wicked people like? They are constant liars.

Proverbs 6:12 (NLT)

Recently, the term "fake news" has become popular to describe false reports that circulate on social media. Have you ever shared a shocking or interesting story, only to find out later that it wasn't true? I know I have. It makes me feel bad for being so easily fooled. I quickly try to delete the post or at least let others know it was a mistake.

Not long ago, terrible wildfires were spreading through the Amazon rainforests in Brazil. A Facebook report claimed that heavy rains were putting out the fires and many shared it with relief. Later it turned out to be false, yet thousands had shared it without checking the facts first. Unfortunately, there are people who create these lies! The consequences are confusion and sometimes panic.

Lies can lead us into sin, just like Adam and Eve were deceived by Satan when he told them, "You won't die!" (Genesis 3:4, NLT). Fake news spreads quickly, and even when it's proven false, it's often too late to fix the damage. Yet, those who spread fake news keep lying, just as today's proverb points out.

Lies can cause irreparable harm. They seem to spread faster than the truth! Let's make sure to check our sources to see if they're trustworthy. And if we make a mistake, let's do everything we can to correct it. Let's be messengers of truth!

Lord, free me from lies and from spreading lies.

MH

February 7

Follow my advice, my son.

Proverbs 7:1 (NLT)

There's a popular saying, "I'm not poor for lack of advice!" In other words, if advice were money, we'd all be rich! How much advice have you received from your parents over the years? The challenge is following that advice, right?

I can picture Joseph in the workshop, teaching young Jesus the trade. "Hold the hammer like this," he might have said. "Pay attention to the wood grain before you cut." Jesus surely valued his father's guidance and probably received advice in many areas of life.

Years later, Jesus fully dedicated himself to his heavenly Father's work, and he was obedient even then. God was so pleased with him that one day a voice from heaven declared: "This is my beloved Son, with whom I am well pleased" (Matthew 3:17, RSV). When fulfilling the Father's will meant facing pain, suffering, ridicule, blood and death, Jesus still said, "I want your will to be done, not mine" (Luke 22:42, NLT). What a beautiful example of obedience!

While our parents are alive, it's a privilege to have their wise guidance, even if we're grown with our own families. If your father is still with you, cherish his words and never take him for granted. If he only lives in your memories, remember that you are not an orphan. You have a heavenly Father who loves you, speaks to you, enlightens you and guides you. Obey him. Follow Jesus' example!

Jesus, today I want to thank you for being the perfect example of an obedient son. I want to be like you.

MG

February 8

Listen as Wisdom calls out! Hear as understanding raises her voice!
Proverbs 8:1 (NLT)

Did you know there are places in the world where people don't know about the Bible or Jesus? Out of the 6,500 languages in the world it is estimated that only around 3,300 have portions of the Bible translated. How can they hear Wisdom?

There was this particular tribe that believed that someday someone would come to teach them to worship a marvelous God. The tribe's chief longed for this moment, but he died before it happened. His son took over and after some years a missionary family arrived on the island. When the chief heard and understood the Bible's message, he asked, "Why did it take you so long to get here? My father waited for you and died without knowing your message."

Some call the eighth chapter of Proverbs "wisdom personified in Jesus." It describes what Christ did during his ministry: he called out and proclaimed God's love in the streets and on the mountains. His lips spoke truth and he cared for the lost world. But then he left! Did his work end there? No! He entrusted it to those he saved, so they could be his voice.

You and I hear the Word of Wisdom and make it our own. We, too, are missionaries. We can bless others with his message. Let's share it with everyone we can, wherever we can.

Beloved Lord, open my mouth so your wisdom can reach others.

YF

February 9

Leave simpleness, and live, and walk in the way of insight.
Proverbs 9:6 (RSV)

David Hume was an English philosopher who concluded that we can't truly know what we know. Regarding creation he suggested that what we see is just a random arrangement of particles that have the appearance of design. What did he mean by that?

Hume argued that if you had a box of Legos and tossed the pieces in the air, chance could make them land perfectly together to build a plane, a train, or whatever the box showed.

Crazy? Foolishness? Truth? What do you think? In Proverbs 9, wisdom is personified as a woman calling out from the city's heights, urging us to leave behind foolishness and embrace intelligence. The beautiful world around us cannot be the result of chance. I bet if you conducted the Lego experiment hundreds of times they would never land in the right spot without a designer—a guiding hand.

Let's thank God for being the Creator of this world and for giving us minds capable of understanding and praising his greatness. Take a moment today to enjoy the design of this world and your own body. Choose good judgment!

Lord, I praise you for the beautiful world you have created.

KO

February 10

We have happy memories of the godly (the just), but the name of a wicked person rots away.

Proverbs 10:7 (NLT, with translator's note)

"Create a good reputation, find sleep, create a bad reputation, find your escape." This saying reminds us that our reputation is tied to our actions—and it has consequences, either good or bad. How will we be remembered in the future?

A common essay prompt begins, "Describe the person you most admire." For me, I'd choose a woman who was an example to me, known for her kindness, unwavering faith and Christian service. She excelled at giving advice, especially because she knew the Word of God and how to apply it. She was righteous because she genuinely followed Jesus Christ. Her intelligence and grace shone through in her missionary work and her role as a university professor.

Indeed, "we have happy memories of the just." The word "just" has multiple meanings in both Hebrew and Spanish. In Spanish, it refers to someone who "acts according to justice, morality, or reason." In the Bible, a just person is described as upright and justified before God. The Patriarch Abraham "believed the Lord, and the Lord counted him as righteous (just) because of his faith" (Genesis 15:6 NLT, with translator's note). As Christians, we recognize that true justice in our lives is a gift from the Lord.

Do you want your children, friends, and relatives to have good memories of you? Follow the example of admirable people so you can become like them. Above all, clothe yourself in the justice of Christ. With his strength, make choices that lead you down the right path. May your words and actions reflect his presence in your life.

My Father, help me reflect Christ and his justice today.

MH

February 11

A gossip goes around telling secrets, but those who are trustworthy can keep a confidence.

Proverbs 11:13 (NLT)

When Barack Obama was President, he had to keep a secret from his wife Michelle. During a visit to Buckingham Palace, while he was preparing a speech, a butler told him, "Mr. President, there's a mouse in the bathroom." Obama responded, "Please don't tell the First Lady."

There's a saying that goes, "Sooner or later everything comes to light." In a study commissioned by Michael Cox, UK director of Wines of Chile, researchers surveyed 3,000 women and found that the average time a lady is able to keep a secret is just 22 minutes, though some could manage a whole two days. According to the study our modern technologies make it even easier to spill secrets. Benjamin Franklin once said, "Three can keep a secret if two are dead."

Today's proverb shows us there are two types of people: gossips and those who are trustworthy. When someone shares a secret with us it shows they trust us. The best way to return that trust is by guarding that trust and keeping your word. Have you ever felt embarrassed or betrayed when someone revealed your secret?

Let's apply the Golden Rule: "Do to others whatever you would like them to do to you" (Matthew 7:12, NLT). Remember, when someone repeatedly does something, they're creating habits and building a reputation.

Lord, I want to be trustworthy. Help me have a faithful spirit.

MG

February 12

Better to be an ordinary person (a Mr. Nobody) with a servant than to be self-important (a Mr. Important) but have no food.
Proverbs 12:9 (NLT with translator's note)

Many financial problems stem from poor money management. If we look at the lives of famous people who went bankrupt, we often find a pattern of wastefulness. When emergencies arise, they can't stay afloat.

Take one of the greatest boxers of all time, Mike Tyson. He's known for winning many of his fights with quick knockouts. He's held numerous titles and records; he's appeared in movies and in 2011 was inducted into the Boxing Hall of Fame. Throughout his career he earned nearly 300 million dollars. However, his life was a mess. With drug addiction, wild parties, and a lavish lifestyle, he spent $400,000 a month. By 2003 he had $27 million in debt, mostly from taxes, and declared bankruptcy, losing his home. He was a Mr. Important without food!

The essence of our proverb can be summed up in this quote from the Apostle Paul: "But those who won't care for their relatives, especially those in their own household, have denied the true faith. Such people are worse than unbelievers" (1 Timothy 5:8, NLT).

I know many women who aren't famous but work hard to provide for their families. Some even give their money as a gift of love. Who do you relate to more? A Mr. Nobody or a Mr. Important?

Lord, help me be wise in how I use my money.

YF

February 13

Those who control their tongue will have a long life; opening your mouth can ruin everything.

Proverbs 13:3 (NLT)

When Andrew, also known as Brother Andrew, started working in a chocolate factory in Holland after the war, he didn't expect to encounter Greetje, who annoyed the other girls with her crude jokes. Andrew and another Christian girl began inviting their coworkers to church, and Greetje often mocked them. One day, Andrew lost his patience and told her, "Shut up, Greetje. The bus leaves at 9 am on Saturday for the service. You better be there!"

To everyone's surprise Greetje attended the service, although she seemed indifferent. At the end, Andrew offered to bike her home, thinking it would be a good chance to talk about her need for salvation. However, a strong feeling urged him not to mention spiritual topics, so he talked about the tulip fields they passed.

The Bible reminds us that there's "a time to be quiet and a time to speak" (Ecclesiastes 3:7, NLT). On Monday, Greetje sought out Andrew. "I thought you'd pressure me to believe during the bike ride, but you didn't. I wondered if you thought that someone as sinful as me could never find God's forgiveness. So, I asked God to forgive me and now I feel fantastic!" Andrew smiled, relieved he hadn't opened his mouth too soon; otherwise, he might have ruined everything.

Let's ask God for guidance on when to speak and when to stay quiet, so we don't mess things up!

Lord, help me hear your voice clearly when you want me to be silent.

KO

February 14

A peaceful heart leads to a healthy body; jealousy is like cancer in the bones.
Proverbs 14:30 (NLT)

The heart symbol we use today comes from Ancient Greece and resembles an ivy leaf. It's everywhere—on stickers, cards, jewelry and even in emoticons. We often connect the heart with love and emotions.

"Eyes that don't see; a heart that doesn't feel."

"A passionate heart doesn't want advice."

"Full belly, happy heart."

These sayings highlight the heart as the center of our emotions, especially love.

In Hebrew, the word for "heart" has a broader meaning. It refers to the innermost part of a person, encompassing not just feelings but thoughts and reasoning. Emotional and mental peace are linked to overall health. Some believe many illnesses are tied to negative emotions like stress, malice, anger and, as this verse mentions, jealousy. These feelings can be like "cancer in the bones."

Everyone desires peace over suffering. If we spend our time envying those who seem to have more, the only outcome is inner turmoil and bitterness. Instead, let's recognize and appreciate the gifts and opportunities God has given us. Even amid limitations or adversity, if we radiate peace, we show others the power of Christ in our lives.

Lord, thank you for being my peace. Help me reflect this peace in my demeanor.

MH

FEBRUARY 15

The eyes of the Lord are in every place, keeping watch on the evil and the good.

Proverbs 15:3 (NABRE)

One night, as I tucked my daughters into bed, I wanted to teach them that God is always watching over us. I told them, "God is everywhere. He's here in this room right now and he sees everything we do. We can't hide from him. If we go into the closet he sees us, and if we crawl under the bed, he still sees us." Their reaction surprised me; they looked wide-eyed and became aware of God's omnipresence, feeling a bit scared.

Fear of God is a feeling of reverent awe. It is "the beginning of wisdom." It's good to know that God sees us, but he doesn't just watch; he acts according to our circumstances. For the wicked, "It is a fearful thing to fall into the hands of the living God" (Hebrews 10:31, NABRE).

What about the good? The Bible tells us, "The eyes of the Lord search the whole earth in order to strengthen those whose hearts are fully committed to him" (2 Chronicles 16:9, NLT). His goal is to bless us and show his power to those who live with integrity!

As we read God's Word and get to know him better, we realize the depth of his love. Looking back, we see the Good Shepherd has always been there to help, bless, heal, and provide for us. What does it mean to you to know that God's eyes are always on you?

Dear God, show me if there's any wickedness in my ways, and guide me along the everlasting path.

MG

FEBRUARY 16

Commit your actions to the Lord, and your plans will succeed.

Proverbs 16:3 (NLT)

When starting a project, we often seek help from the most qualified experts. For instance, if you're building a house, you'd look for a good architect. You'd want to see their previous work and hear recommendations from others. You wouldn't trust your home to someone inexperienced.

Josh McDowell was once a skeptical student who didn't trust anyone. He was determined to prove that Christianity was a lie, and that Jesus wasn't God and didn't rise from the dead. He investigated history and the Bible until he realized that everything he was trying to disprove was true. His research is compiled in several books, including *Evidence That Demands a Verdict*, where he demonstrates Jesus' divinity and resurrection.

God is trustworthy. Josh discovered this and entrusted all his work to Him. God says in Jeremiah 29:13: "When you look for me, you will find me. Yes, when you seek me with all your heart" (NABRE). He is ready to reveal himself to those who desire it.

Do you want to call on the expert of life? You may have doubts, but if you seek God with all your heart, you'll be pleasantly surprised. He is looking for you!

Thank you, Father, for being the expert in our lives.

YF

February 17

Acquitting the guilty and condemning the innocent—both are detestable to the Lord.

Proverbs 17:15 (NLT)

Darryl Beamish, a blind and deaf man, was wrongfully convicted at age 18 for the death of Jillian Brewer. After 15 years in prison, he was found innocent and exonerated.

David McCallum and Willie Stuckey were sentenced to prison for killing a white man. Twenty years later, DNA tests proved their innocence. McCallum left prison, but Stuckey had already died behind bars. Does injustice bother you?

We all despise it when a guilty person is set free, and an innocent person is wrongly condemned. Sadly, while we may believe that a murderer should pay for their crimes, there are other areas where we've started to call evil "good" and good "evil," referring to sweet things as "bitter" and bitter things as "sweet" (Isaiah 5:20).

Sometimes, we justify lies and deception, using softer words to describe our actions. But God sees human behavior clearly. He detests injustice, lies, greed, and revenge.

How can we tell if our perspective has changed, and we've made the mistake of calling good things evil? We can ask a child for their perspective, we can put ourselves in another person's shoes, or we can analyze what the Bible says. God hates sin and we should too.

Lord, I want to hate what you hate. Help me rejoice when justice prevails.

KO

February 18

Unfriendly people care only about themselves; they lash out at common sense.
Proverbs 18:1 (NLT)

Have you ever wondered why certain birds chatter all day long? Parakeets, for instance, are very sociable and constantly communicate with each other and their owners. Sometimes, you might wish they'd quiet down. What about people?

Do you have a friend who only talks about herself, her problems, and the details of her daily life? She hardly asks about you. Her conversations seem endless, covering everything from her health to her family to her worries about safety. You can't find a way to change the subject, and you dread calling her because ending the conversation is so difficult. Who knows, maybe without even realizing it, we're like that too.

As today's proverb suggests, these people "care only about themselves." They do not listen to reason and often ignore common sense. Their words reflect exaggerated ideas rather than good judgment. Another translation says they "spit on the common good."

Before pointing fingers at someone who talks non-stop, let's reflect on ourselves. Do we listen more than we speak? If we know people who are self-absorbed, let's ask God for wisdom to be patient and guide the conversation toward gratitude and praise. There's no better antidote for complaining than gratitude.

Lord, help me avoid being unfriendly, and grant me wisdom to treat those still learning with love.

MH

February 19

Enthusiasm without knowledge is no good; haste makes mistakes.

Proverbs 19:2 (NLT)

One afternoon, I took a cake out of the oven, eager to decorate it for dinner. Even though it wasn't completely cooled, I started to remove it from the pan. An experienced baker knows that a warm cake is likely to crack and that's exactly what happened. Some pieces fell apart, the middle stuck to the pan and I ended up spending twice as long decorating the little squares I managed to salvage.

I learned my lesson: I had enthusiasm but lacked experience. Now, I need to work on being patient. Every day, we make many decisions, and our successes and failures stem from those choices. Today's proverb emphasizes two vital factors for making good decisions: be informed and take your time.

Jesus also taught the importance of gathering and analyzing information before starting a project. He asked, "For which of you, intending to build a tower, does not first sit down and estimate the cost, to see whether he has enough to complete it? Otherwise, when he has laid a foundation and is not able to finish, all who see it will begin to ridicule him, saying, 'This fellow began to build and was not able to finish'" (Luke 14:28-30, NRSVUE).

Some decisions in life are more significant than others, like choosing your life partner, deciding when to start a family, buying your first home or whether to use a credit card. Take your time, make your calculations, and always place your decisions in God's hands. Don't act hastily!

Lord, may I honor you with each decision I make.

MG

February 20

The lazy person does not plow in season; harvest comes, and there is nothing to be found..

Proverbs 20:4 (NRSVUE)

In Mexico, it's common to see people board buses and ask for money, often sharing emotional stories. One time, a man got on and said he had a daughter in the hospital. He claimed he was working hard but couldn't afford her medicine. Many of us felt moved and gave him money. However, when he got off, someone next to me revealed, "I often see that man asking for money, and every time his story changes. Yesterday, it was his grandmother."

We've all felt lazy at times, but it shouldn't define our lives. Some people have found a way to live fully off the generosity of others. A lazy person doesn't work when they should. This verse is about more than just enjoying the fruits of our labor; it also speaks to our future. What will lazy people do when they grow old? Will anyone take care of them after they've spent their lives living off others?

While we trust that God will provide for our needs, that doesn't mean we shouldn't work. If we put our hands to the plow, the Lord will bless our efforts and provide for us in old age.

Lord, deliver me from laziness.

YF

FEBRUARY 21

We can justify our every deed, but God looks at our motives.
Proverbs 21:2 (TLB)

You've probably bought fruit that looked fantastic on the outside—great color, size and texture. But when you got home, washed it, and peeled it, you found it bland or unripe. What a letdown! Today's proverb reminds us that we can sometimes be like that deceptive fruit.

In our own eyes, we may think we're good people doing good things for the good of our community. But God sees deeper and knows the true motives behind our actions. Maybe we offer to help at an event thinking it will make us look good, or maybe we offer flattering comments hoping to gain favors or perhaps we smile at someone while harboring negative feelings.

The Bible reminds us, "Nothing in all creation is hidden from God. Everything is naked and exposed before his eyes, and he is the one to whom we are accountable" (Hebrews 4:13, NLT). Others may not see our true motives, or they might praise us for our actions, but our souls are laid bare before God.

Let's not view this proverb simply as a warning but let us view it also as a motivation. Perhaps you're quietly helping others, caring for your home and striving for healthy, respectful relationships. God sees it! Let's not justify our actions, even to ourselves. May God examine our hearts and guide our intentions.

Lord, probe my heart and help me not to be deceived by my own opinion.

KO

February 22

In this way, you may know the truth and take an accurate report to those who sent you.

Proverbs 22:21 (NLT)

An African queen arrived with a large entourage and a caravan of camels carrying gold, jewels, and spices, fitting for the king she was about to visit. The Queen of Sheba had heard about Solomon's wisdom and came to test him with tough questions. What might she have asked?

Perhaps she inquired about the mysteries of nature or the fundamental questions of life: where we come from, why we exist, who determines good and evil, and what happens after death. The Bible tells us that Solomon had answers for all her questions, and she was left astonished.

Today's proverb reminds us that God has answers to all our questions. Like the Queen of Sheba, we need to seek him out and ask. If we don't, we won't learn anything. When we hear what God has to say, we might find ourselves saying, "The report I heard about you is true, Your wisdom and prosperity even surpass what I heard" (cf 1 Kings 10:6-7).

The Queen of Sheba returned home laden with gifts and a report of a king with an incredible God. You and I can know this God. Speak with Him about everything on your mind and you will discover the truth.

Lord, dispel my doubts.

KO

February 23

Listen to your father who begot you, and do not despise your mother when she is old.

Proverbs 23:22 (NRSVUE)

Gerontocracy is a form of government where power is held by the elderly. Some indigenous peoples in Mexico, like the Mixes of Oaxaca and the Zoques of Chiapas, still practice this form of governance. In the Zoque language, *Kubguy jyara* means "father of the people," referring to a respected elder with wisdom and leadership. This system has intrigued ethnologists who believe it's becoming rare. In Japan, every third Monday in September is dedicated to honoring the elderly.

The Bible warns us about the know-it-all attitude we often adopt toward our parents and grandparents. As we age, we may begin to overlook their wisdom. Few are willing to listen to those who have so much to share, and fewer still are ready to support those who may no longer be strong.

What's the opposite of disdain? Romans 13:7 teaches us to honor: "Pay to all what is due them: taxes to whom taxes are due, revenue to whom revenue is due, respect to whom respect is due, honor to whom honor is due" (NRSVUE).

We can cultivate a more empathetic culture toward the elderly. There are many ways to show honor, and respect is a language understood at any age. What can you do today to honor someone older than you?

God, may your arms embrace the elderly through me, and may I hear your wisdom through their voices.

MG

February 24

Don't envy evil people or desire their company.

Proverbs 24:1 (NLT)

Mother Teresa of Calcutta tops Gallup's list of the most admired people of the 20th century. Yet, even though we may say that she is a woman worthy of imitation, we often find ourselves admiring others, the beautiful and successful women with glamorous lives. We secretly wish we could be like the magazine models, pop stars or actors who dominate the entertainment industry.

I knew a girl who dreamed of working for a major television network. She prayed for God's help to become an artist and asked her church to pray for her too. She grew frustrated with warnings about the dangers of the entertainment industry and the fleeting nature of fame. When the job didn't materialize, she found herself settling for something else. Years later, she realized God had protected her from many dangers.

It's easy to envy those who seem to have it all and want to be in their company. But David echoes today's proverb, reminding us, "Don't worry about the wicked or envy those who do wrong. For like grass, they soon fade away. Like spring flowers, they soon wither" (Psalm 37:1-2, NLT).

If you admire a celebrity, pray for them. You don't know what their life is truly like. Surely, they need someone to share the Lord with them and give them his Word.

Lord, today I pray for _____ that they may come to know you.

YF

February 25

To one who listens, valid criticism is like a gold earring or other gold jewelry.

Proverbs 25:12 (NLT)

Costume jewelry is just that—fake! These are pieces that look like gold, silver, or precious stones, but are made of cheap materials.

My daughter enjoys making bracelets and necklaces with plastic beads. When I attend a wedding, I prefer to wear a pearl necklace or a gold chain. However, for everyday wear, I don't mind sporting the little "jewels" she creates. In both cases, they add a nice touch.

Today's proverb tells us that listening to criticism is like wearing jewels. Criticism is a thoughtful opinion we share after analyzing a situation. The difference between constructive and destructive criticism lies in the intent. Are we sharing feedback to encourage someone or to bring them down? Constructive criticism aims to help "others do what is right and build them up in the Lord" (Romans 15:2, NLT).

Let's learn from the "gold" criticism that comes from those who love us. Always accept and treasure constructive feedback but also learn to discern the "plastic" criticisms that may stem from envy. Use both to become a better person. Adorn yourself with insights of a wise heart that learns from criticism.

Father, I don't want to only hear the good about what I do, but also what can help me improve.

KO

February 26

Interfering in someone else's argument is as foolish as yanking a dog's ears.
Proverbs 26:17 (NLT)

Have you heard the term busybody? It refers to someone who meddles in another person's affairs or even gossips. They often want to know the private happenings of other people and enjoy giving their unsolicited opinions. In our culture, when someone pries into things that don't concern them, they might be told, "Why do you care?"

It's easy to give advice about others' children, marriages or fashion choices, but our guidance may not be as helpful as we think.

Today's proverb warns us against getting involved in other people's disputes. Another translation describes a meddler as someone who "gets carried away by rage in another's fight." Taking sides in an argument can lead to trouble, much like yanking a dog's ears can cause pain and get you bitten.

Is it too easy for us to take an interest in other people's affairs and share our opinions when nobody asks? Beware: we might favor one side in a conflict without knowing the full story. Instead, with the help of the Lord, we can stay quiet and do something much more valuable: pray for them and see what God can do!

Father, it's hard for me not to meddle in other people's affairs. Teach me to put them in your hands.

MH

February 27

Oil and perfume make the heart glad, and the sweetness of a friend comes from his earnest counsel.

Proverbs 27:9 (ESV)

Essential oils and diffusers are becoming increasingly popular in homes. Influencers on YouTube recommend the best combinations for creating a harmonious atmosphere. Scents like lavender, bergamot, verbena, orange blossom and jasmine are known to promote good moods and positive emotions. Aromatherapy has been practiced since ancient times.

Can you recall the delightful feeling of breathing in a beautiful aroma that transports you to a cherished childhood memory or simply brings you a sense of peace?

Today's proverb tells us that receiving a friend's counsel can evoke a similar feeling. It's not always easy to accept advice, but the key lies in how it's delivered. Good advice isn't packaged as a scolding; it's offered gently and with the best intentions.

If you want your advice to be like a pleasant fragrance, be mindful of how you give it. And if you're looking for a warm scent that brings peace today, listen to the guidance of a friend.

Lord, may my words always bring joy to my friends' hearts.

MG

February 28

When a country is rebellious, it has many princes, but by someone who is discerning, and knowledgeable order is maintained.
Proverbs 28:2 (NET)

The more political divisions there are, the greater the problems, as this can further divide a country and allow corruption to thrive. Sadly, almost every country today faces various political issues.

When the people of Israel asked Samuel for a king, he was saddened and prayed to the Lord, presenting the problem. God told him, "Obey the voice of the people in all that they say to you, for they have not rejected you, but they have rejected me from being king over them" (1 Samuel 8:7, ESV). They didn't want God to be their king; they wanted to be like other nations.

What does it take for a country to have a good leader who maintains order? It requires our God to reign. Jesus promised to return to rule and that is our hope. Revelation 11:15 assures us that in the not-too-distant future, this world will become the kingdom of "Our Lord and of his Christ, and he shall reign forever and ever" (NLT).

The world's problems won't be solved by human leaders. What can we do? We can pray for the Lord's swift return and eagerly await His coming. Let's remember: "And now the prize awaits me—the crown of righteousness, which the Lord, the righteous Judge, will give me on the day of his return. And the prize is not just for me but for all who eagerly look forward to his appearing." (2 Timothy 4:8, NLT).

Come quickly, Lord Jesus.

YF

February 29

Pride ends in humiliation, while humility brings honor.

Proverbs 29:23 (NLT)

Edwin Stanton, Secretary of War under Abraham Lincoln, was openly disrespectful toward the president. At a critical moment during the Civil War, Lincoln issued an order that Stanton refused to follow. He even publicly called Lincoln a fool. What would a president do today?

Most likely, he would be angry and might remove Stanton from his position or try to discredit him. Lincoln did neither. Instead, he said, "If Stanton thinks I'm a fool, then I must be." He then arranged a meeting with Stanton, where he listened carefully to his concerns. Lincoln ultimately concluded that Stanton was right and withdrew the order. This wasn't the only time Lincoln showed he was willing to reconsider his opinions if he was wrong.

Lincoln exemplified humility. Humility means having a clear understanding of oneself, including recognizing that we don't know everything and we're not perfect. A humble person can say, "I don't know," "I was wrong," or "You're right." And so, we follow these instructions, "Always be humble and gentle. Be patient with each other, making allowance for each other's faults because of your love" (Ephesians 4:2, NLT).

Today, find ways to demonstrate humility. How? Admit when you don't know something and be open to learning. Acknowledge your mistakes and ask for forgiveness. Recognize that others might know more than you. Lincoln's humility led him to be regarded as one of the greatest leaders in history.

Lord Jesus, I want to be humble like you.

KO

March 1

My child, listen when your father corrects you.

Proverbs 1:8 (NLT)

These days having a personal trainer is quite popular. Just going to the gym isn't enough, people seek help from *fitness* professionals to achieve better results.

I admit I can be rebellious when it comes to exercise. I often prefer to quietly hop on the stair climber or treadmill for 20 minutes to ease my conscience rather than follow a structured routine. However, I once had a personal trainer who monitored me closely throughout the entirety of a workout session. She stood right next to me, at times encouraging me, at other times challenging me—sometimes it was hard to tell the difference between the two—during sets of crunches. Her constant presence created accountability and I was able hit my ideal weight goal and improve my cardiovascular fitness.

In today's proverb, the word "correct" comes from the Hebrew word "musar," which implies training with supervision. Do you see who is responsible for this training? Our parents!

If you're still under your parents' guidance, take this advice seriously. Even if it feels like they're pressuring you or as if they're watching over you too closely, be wise and receive their instruction. If you're a mother, don't neglect your role as your child's personal trainer. It takes time and commitment, but it's part of your responsibility. Correct, instruct, and love them.

Thank you, Lord, for my parents. Help me imitate the good things they've done and learn from their mistakes.

KO

March 2

She has abandoned her husband and ignores the covenant she made before God.

Proverbs 2:17 (NLT)

According to data from the National Institute of Statistics and Geography, the number of divorces in Mexico has quadrupled since 1986. This trend is also rising in other Latin American countries, with more couples choosing not to marry.

When Ian and Larissa were dating, they faced a significant challenge. Ian had a severe accident that caused brain damage, leaving him disabled. It took him a while to learn how to speak again, and speaking is still difficult for him. They waited four years after graduation to marry, wanting to be sure that marriage was the right thing for them to pursue. Even though Ian still uses a wheelchair and has many physical limitations, they understand that love goes beyond traditional expectations.

Larissa's commitment is the opposite of the woman who has "abandoned her husband and ignores the covenant she made before God." This verse emphasizes that marriage is a covenant before God, not just a contract between people. Jesus reiterated the message of Genesis 2:24, that man and woman become one flesh, adding, "Therefore what God has joined together, let no one separate" (Matthew 19:6, NRSVUE).

In marriage vows, couples promise to love each other in sickness and in health, for richer or poorer. We commit to weathering life's storms together. When challenges arise, let's remember that we made our covenant before God! He will give us the strength to continue loving and supporting our spouses.

Lord, I trust that today you will help me be faithful to my promises.

MH

March 3

Trust in the Lord with all your heart; do not depend on your own understanding.
Proverbs 3:5 (NLT)

I invited a couple of friends over for breakfast and served food on a beautiful gold-rimmed china set we received as a wedding gift. When I went to put a dish that had cooled into the microwave, one of my friends noticed the metallic edge and warned me not to do it. I didn't listen, and, as expected, sparks started flying.

Sometimes, we choose to do things our own way because we think we know best. Just like Abraham and Sarah, who thought God would give them a child through her handmaid. They acted on their own understanding and the consequences were painful for Sarah, Hagar, and their descendants, who have been at odds ever since. God had a better plan though, they just needed to trust and wait.

Psalm 37:5 is a great verse to memorize: "Commit your way to the Lord, trust in him, and he will act" (NRSVUE). We must fully trust that God always desires what's best for us. Impatience can cloud our judgment—much like when I ignored the warning about the plate.

This is how Rita ignored the advice "Do not be yoked together with unbelievers," only to find herself years later in a troubled marriage. Or Robert, who dismissed the warning "Do not look on the wine when it is red," thinking he could enjoy a few drinks without consequences, only to become an alcoholic who lost his health, job, and family.

God doesn't want our lives to be marked by the sparks of sin. Following His counsel is the best way to show our love and trust.

I entrust my plans to you, God. I hope and trust in you.

MG

March 4

She will place on your head a graceful garland; she will bestow on you a beautiful crown.

Proverbs 4:9 (ESV)

In the animal kingdom males are the ones that seek after the females. Male birds display beautiful plumage, while females are usually plainer. However, when it comes to people, it's often women who try to catch the attention of men, doing so by following the patterns of our cultural. In a tribe between Myanmar and Thailand, women are considered beautiful because of the brass rings they wear around their necks from the age of five. Each year, they add a ring as thick as a finger. They are called "the Giraffe Women." The longer their necks, the more attractive they are thought to be. Some women wear as many as 27 rings, which also indicates their economic status.

Our proverb tells us that wisdom gives us a garland of grace and a beautiful crown. It's always a pleasure to meet someone who is sensible, trustworthy, kind, pure, joyful, prudent and filled with the Holy Spirit! Such individuals are often described as beautiful inside and out. They radiate peace, have a special sparkle in their eyes and love the Lord above all else.

You and I can be beautiful both inside and out. Proverbs reveals the secret to true beauty: seeking wisdom as if it were gold. Loving what God loves and immersing ourselves in it will bestow upon us a crown of grace admired by others.

Father, I want to be beautiful inside and out.

YF

March 5

My son, pay attention to my wisdom ... Then you will show discernment.
Proverbs 5:1-2 (NLT)

My friend Nicola is an artist who can distinguish between two shades of light blue that look the same to me. Meanwhile, I can easily detect when someone is out of tune when we sing. Nicola looks at me as if I've lost my mind! This skill is called discernment—the ability to perceive subtle differences. Nicola excels in art, while I stand out in music. In life, we all need discernment.

We can learn to discern by giving our attention to Jesus, the Wisdom of God. By understanding the priorities that guided Jesus during his time on earth, we can learn which path to take.

Paul prays that our "love may abound more and more, with knowledge and all discernment, so that you may approve what is excellent" (Philippians 1:9-10, ESV). In other words, Paul wants us to learn to differentiate between good and bad, and between good and better. I often choose good things, like taking a break, but sometimes I neglect to choose the best: a break that includes time spent in God's Word.

May God help us see the fine distinctions that we often overlook. Let's learn to recognize what is good and, more importantly, what is better. What "good" thing will you do today? Is there a "better" option available?

Father, give me eyes that recognize the "best" in every person and situation.

KO

March 6

There are six things the Lord hates... haughty eyes...

Proverbs 6:16-17 (NLT)

"Pride is a ruinous architect; it lays the foundations on top and the tiles on the foundations," wrote Francisco de Quevedo. Pride, or arrogance, is the sense of superiority one person feels over another, revealing the lowness of that individual. We've seen racism in the United States, where skin color separates people. And what about in our Latin American countries? The most marginalized groups are often the Indigenous Peoples.

The author of Proverbs emphasizes that "the Lord hates ... haughty eyes." Arrogance is defined as "haughtiness, pride or a feeling of superiority." This attitude is the opposite of that of Moses, who was "very humble—more humble than any other person on earth" (Numbers 12:3, NLT). When his siblings Aaron and Miriam criticized him for marrying a Cushite woman, God became angry and punished Miriam by making her skin leprous.

The Cushites were likely of African descent, possibly Ethiopian. Moses pleaded with the Lord, "Oh, my master! Please don't punish us for this sin we have foolishly committed" (Numbers 12:11, NLT). Despite the arrogance of his siblings, he remained humble and took partial responsibility for their sin, asking God to heal Miriam.

Do we sometimes act with pride and a sense of superiority? Perhaps we've looked down on someone for being less educated, or for being a foreigner, or because they're poor or because they have a disability. If so, let's confess our mistakes. As mothers and teachers, let's instill respect for others in our children and students.

Father, help me reflect the humility of Christ in my daily life.

MH

MARCH 7

Bind them on your fingers; write them on the tablet of your heart.

Proverbs 7:3 (ESV)

The Code of Hammurabi is a set of laws engraved on diorite stone, written around 1750 B.C. by the Babylonian king Hammurabi. It was phrased as if it were dictated by his god Marduk or Shamash. In ancient times, laws were believed to be sacred, dictated by the gods. A stela of this code is preserved in the Louvre Museum in Paris. Hammurabi understood that inscribing his laws in stone would ensure their permanence.

Jehovah, the one true God, wrote commandments with His own finger on tablets of stone, given to Moses so the people could remember and obey them. Yet, humanity still disobeyed.

God wants us to keep and treasure His commandments, and the only way to do that is to engrave them in our hearts and minds. This can only happen through the presence of the Holy Spirit within us. Paul writes, "You show that you are a letter of Christ, prepared by us, written not with ink but with the Spirit of the living God, not on tablets of stone but on tablets that are human hearts" (2 Corinthians 3:3, NRSVUE).

It would serve no purpose to engrave the law on our hearts if our actions do not demonstrate our obedience. May your life be a beautiful letter, where you write an eternal poem of adoration and joy, serving as a testimony and blessing to all who read it.

Lord, I have kept your words in my heart, that I might not sin against you.

MG

March 8

For whoever finds me finds life and obtains favor from the Lord.

Proverbs 8:35 (ESV)

As I write this, I've learned that many people that I know have become sick with Covid-19, and some have died. A doctor mentioned that with this virus, we all need to be prepared to lose someone in our families. Some, I'm sure, are thinking of giving everything they have to avoid losing their own lives or those of loved ones.

There was a certain woman who desperately wanted to be healed. She put herself at risk, the risk of rejection and even the risk of being stoned for the sin of "defiling the men" with her illness. According to the Law of Moses, a menstruating woman could not leave her house. Yet, she had been confined for 12 years due to a flow that wouldn't stop. She spent all her money on doctors, but no one could help her—until she found Jesus!

For her, meeting the Lord was truly finding life. She encountered wisdom personified, the God made man who showed her favor and healed her! The very words of today's proverb echo the Lord Jesus when he said, "I am the resurrection and the life" (John 11:25, NLT).

We have found the source of life. A virus, a health issue or any other challenge cannot stop Him. He continues to bring life today. We have examples in our congregation of people who have triumphed over Covid-19 and other serious illnesses, expressing gratitude for the Lord's favor. But the greatest victory is when a sinner repents and receives eternal life!

Father, in you, I find life. Thank you!

YF

March 9

She has prepared a great banquet.

Proverbs 9:2 (NLT)

There's a story about two enormous tables with guests seated around them. Food is placed in the center and long forks are handed out. At one table, the guests starved because they couldn't get the food to their mouths, despite being able to reach it with their forks. At the other table, the guests decided to feed one another, and they enjoyed the feast! Which table do you want to be at?

In Proverbs 9, there are two banquets. The first is prepared by wisdom, who sets out food and mixed wines, inviting everyone to come and enjoy. The second banquet is hosted by the foolish woman, who calls to the busy and offers them stolen water and secret food. Which invitation sounds appealing to you?

The Bible often refers to two paths, two doors and two masters. Sadly, it reminds us that "no one can serve two masters" (Matthew 6:24, NLT). We can't attend both tables or both banquets. In life, we must choose. Will we go to the table of generosity and wisdom, or will we starve because we refuse to share and choose stolen bread?

Every decision presents us with two alternatives. Each day, we must choose between wisdom or foolishness. It's unfortunate that we often prefer the path of folly and selfishness. But today, we can make a difference. Let's choose wisdom!

Lord, I want to attend the banquet of your love. Thank you for inviting me!

KO

March 10

The Lord will not let the godly go hungry.

Proverbs 10:3 (NLT)

A Mexican couple dedicated themselves to training youth and taking them to indigenous areas for internships. They promoted intercultural missions before it became common in many churches. They lived by faith, with the occasional donation and no steady income. One day their daughter came home from school and was asked to set the table. When she inquired about dinner, her mother explained that there was no food in the house, not even cereal. But she assured her daughter that God would provide.

While they were giving thanks for the food that wasn't there, the doorbell rang. It was the gardener of their housing complex; the mother had occasionally offered him a glass of water. Grateful for her kindness he brought in a basket filled with barbecue and tortillas from a party in his town.

The promise of this proverb was fulfilled. Similarly, King David wrote in his old age, "Yet I have never seen the godly abandoned or their children begging for bread" (Psalm 37:25, NLT). These words can offer strength to those who face material hardship yet still trust in God to provide. Jesus taught that the Father provides for those who seek His kingdom first (Matthew 6:25-33).

In Latin America, we are familiar with poverty. In some countries the poverty rate exceeds 60%. Many families in our faith communities struggle to make ends meet daily. Yet, we have seen how God provides for them. If you're worried about a particular need, turn your eyes to your heavenly Father and trust in His promises.

My Father, I know that you will provide what I need, for I am your daughter.

MH

March 11

Where there is no guidance, a people falls, but in an abundance of counselors, there is safety.

Proverbs 11:14 (ESV)

An international organization of global leaders called "The Elders" was founded by Nelson Mandela with the goal of leveraging their collective experience and influence to address global issues related to peace, human rights, and poverty. Most of the members have received the Nobel Peace Prize and have demonstrated through their work their ability to lead by example and create social change.

Every government, church, family, and individual needs wise leaders to guide them in the right direction. Counselors are essential for solving both personal and collective problems. Kings, presidents, and anyone who understands the importance of making not just good decisions, but the best ones turn to counselors.

One of Jesus' names is Counselor (Isaiah 9:6). He has given us His Word as a lamp to guide us—the counsel we need to help us see clearly. If we want the best advice, it can only come from the one who knows everything, sees everything, and can do everything.

Have you considered that you can share this light with others? Sometimes you'll be the one seeking advice, and other times you'll be in the position to give it. Both roles are necessary and important. May our wisdom come from the divine Counselor.

Lord, help me give wise counsel.

MG

MARCH 12

The righteous know the needs of their animals, but the mercy of the wicked is cruel.

Proverbs 12:10 (NRSVUE)

Since the Lord gave Adam dominion over the earth, humanity has often abused that power, showing the cruelty that exists in the human heart. Indiscriminate killings and hunting are common. In recent years, organizations advocating for animal rights and animal welfare have emerged. Some countries have banned hunting certain species and using animals in circuses.

I was saddened to see a video of a blind, pregnant dog who had been beaten and abandoned in the mountains. Can you believe a human could do that? Fortunately, a family found her and contacted an animal rescue organization. The rescuers took her to the hospital, where they discovered the puppies had died. They immediately removed them and focused on healing the dog, managing to save one eye thanks to their efforts and kindness. Today, this little creature is safe with a loving family.

The righteous understand that animals have feelings. Their expressions of pain and love are God-given abilities to communicate with us. Only twisted minds fail to see this wonder.

We may not need to join an animal rights organization, but we do have a responsibility to help protect the lives around us. If we consider ourselves righteous daughters of God, we must help the defenseless, including animals. Let's cherish God's creation!

Lord Creator, make me an ambassador for your creation.

YF

March 13

Wise people think before they act; fools don't—and even brag about their foolishness.

Proverbs 13:16 (NLT)

Five hours of sleep isn't enough. Doctors and sleep experts recommend at least eight hours of uninterrupted sleep for optimal functioning. Yet, we often go to bed late, thinking it won't affect us. We act as if we're invincible and even brag about it to others. Isn't that foolish?

When I was younger, it felt like a competition in college to see who could sleep the least. Folly, often equated with foolishness, is characterized by a lack of prudence and maturity, something we often see in others but fail to recognize in ourselves. We should take a moment to analyze our own behaviors. Smoking and believing it won't lead to cancer, mistreating someone who is your junior and expecting loyalty, or indulging in junk food without considering the consequences are all clear signs of a lack of wisdom.

Jesus illustrated the folly of a man who builds a house on sand without a foundation or preparation for rain. This man acted recklessly, and we shake our heads when we read about his house collapsing, thinking, "I knew it." Yet, how often are we blind to our own foolishness?

Doesn't the doctor shake his head when we complain about low energy or weakness only to confess that we sleep four to five hours a night? Let's examine where we show foolishness and make corrections. As today's proverb states, "wise people think before they act."

Lord, I have unhealthy habits that I refuse to give up, even when I know I should. Give me the strength to change.

KO

MARCH 14

The wise are cautious and avoid danger; fools plunge ahead with reckless confidence.

Proverbs 14:16 (NLT)

In March 2019, a group of students ignored warnings and climbed Mexico's Popocatepetl volcano. Their "prank" came to light when they posted a video on social media. Days later, the volcano erupted violently, startling residents in nearby cities and causing windows to rattle. Incandescent fragments flew out, igniting a forest fire on the mountain slopes.

What must those young people have felt? On one hand, they probably sighed in relief that they weren't at the top when the eruption occurred. On the other hand, they must have realized they had put their lives at risk, even if their reckless adventure initially seemed fun. In fact, in 1996, five climbers died while attempting to scale that same volcano without permission.

Our proverb reminds us that the wise are cautious and avoid danger. If they knew something could harm them, they wouldn't dare do it. In biblical times, they might have worried about lions; today, we might think of drugs or premarital sex. Danger shouldn't be taken lightly. Even Jesus knew to withdraw to another region when people plotted to kill him before the appointed time (Mark 3:6-7).

While we may not engage in the same recklessness as those students, we might still do things that endanger our health or the well-being of our families. God's Word guides us to make the best decisions.

Father, guide my steps and my decisions so that I act with prudence.

MH

March 15

All the days of the poor are hard, but a cheerful heart has a continual feast.
Proverbs 15:15 (NRSVU)

Irma was born into a large family with limited resources. In conversations, she often mentions what they lacked and expresses resentment toward her father for abandoning them. Now at 50, she remains single. Rosa, on the other hand, loved having many siblings because they could team up for games. Although she misses that camaraderie, she has formed her own family. Interestingly, they are sisters who experienced the same childhood. If you show them a glass with a little water, Irma sees it as half empty, while Rosa sees it as half full.

Irma and Rosa had difficult childhoods, but Rosa chose to adopt the attitude of the prophet Habakkuk, who declared:

Even though the fig trees have no blossoms,
   and there are no grapes on the vines;
even though the olive crop fails,
   and the fields lie empty and barren;
even though the flocks die in the fields,
   and the cattle barns are empty,
yet I will rejoice in the Lord!
   I will be joyful in the God of my salvation!

(Habakkuk 3:17-18, NLT)

We can have something better than a happy heart; we can have a joyful heart!

Your joy, O God, is the strength of my life.

MG

March 16

All the words of my mouth are righteous (just); there is nothing twisted or crooked in them.

Proverbs 8:8 (NRSVU, with translator's note)

During the Covid-19 pandemic, many people said, "It's not fair that people don't wear masks. We're tired of this lockdown." After the U.S. elections, we heard, "It's not fair; they cheated." When a journalist investigating a body dumped on a highway in Guanajuato, Mexico, was assassinated, his family declared it was not fair.

Everywhere we hear about unjust deeds. When we exclaim, "It's not fair!" we express our feelings of powerlessness in the face of so much wrong. In essence, we long for justice.

We desire justice in this world. But true justice will only come when humanity chooses to follow the one who declares, "all the words of my mouth are just." Justice will prevail when we heed the righteous principles found in God's Word.

How blessed are we who listen to and love His words! We understand that while injustice may exist in this world, the Lord is just and will bring justice for us when the time is right.

Lord, you are just. Thank you for being just.

YF

March 17

It is painful to be the parent of a fool.

Proverbs 17:21 (NLT)

Hudson Taylor grew up in a Christian family, dedicated to God from birth, especially to serve in China. However, at 15 he began working in a bank and soon fell into a lifestyle of partying and cursing. He lost interest in prayer and Bible reading. By age 17, Hudson had developed a violent temper. As the proverb suggests, his foolishness caused his parents great suffering; nothing they said could change him. What happened next?

His mother, Amelia, decided to take a short trip to pray for her son. She shut herself in a room and vowed not to stop interceding for his salvation until God gave her peace. And peace did come. While she prayed, Hudson read a pamphlet about salvation and came to believe in Jesus. Interestingly, his younger sister, only 13 at the time, was also praying for him.

The rest is history. Hudson Taylor traveled to China and dedicated much of his life to sharing God's love. The prayers of his mother and sister made a difference. We should never underestimate the power of a mother, sister, aunt, niece, cousin, grandmother, or sister-in-law who prays: "The earnest prayer of a righteous person has great power and produces wonderful results" (James 5:16, NLT).

If you don't want to be a mother who suffers from her children's foolishness, don't lose heart—keep praying for your loved ones. Our children are worth the effort, time, and love we invest in bringing them to the one who can change their hearts: the Lord.

Father, sometimes I falter in praying for my children, but renew my strength.

KO

MARCH 18

Wise words are like deep waters; wisdom flows from the wise like a bubbling brook.

Proverbs 18:4 (NLT)

In central Mexico, near the Popocatepetl and Iztaccihuatl volcanoes, there are abundant springs of pure, fresh water from melting snow. In one town, where people can fill their water bottles directly from the spring, a sign announces the water's purity, chemically certified.

The proverb states that "wise words are like deep waters." To access them we might say we need a bucket with a long rope. Jesus' stories, which we call parables, are like this. Only those who truly seek to understand can grasp their real and hidden messages— those who hunger for wisdom and God.

For example, after Jesus told the Parable of the Sower and after the crowd left, the disciples asked him what it meant. Only those who sought understanding were able to learn the application. After giving another illustration, Jesus urged, "Pay close attention to what you hear. The closer you listen, the more understanding you will be given—and you will receive even more" (Mark 4:24, NLT). Listening here means going beyond the surface to understand the deeper meaning, where "wisdom flows like a bubbling brook."

In today's fast-paced world, do you find it hard to stop and truly listen to God? To pay attention you need time and silence. Seek these moments in your daily routine so you can drink from the stream of God's wisdom.

Father, I want to hear your voice and your wisdom; give me understanding to dive deeper into the "deep waters."

MH

MARCH 19

Slothfulness casts into a deep sleep, and an idle person will suffer hunger.
Proverbs 19:15 (ESV)

One of my favorite moments is that feeling of "task completed!" After a day of chores, when everything is in order and smells clean, I feel satisfied. I've studied the techniques from the Japanese organization expert Marie Kondo on keeping a clutter-free home. Sometimes, things accumulate, and it becomes difficult to know where to put everything. That's when it's harder to get started.

Laziness and procrastination rear their heads when we see a mountain of clothes or a stack of papers. We must fight against our neglectful tendencies. We know we shouldn't leave for tomorrow what can be done today, but distractions like social media or Netflix pull us away from our goals.

Ephesians 6:7 serves as motivation: "Work with enthusiasm, as though you were working for the Lord rather than for people" (NLT). Focusing on who we are doing things for can give our work new meaning.

Once we start moving, our bodies respond, filling us with energy. The first step is overcoming laziness to get going. Do you have a pending project? Don't put it off any longer. What can you do today to address it?

Father, thank you for this day. Help me use it wisely and live with enthusiasm.

MG

MARCH 20

Many a man proclaims his own loyalty, but a faithful man who can find?

Proverbs 20:6 (RSV)

In the novel The Great Gatsby the millionaire Jay Gatsby lies constantly. He fabricates stories about his wealth, his love life and even claims to have read all the books in his library. He lies so much in the story that today his character symbolizes people who aim to be something they aren't. Our proverb reminds us that while many promise loyalty, finding a truly trustworthy person is rare.

This verse complements Proverbs 31:10 which asks, "Who can find a woman of worth?" (NABRE). Men are seeking exemplary women, and women need loyal and trustworthy men. Where can he be found? Isn't this a question many single women ponder?

We have the ultimate example in Jesus. What should you seek in a partner? If a man's heart is obedient to God's Word and he loves the Lord wholeheartedly, a woman has nothing to worry about. She will have a man who loves her as Christ loves the Church, treating her with care and respect.

If you desire a faithful partner, start by praying for the Lord to send him into your life. Make sure to include a sincere and trustworthy man on your list of qualities for a future partner. Remember, only someone with God in their life can truly exhibit these qualities.

Father, today I pray for my mate. Prepare me to be the person he needs, and may he be your servant.

YF

March 21

To do righteousness and justice is more acceptable to the Lord than sacrifice.
Proverbs 21:3 (NRSVUE)

In the temples of the goddess Kali in southern India, the god Garuda is celebrated with the Garudan Thookkam. At the annual festival devotees are hung from hooks through the skin on their backs and legs. They advance in procession to the temple while others pray, dance and sing. These images are not pleasant, but perhaps we aren't far from this kind of behavior ourselves.

Every human seeks to earn divine favor regardless of their religion. Some make pilgrimages, others offer sacrifices; even those who claim to believe in nothing may deprive themselves of certain things in hopes that their acts of deprivation will allow their dreams to come true. However, today's proverb reminds us that there is something more important than sacrifices.

Imagine a devotee of Kali, after his pious display, removes himself from the painful hooks and then begins arguing with his wife, he steals coins offered to the goddess and then spends that money getting intoxicated with alcohol. What good was that spectacle? That's the point God wants to make. It's not about appearing religious; it's about practicing what God commands (James 1:22).

He desires a humble and repentant heart over outward, hypocritical displays. Let's not fall into the trap of doing things to be seen by others while lacking goodness or love within. When we do what is right, we please God. A clean and honest life is worth far more to Him than "hanging from hooks."

Lord, help me practice righteousness and avoid pretense.

KO

March 22

Choose a good reputation over great riches; being held in high esteem is better than silver or gold.

Proverbs 22:1 (NLT)

I worked part-time at the same institution for many years and loved the environment and my coworkers. However, one year, they pressured me to sign something that was untrue, a false declaration that would financially benefit the owners. I refused. My boss begged me to reconsider. Friends reminded me that "that's life" in Latin America.

I thought about my students and how I had insisted on honor. How could I compromise my principles for financial gain? How could I teach one thing and do another? It's possible no one would have noticed, but my conscience would have condemned me if I signed it. In the end, I had to find another job.

Material wealth has long been seen as a sign of success, but it often leads to downfall. Even the disciples were surprised when Jesus said it's nearly impossible for the rich to enter the Kingdom of Heaven (Matthew 19:24-25). The young rich man who wanted to follow Jesus discovered he loved his possessions more than Jesus and went away sad (Matthew 19:22).

In moments of craziness, we might prioritize being "rich" over being held in high esteem. But true success comes from integrity. In critical moments, seek out people who live by their principles and have good reputations, rather than those who hoard wealth. How can you demonstrate integrity today?

Father, help me yearn for the true wealth of a good reputation that honors you.

MH

March 23

Everything in me will celebrate when you speak what is right.
Proverbs 23:16 (NLT)

My friend Mayra has experienced stages of life that I can only glimpse in the future. My daughter is only seven, while Mayra's oldest daughter has graduated from university and gotten married. I could see the joy on Mayra's face during both occasions, expressed through smiles and tears. Her entire being celebrated her daughter's achievements. What do we celebrate in life?

We celebrate our children's birthdays and their milestones, from preschool to graduate school. We cheer for them when they win soccer games or earn medals in poetry contests. We applaud their first piano recitals and dance performances. The author of Proverbs rejoiced when his son spoke what was right. But let's not forget the most important celebration.

The most significant moments in our loved ones' lives don't go unnoticed by the angels. Jesus told a story about a woman who lost a silver coin and rejoiced with her friends when she found it. He concluded, "In the same way, there is joy in the presence of God's angels when even one sinner repents" (Luke 15:10, NLT).

I know that my friend Mayra has also celebrated the new birth and salvation of her eldest daughter. So many wonderful celebrations! When our loved ones come to God, it becomes the most beautiful occasion, making our hearts rejoice!

Lord, today I pray for _____ who still does not know you.

KO

March 24

By knowledge, the rooms are filled with all precious and pleasant riches.

Proverbs 24:4 (ESV)

I have many beautiful paintings and meaningful decorations on the walls of my home that I want my visitors to see. I also have ceramic tiles I painted myself and souvenirs from my travels that adorn my living space. I love hearing my guests comment on how lovely they believe my home is. I've been collecting these treasures for a long time and now that I have my own place, I can use these items to fill all my rooms.

When the Word of God speaks of filling rooms with precious and pleasant objects, it refers to the rooms of our hearts. We should fill them with valuable knowledge! Just as we decorate our homes with beautiful items, the right knowledge chosen and treasured will adorn our hearts.

Paul writes, "I regard everything as loss because of the surpassing value of knowing Christ Jesus my Lord" (Philippians 3:8, NRSVUE). Knowing Christ is the ultimate treasure. When we search the Scriptures or seek the biblical insights of wiser people, we are gathering and collecting precious insights that others will notice and benefit from.

We need to fill our hearts with upright teachings and Scripture that will strengthen us in the right moments. These truths will be ornaments that beautify our souls before others. Decorate the rooms of your heart today!

Father, I know that out of the abundance of my heart, my mouth speaks. May my soul be filled with beauty.

YF

MARCH 25

Timely advice is lovely, like golden apples in a silver basket.

Proverbs 25:11 (NLT)

According to one website, the song "Amazing Grace" has been recorded more than 6,600 times. It's sung at funerals and after tragedies, like the events of September 11, 2001. It was a regular song sung during the 2020 pandemic and is embraced by Christians and non-Christians alike, as well as being sung in a multitude of languages. But where did this song come from?

The composer, John Newton, wasn't always a Christian, he was once a rough seaman who smuggled slaves. But he met Christ, and his life was transformed. His journey with God didn't begin at that moment though, it started much earlier, at the feet of his mother, Elizabeth Newton, a committed Christian. While she suffered from tuberculosis, she spent her time reading the Bible and teaching her young son about Jesus. Elizabeth passed away when she was 27 and John was just seven, but the lessons she imparted stuck with him and eventually bore fruit. Elizabeth's story fulfills the wisdom of this proverb and the scripture that encourages us as mothers to instruct our children from an early age (Proverbs 22:6).

If you are a young mother, take the time to read the Bible with your children and discuss God with them, even amid the chaos of parenting. We don't know how much time we have on this earth, so every moment is precious. If you have a child who has drifted away from God, don't lose hope. Keep offering timely advice and trust that one day their heart will recognize God's love. In the meantime, love them and continue providing guidance.

Father, may my words be fitting for my children during their childhood and youth, engraving your Word in their hearts.

KO

March 26

Guide a horse with a whip, a donkey with a bridle, and a fool with a rod to his back!

Proverbs 26:3 (NLT)

Did you know that beasts of burden didn't exist in America until the Spaniards arrived? In ancient Mexico, people relied on *tamemes*—men who carried heavy loads. The first four donkeys arrived in Hispaniola with Christopher Columbus. Have you ever traveled on one of these animals?

When I participated in missionary training in the jungles of Chiapas, we faced a challenging 13-mile trek, with our feet sinking into muddy trails. It was exhausting; and so, we were thrilled when it was our turn to ride a mule. But I also felt anxious when the mules took us up steep paths or stubbornly refused to move. This is why bridles and whips are necessary, it makes them obey.

Just as some animals require force to comply, some foolish people do too. In biblical times, corporal punishment was common. If someone wouldn't learn through reason, they faced consequences. Today, in many countries, hitting people like this is a crime, but sometimes strong measures are necessary to address foolishness.

We know that if we act selfishly and rebelliously, God may use illness, accidents, or job loss to get our attention. Not every trial we experience is meant for correction, but if we have done something that displeases the Lord, we should recognize it! Let's not be like animals that need a "whip" to listen. Instead, let's heed the gentle voice of the Spirit of God guiding us.

My Father, sometimes I'm a daughter who doesn't listen to you. Help me to understand and obey you.

MH

MARCH 27

A continual dripping on a rainy day and a quarrelsome wife are alike...
                                          Proverbs 27:15 (ESV)

In my city there's a saying, "You seem like pottery from Amozoc." It refers to an overly sensitive person who gets upset over minor issues. We say she is "touchy," as if her heart could crack like fragile pottery.

A disagreeable person is often quarrelsome, and the root of her anger may come from deep-seated resentment. Resentment is a grudge that lingers even as time passes. It's like a woman who keeps a safe in her heart filled with hurtful words, offenses and betrayals. She keeps it locked because she doesn't want to forget or forgive what happened. Sometimes, she even revisits the contents, which only keeps her wounds open.

Mark 11:25 offers a cure for this heart: "And whenever you stand praying, forgive, if you have anything against anyone, so that your Father also who is in heaven may forgive you your trespasses" (ESV). Prayer can heal old wounds. Some pains can only be healed by God and forgiveness is the best balm.

Most of us want our homes to be pleasant, especially for those we live with. Are you holding onto something in your heart's safe? Decide to empty it and leave the past behind.

Lord, I open my heart so you can remove all that hurts. Heal my wounds.
   Today, I choose to forgive _____ for _____.

MG

MARCH 28

Whoever heeds instruction is a wise son, but whoever joins with wastrels disgraces his father.

Proverbs 28:7 (NABRE)

I once loved the show featuring Topo Gigio, a little mouse who sang, "Like my dad, like my dad, how nice it would be to look like my dad." As a girl, I admired my father and dreamed he would become president or something equally fantastic like that. I often boasted about him to my friends, inventing tales of his heroic deeds. But as I grew older, I realized he wasn't a hero and I longed for freedom from his authority.

Yet, I think of Jonathan, the son of Saul, who remained loyal to his father until the end, despite having a father who was not a good example. Jonathan performed great military feats, even though his father's impulsive decisions harmed his army and family. Johnathan may have had legitimate reasons for abandoning his father, but it seems Jonathan remembered the fifth commandment, the instruction that we would honor our parents.

Jonathan, the crown prince, knew that God would give the kingdom to David, and he supported that. His friendship with David was sincere, yet he stayed by his father's side until the last battle. David later lamented, "How beloved and gracious were Saul and Jonathan! They were together in life and in death" (2 Samuel 1:23, NLT).

Let us learn this lesson from Jonathan's life, that we would obey God's law, regardless of whether our parents deserve our respect or not. Always remember that we have the perfect Father in God and let's aspire to be like Him. If we wish to mirror our Father, what better way than to submit to His Word?

Lord, I want to be like you.

YF

March 29

The rod and reproof give wisdom, but a child left to himself brings shame to his mother.

Proverbs 29:15 (ESV)

The first mirrors were made from obsidian, copper, gold, and bronze. More than 6,000 years ago they existed in Persia and Turkey. By 400 BC glass was first used to reflect images in Lebanon. Today, we have multiple mirrors in our homes and even in our handbags to check our appearance. However, the most powerful mirror for truly seeing ourselves is our children.

Have you ever been told that your child is the spitting image of you? Children resemble us in many ways, not just physically. Their behaviors, preferences and values often reflect ours. They speak like us and share our priorities. They serve as real-time report cards—and not always for our positive traits.

Our proverb tells us that a spoiled child brings shame to their mother. So how can we be good mothers? If our children are our mirrors, then the answer lies in being good daughters of God. If He teaches, changes, and shapes us, our children will reflect Him too. In other words, let's be mirrors of Jesus, and we can say to our children what Paul said, "You should imitate me, just as I imitate Christ" (1 Corinthians 11:1, NLT).

How can we be good daughters of God? By accepting correction, being disciplined in studying the Bible and praying, and seeking God's guidance in our actions. Let's be worthy mirrors that others can look up to.

Lord, I want to be a good daughter of yours. Help me.

KO

March 30

Give me neither poverty nor riches! Give me just enough to satisfy my needs.

Proverbs 30:8 (NLT)

In 2019, it was reported that 184 million people in Latin America lived in poverty with 62 million living in extreme poverty. These numbers have likely risen in recent years. Do you consider yourself poor?

When my children were young there was a time, we felt poor. For several months, we couldn't afford gas for our stove, which limited our meals. We had to find creative ways to heat water for baths, which challenged us to walk more and explore new scenery outside the city. This period of our lives taught us to appreciate small blessings. We didn't have much, but we had enough to meet our needs.

The author of this proverb didn't want poverty or riches. He knew that extreme poverty endangers life and health. He also recognized that material abundance can lead us away from God and fill us with pride. Materialism often diminishes our appreciation for relationships and the daily delights God offers. The apostle Paul reminded Timothy, "So if we have enough food and clothing, let us be content" (1 Timothy 6:8, NLT).

Let this be our daily prayer: neither poverty nor riches, but just enough to live and be content.

Father, I thank you for the daily blessings you provide. Teach me to be content with them!

MH

March 31

An excellent wife who can find? She is far more precious than jewels.

Proverbs 31:10 (ESV)

The crown jewels are housed in the Tower of London: tiaras, crowns and scepters belonging to the kings and queens of England. Visitors can admire the world's largest diamonds, like the Cullinan and the Koh-i-Noor, which are part of Queen Elizabeth's crowns.

Legend has it that one of the wives of the Persian emperor Nader Shah described the "Koh-i-Noor" as follows: "If a strong man were to throw five stones—one to the north, one to the south, one to the east, one to the west, and one straight up—the space they create filled with gold and gems would equal the value of the Koh-i-Noor."

Can you imagine the value of a virtuous woman? Virtue is defined as a person's habitual disposition to do good, acting according to truth, justice and especially the fear of God. The writer of Proverbs believed that a woman of honor, integrity and excellence is hard to find, much like discovering a great diamond. Yet her worth far surpasses that of the most precious gems.

Polishing our character, qualities, and skills—along with our daily relationship with God—makes us even more valuable. Just as the value of precious stones depends on the cutting process, God wants to refine us like rough stones, revealing our royal worth. He removes our dullness and helps us shine as His daughters of royal lineage and as true precious stones.

Lord, help me to be prudent and virtuous. Like a diamond, I want to reflect your light.

MG

April 1

Because they hated knowledge, and the fear of the Lord they did not choose.

Proverbs 1:29 (NABRE)

The conquistador Hernán Cortés noted that when people entered the presence of Moctezuma, the emperor of Tenochtitlan, they lowered their heads and eyes, bowed before him, and spoke to him without looking at his face. When this proverb uses the phrase "the fear of the Lord," do you think this is the type of attitude the writer is imagining?

When we think of "fearing" a superior, we often associate it with words like reverence and respect. Humility also reflects how we should approach an all-powerful God. We can't be wise without cultivating humility before God's authority.

Eugene H. Peterson reminds us that humility comes from the Latin word for man, "humus," which reflects our origins: "For you were made from dust, and to dust you will return." (Genesis 3:19, NLT). Acknowledging our limitations, our smallness and our transient nature leads us to fear of God.

Many today reject wisdom because they choose not to fear God and ignore the reality that there is a Superior Being. In the past, the Aztecs showed humility before a mere man, but you and I can bow our hearts before the King of the universe, thus becoming wise.

Lord, grant me the humility to recognize your authority.

KO

April 2

For only the godly will live in the land, and those with integrity will remain in it.
Proverbs 2:21 (NLT)

The first time my family and I stayed in a five-star hotel my kids shouted, "We should live here forever!" Five days later, they wanted to go home. On another occasion, we stayed in a two-star hotel and the difference was stark. My husband encouraged us, "Be strong. It's only for two nights." Is your life more like a two-star hotel or five-star hotel?

You might be fortunate enough to live comfortably, or perhaps your life feels more like a one-star experience. Regardless, our life on Earth resembles a hotel stay—we are merely passing through. C.S. Lewis said, "Our Father refreshes us on the journey with some pleasant inns, but will not encourage us to mistake them for home."

Today's proverb reminds us that the godly will dwell in the land and remain in it. What land does this refer to? In Revelation we read, "Then I saw a new heaven and a new earth. The former heaven and the former earth had passed away… I heard a loud voice from the throne saying, 'Behold, God's dwelling is with the human race. He will dwell with them, and they will be his people, and God himself will always be with them [as their God]'" (Revelation 21:1, 3, NABRE).

If you have faith in Jesus, you are among the godly mentioned in this proverb. We are pilgrims on this Earth, here for only a brief time compared to eternity. Your hotel may be old or new, luxurious, or modest, but what truly matters is that your eternal home awaits you.

Father, help me remember that this is not my forever home. This house is temporary, but I have an eternal place prepared for me!

KO

APRIL 3

Honor the Lord with your wealth... Then will your barns be filled with plenty.

Proverbs 3:9-10 (NABRE)

What can you give someone who has everything? This is what the Duchess of Cambridge wondered when spending Christmas with Queen Elizabeth II, her husband's grandmother. She thought about what to give her own grandparents and decided to prepare something herself. She made homemade chutney, a sweet and spicy sauce from India that is quite popular in the UK. "I was a bit worried about it, but I noticed the next day that it was on the table," she recounted in her first television interview.

Something similar happens when we consider giving something to our Creator. There's nothing we can give to God that He needs. However, when we offer Him gifts, we're saying, "God, I love you. You are my priority," as Rick Warren puts it. Tithes and offerings are acts of worship. God doesn't want our leftovers; He wants to be at the center of our lives. When we do this, we see His promises fulfilled.

Malachi 3:10 is a promise: "Bring the full tithe into the storehouse, that there may be food in my house. And thereby put me to the test, says the Lord of hosts, if I will not open the windows of heaven for you and pour down for you a blessing until there is no more need" (ESV). When He sees our desire to obey His Word—even in our finances—He assures us, "I will bless you."

Our Father always gives us more than we can imagine. The King of kings provides according to the riches of His glory.

May my offering be a sweet aroma to you.

MG

April 4

Keep your heart with all vigilance, for from it flow the springs of life.
Proverbs 4:23 (ESV)

Marcela was a single mom. The man with whom she had two daughters abandoned her for another woman, leaving her heart bitter against him. When Marcela heard the Gospel, she wanted to follow Christ and for her daughters to love Him too. Initially, her relationship with God was strong and stable. However, resentment lingered in her heart against the man who deceived her. And although what she needed most was to depend on the Lord to learn wisdom, she chose to give her heart to someone else who promised her the moon and stars, again. Did that work out?

She thought her economic and emotional situation would finally improve, but her new partner took advantage of her, leading to problems and ultimately separation. Afterward, she trusted another man but faced the same outcome. She grew distant from the Lord and experienced more disappointment.

I believe this verse warns us about the dangers of giving others our hearts thoughtlessly. How wise is the Lord to instruct us to guard our hearts! We can't give our hearts to just anyone without ensuring they will be well cared for.

You may have experienced disappointment as well. If you've come to believe that no man is worthy of your heart, you're right—only the Lord, who created it, is deserving. Give your heart to Him and love Him above all else. You'll find that He cares for you and shows His love daily.

FaLord, may my heart be hidden in you, so that when a man finds me, he finds you first!

YF

April 5

You should reserve it for yourselves. Never share it with strangers.

Proverbs 5:17 (NLT)

Russell Conwell, in his book Acres of Diamonds, tells the story of a young man who searched for fortune only to die in the process. Meanwhile, someone else discovered diamonds in the yard behind his house. It's tragic because this young man wasted his energy and life, searching for something that was already at his home!

A colleague who has been divorced three times now admits that she shouldn't have given up on her first marriage. In seeking her soulmate, she abandoned the one who was her better half. When faced with the first issue, she neglected to appreciate the commitment and effort marriage requires, choosing separation instead.

Proverbs 5 warns us about what happens when we allow ourselves to be captivated by someone other than our spouse. What may seem like an exciting adventure can lead to loss of honor, anguish and even illness. That's why the wise writer advises us to "share your love only with your wife" (Proverbs 5:15, NLT), which can also apply to husbands.

Perhaps your marriage isn't what you envisioned at the start, but have you made any efforts to improve it? Don't search for precious jewels outside your home when you can find the diamond of a fulfilling relationship right under your roof. It takes effort, time, and determination, but with God, anything is possible!

Lord, help me recognize the diamonds in my home.

KO

April 6

Too much talk leads to sin. Be sensible and keep your mouth shut.
Proverbs 10:19 (NLT)

In the year 2000, I visited England for the first time and enjoyed afternoon tea. We were served small cucumber sandwiches and a variety of cookies on fine china. Between sips, we chatted about the weather—a common topic in England—and my future plans. What I remember most about my host, a woman in her 70s, is her willingness to embrace silence without rushing to fill the void.

I love the quote from Alice in Wonderland where the Mad Hatter asks, "Would you like an adventure now or shall we have tea first?" Have you ever shared a cup of tea or coffee with friends? Isn't it true that we often talk too much and share things that aren't ours to disclose?

Let's heed this proverb and learn to enjoy moments of silence. Friendship isn't defined by the number of words exchanged or the bustling atmosphere of a party; it can flourish in those comfortable moments of silence over a warm drink, where we listen, empathize and pray for one another.

Not every moment in life is an adventure, as the Hatter suggests. Sometimes, all we need is a cup of tea with a friend. Perhaps we can plan such a gathering this week, while remembering to be prudent and avoid excessive chatter.

Lord, teach me to watch over my words.

KO

APRIL 7

I saw among the simple ones, I observed among the youths, a young man without sense.

Proverbs 7:7 (NRSVUE)

Martha, a Christian girl, began dating a boy she met at church. Just days later, he left to study in another city. One day over the phone, he jokingly mentioned that he had new friends who decided to "welcome" him by hiring a prostitute. The boy bragged about his adventure, pressuring Martha to do the same the next time they met. Fortunately, she realized he was not a young man who loved God and ended the relationship. This boy resembles the foolish young man in Proverbs 7, who, enticed by the words of a beautiful but deceitful married woman, falls into sexual sin—a scenario Martha never imagined.

Years later, Martha was careful to thoroughly evaluate the young man she would eventually marry. She made sure to get to know him well and look for signs of integrity in his life. The Bible teaches us how to discern a person's true nature in Matthew 7:15-16, "You can identify them by their fruit, that is, by the way they act. Can you pick grapes from thornbushes, or figs from thistles?" (NLT).

One of today's most profitable underground businesses is prostitution and human trafficking. These industries wouldn't exist without high demand. Let's pray for women trapped in these networks and remain vigilant against the temptations that affect all men. If you're searching for a partner, ask God for wisdom to choose someone who demonstrates their faith through their actions.

Lord, we are in the world but not of it. May my light shine in the darkness that surrounds us.

MG

April 8

Mine is strength; I am understanding.

Proverbs 8:14 (NABRE)

Do you remember Moses before the burning bush? God gave him a mission, but he felt so insecure that he started making excuses and asking questions. "If I go to the Israelites and they ask me, 'What is the name of God?' what should I say?" God replied, "I am who I am. ... Thus, you shall say to the Israelites, 'I have sent me to you'" (see Exodus 3:13-14). Some think God avoided revealing His name, but "I am" is actually perfect. Our God exists in the present moment. It's said that for Him, there is no past or future—He simply is.

When Moses reminded the Israelites in Deuteronomy 4:15, "Since you saw no form when the Lord spoke to you at Horeb out of the fire, watch yourselves closely" (NRSVUE), God didn't want an image of Himself. Why? Because the perfect image of God, and the only one we truly need to remember, is the Lord Jesus.

Jesus embodies the image of God and is also the I AM. Do you remember what He said? "I am the vine." "I am the bread of life." "I am the gate." "I am the way." But we often forget today's verse: "Mine is strength; I am understanding." In our quest for wisdom, let's not forget to turn to the eternal I AM, the source of all understanding.

Don't make the mistake of following anyone else. No created being can match the greatness of this title—only our Lord Jesus can.

Lord Jesus, thank you for being the great I AM.

YF

April 9

She has sent her servants to invite everyone to come.

Proverbs 9:3 (NLT)

The British explorer Ernest Shackleton once recruited his crew with an advertisement that read: "Men wanted for hazardous journey. Low wages, bitter cold, long hours of complete darkness. Safe return doubtful. Honor and recognition in event of success." Despite the risks, he managed to gather an incredible group, and his story of survival remains well-known.

In today's proverb, Wisdom has prepared a banquet and sent out invitations to everyone. This invitation is even more inclusive than Shackleton's, with no preferences regarding gender, age, marital status, or occupation. It's open to all! The next verse even suggests that the naiver and lacking in judgment we are, the more welcome we'll be.

Shackleton didn't sugarcoat his invitation and neither does the Bible. The message of wisdom reminds us that the straight path is often fraught with challenges. We will face afflictions, both good days and bad. We won't be exempt from illness or financial struggles. We might encounter earthquakes, hurricanes, or tsunamis. Yet, Jesus, who invites us, adds an important note: "And be sure of this: I am with you always, even to the end of the age" (Matthew 28:20, NLT).

Life is not easy; no one escapes trials, problems, and disagreements. Illness and the loss of loved ones are unavoidable. Nevertheless, Wisdom invites us to her banquet, where we find a significant difference: God's presence is with us, through both good and tough times. Do you accept?

Lord, we are in the world but not of it. May my light shine in the darkness that surrounds us.

KO

April 10

The blessing of the Lord makes a person rich, and he adds no sorrow with it.
Proverbs 10:22 (NLT)

John Ruskin, a leading art critic in England in 1876, believed that Lilias Trotter could have been one of the most famous painters of her time if she had dedicated herself to art. However, God had other plans. Lilias realized she couldn't pursue art and seek God's kingdom simultaneously, so she followed His call and traveled to Algeria as a missionary. Was this a waste?

Perhaps Ruskin thought so, but her work with girls and women in Algeria made a lasting impact. For 40 years, she brought light and life to the Arab Muslim people. Her art continues to inspire us, as well as her writings which offer comfort.

Today's proverb tells us that God's blessing brings true riches. These riches might not be material; instead, they could be the hearts we've touched and the lives we've changed. The proverb concludes by stating that God does not add sorrow to His blessings, as what He gives us comes as a divine gift. The question is: Are we able to recognize God's blessings?

Lilias could have filled galleries with her paintings, but she chose to seek lost souls instead. She faced challenges and health issues, and her ministry was not without pain. But throughout her life she experienced the blessings of God, which bring no sorrow, until her dying day.

Lord, thank you for the blessings you give me. Help me to recognize and appreciate them.

KO

April 11

The crooked in heart are an abomination to the Lord, but those who walk blamelessly are his delight.

Proverbs 11:20 (NABRE)

Human beings often seek to impress those we consider important or of higher status. The peoples conquered by Pharaoh sent tributes to win his favor. The Aztecs sacrificed beautiful maidens to please their gods. In medieval times, jesters entertained kings to keep them happy. Today, devotees of the Virgin of Fatima in Portugal or the Virgin of Guadalupe in Mexico walk long distances on their knees to earn her favor or fulfill a vow.

Our good God doesn't require any of this. He takes pleasure in those who walk with integrity. God the Father was so pleased when Jesus was baptized by John that He publicly expressed His delight.

"For it is loyalty that I desire, not sacrifice, and knowledge of God rather than burnt offerings," says Hosea 6:6 (NABRE). The self-punishment some people inflict during Holy Week serves no purpose, nor do the fasts we undertake while harboring "little sins" and "white lies."

"This is my beloved daughter, in whom I am well pleased." Will those be the words the Lord says about us?

I want to please you, Lord Jesus, and to express my love through my actions.

MG

April 12

From the fruit of their mouths people have their fill of good, and the works of their hands come back upon them.
Proverbs 12:14 (NABRE)

Charles Perrault told the story of a widow with two daughters. The older daughter was moody and selfish, while the younger resembled her father, being sweet and friendly. One day, the younger daughter, who was often mistreated, met an old woman at the spring where she collected water. The woman asked for a drink and the girl immediately offered her some. The old woman then transformed into a fairy and gave the girl a gift: every time she would speak a flower, or a jewel would come from her mouth. When the mother saw the diamonds coming out of her younger daughter's mouth, she sent the older daughter to fetch water. What happened next?

The older daughter refused to give the old woman water, and because of her poor attitude, the old woman cursed her: every time she opened her mouth, snakes or toads would come out. Which daughter do you identify with?

God places immense value on our words. He wants us to use our speech to gather blessings, like flowers and jewels. Romans 10:9 reminds us that "if you confess with your mouth that Jesus is Lord and believe in your heart that God raised Him from the dead, you will be saved" (ESV). By confessing with your mouth that Jesus is your Lord you can receive salvation.

Heavenly Father, help me to watch my words.

YF

APRIL 13

The righteous have enough to satisfy their appetite, but the belly of the wicked is empty.

Proverbs 13:25 (NRSVUE)

According to statistics, 38% of women and 27% of men in Mexico suffer from obesity. In Peru, one in four women is overweight. The Dominican Republic has the highest obesity rate in women after Mexico. In the United States, nearly 35 million women are overweight. Let's carefully consider today's proverb. How can we apply it to our daily lives?

Notice what it tells us about food. The righteous person eats until they're satisfied. We know that we gain weight when we consume more than we should. Our bodies are designed for a certain amount of food, but due to stress, bad habits or cravings, we often eat more than we need. Eating more leads our bodies to demand even more.

A fool will always find themselves in need. When we act foolishly and don't monitor our weight, we'll always feel "hungry." Let's examine our habits and emotions. Many eating problems—whether obesity or anorexia—arise when we feel anxious or sad and we try to fill that emptiness with food. What can we do? We should remember that God "gives life and breath to everything, and he satisfies every need" (Acts 17:25, NLT).

Let's ask God for help daily regarding our eating habits. Let's listen to our bodies and eat until we're satisfied. And when we feel that "there is still a little room," let's pray and ask God to fill it with His love, peace and self-control. Obesity is a complex issue, but if we are wise, we should seek help and learn to manage ourselves.

Lord, you satisfy me more than a sumptuous banquet.

KO

April 14

Whoever walks in uprightness fears the Lord, but he who is devious in his ways despises him.

Proverbs 14:2 (ESV)

In the 21st century it's hard to get lost with mobile apps that guide us to our destinations. These apps indicate the most direct route or the one with the least traffic and can alert us to roadblocks. It's no longer necessary to memorize routes or jot down directions. But things can still go awry!

Once, an Uber driver, following his app's instructions, took me down an unpaved street and ended up in a pothole so deep that we couldn't move forward. The road construction wasn't finished! At other times, inaccurate Google Maps directions made me difficult to find, leaving me stranded while I waited for a ride. Even with all this technology there are no guarantees.

With God, there are no mistakes. He always leads us along the right path if we fear the Lord and trust in His Word. In John 10, Jesus describes Himself as the Good Shepherd whose sheep hear His voice and follow Him. His voice is more reliable than any app and He provides direction in all areas of our lives. Those who only follow their own internal app or personal instincts will make mistakes and face difficulties.

You and I have probably ignored the Lord's teachings at some point and suffered the consequences. Sometimes we take the easy way out instead of waiting for God to reveal the best route to reach our destination. In the decisions we make today, let's be careful to seek God for "the right way."

Master, teach me and guide me to follow your path and not mine today.

MH

April 15

The sacrifice of the wicked is an abomination to the Lord, but the prayer of the upright is his delight.

Proverbs 15:8 (NRSVUE)

One of the things I cherish most in life is chatting with my best friend, my husband. I remember when we were dating and spent hours on the phone without realizing how much time had passed. We only noticed when dawn broke and the birds began to sing!

Spending time with someone you love and can open your heart to is a beautiful experience. You know they genuinely care about you and enjoy your company as much as you enjoy theirs.

This is precisely what happens when we pray. Our Lord rejoices in this communion. Although we are imperfect, He sees us as redeemed, justified, and sanctified through His Son. He is a friend who knows us and calls us by name. "I do not call you servants any longer, because the servant does not know what the master is doing, but I have called you friends, because I have made known to you everything that I have heard from my Father" (John 15:15, NRSVUE).

How much do you enjoy talking with Jesus? Do you keep your appointments with Him? He reaches out His hand to support and rejoice with you. He knocks on the door and invites you to dine with Him. What could be more important than that? Open the door every day!

Thank you, Jesus, for showing me your friendship. I want to reciprocate and grow closer to you each day.

MG

April 16

For I speak the truth and detest every kind of deception.
                                      Proverbs 8:7 (NLT)

It's common to hear the phrase "on my honor." This expression implies that a person's reputation is at stake if they fail to keep their word.

Once, I was with a group of women and we were discussing who was more reliable in keeping promises. One of the ladies with great enthusiasm said, "We women have a 'woman's word.'" We laughed at her funny way of saying it, but in the end, we agreed that if we, as ladies, keep our word to protect our reputation, how much more will God keep His?

In this proverb, God addresses us with seriousness: "I speak truth and detest every kind of deception." God cannot lie; it goes against His very nature. If we feel insulted when others accuse us of lacking integrity, how much more does it hurt our Lord when we doubt His Word?

I wish our hearts were sheets of gold where we engrave this proverb with a chisel. While we may be committed to our reputation, believing what God says in the Bible means recognizing it as the "Word of God." God's reputation is tied to everything He tells us in the Bible, for "God is not a man, so he does not lie. He is not human, so he does not change his mind. Has he ever spoken and failed to act? Has he ever promised and not carried it through?" (Numbers 23:19, NLT).

Lord, thank you for your unwavering truth. I can trust your words completely.

YF

APRIL 17

Grandchildren are the crowning glory of the aged.

Proverbs 17:6 (NLT)

Do you know when Grandparents' Day is celebrated? Surprisingly, there's a special day dedicated to honoring our grandparents! In the United States it falls on September 8, in Mexico it's celebrated on August 28 and in Argentina on July 26. Despite these dates on the calendar, many of us often overlook this occasion. However, even though I'm not a grandmother yet, I believe every day is a wonderful opportunity to celebrate grandchildren!

I vividly remember the day my grandfather Ronaldo passed away. The pain, tears and shock of that moment are forever etched in my heart. I can recall every detail of that day, from the morning's calm to the afternoon's heart-wrenching goodbye as he took his last breath. Yet, amidst the sorrow, I hold onto the memory of hugging my *abuelita*, who whispered to me, "He was so proud of you."

Lois, a grandmother mentioned in the Bible, must have felt a similar pride for her grandson Timothy. He remained faithful to the teachings he received, knowing they were true because he trusted his mother and grandmother, who instilled in him "the holy Scriptures from childhood, and they have given you the wisdom to receive the salvation that comes by trusting in Christ Jesus" (2 Timothy 3:15, NLT).

You may not have had a grandmother like Lois, or perhaps you haven't been the pride of your grandparents. However, God willing, you may have the opportunity to become a grandmother one day, imparting the Word of God to your grandchildren. Seize every chance to be a model of faith, nurturing them with biblical knowledge and being an example of sincere faith.

Father, may my grandchildren crown me with glory, not through their achievements, but by being faithful to Your Word.

APRIL 18

Whoever is slack in his work is a brother to him who destroys.

Proverbs 18:9 (ESV)

In biblical times many people lived by manual labor, either in the fields or in the trades. Today, however, many work in offices, schools or behind computers. The home office has become extremely popular.

Seventy-seven percent of employees say they are more productive working from home, while 23% say they actually work longer hours in that environment. While there are advantages to remote work, there can also be more distractions, making it harder for supervisors to monitor productivity.

This proverb highlights two types of workers: the destructive and the negligent. In Matthew 25:14-30 we read about the parable of the talents where a servant buried the money given to him by his master instead of investing it. The master rebuked him saying, "You wicked and lazy servant!" (Matthew 25:26, NLT). Often, the less obvious but all too common sins are those of negligence—failing to obey the Lord's commands.

Consider this: Did I help that person in need on the street? Did I promise to check in on a lonely elderly person and then forget? Did I neglect to tell a desperate friend that God can help her and that I would pray for her? Did I avoid volunteering for that needed role at church? Each of us knows where we've been negligent. Let's reflect on our progress in the most important area: advancing God's kingdom on Earth!

My Father, I often struggle with disobedience. Help me understand, help me trust you and help me do your will.

MH

April 19

My child, stop ignoring instruction, straying from words of knowledge.

Proverbs 19:27 (NRSVUE)

A century ago, high school students studied Oparin's theory of the origin of life and Darwin's theories on evolution. Today, students debate cloning and surrogacy as means of procreation. What was once new is now commonplace. It is a part of life to read horoscopes, to decorate homes according to feng shui and seek daily motivation in New Age books.

Society has strayed from true wisdom. The enemy of our souls has cleverly used media as a tool of indoctrination. Films subtly introduce ideas that seem appealing but can lead us away from God's truth. These concepts gradually take root in our minds until we accept them as the new normal.

The reality is that our citizenship is in heaven. We don't have to live like "normal" people in this postmodern world. The apostle Peter recognized the struggles believers face when he wrote: "I urge you as aliens and sojourners to keep away from worldly desires that wage war against the soul" (1 Peter 2:11, NABRE).

It is television shows with flashy plots, movies with high-tech effects and music that stirs our emotions. Not everything is harmful, but not everything is edifying either. Let's ask for divine wisdom to sift through it all and retain only what is good.

I will guard my eyes, my ears, and my mind so I do not sin against you.

MG

April 20

Take the garment of one who has given surety for a stranger; seize the pledge given as surety for foreigners.

Proverbs 20:16 (NRSVUE)

Surety is a term used in civil matters. It is a person who agrees to pay a debt if the debtor fails to do so.

In a seminar on finance, I learned that people often assume they can manage the future, making business decisions based on what they hope will happen. When we act as someone's guarantor, we risk our wealth, our relationships and even our emotional well-being—especially if we die and our family is left to pay the debt.

Today's verse teaches us that to achieve financial freedom, we must avoid acting as guarantors for others. This can be difficult, especially when close friends ask for help. It's essential to explain to them why God's Word advises against this.

If you're currently a guarantor for someone, seek God's wisdom for your specific situation. Ask for guidance and look for ways to extricate yourself from the arrangement.

Father, grant me wisdom in financial matters.

YF

APRIL 21

The wise man saves for the future, but the foolish man spends whatever he gets.

Proverbs 21:20 (NLT)

In 2014, I watched a documentary about lottery winners. Many of them became instant millionaires but ended up broke just a few years later. They spent their money on extravagant purchases, lavish lifestyles, and helping friends and family, only to find themselves in dire financial situations again. Many regretted not having saved any of their winnings.

This illustrates today's proverb, which emphasizes the importance of saving for the future. Wise individuals recognize that financial security requires planning and discipline. They understand that true wealth isn't just about what you have right now; it's about preparing for tomorrow.

On the other hand, the foolish person spends every penny they receive without considering the future. This kind of mindset can lead to unnecessary stress and hardship down the road.

Are you being wise with your resources? Are you saving for emergencies or future needs? It's essential to strike a balance between enjoying what you have now and preparing for what lies ahead.

Lord, help me to be wise with my finances and to save for the future.

MG

April 22

A fool takes no pleasure in understanding, but only in expressing his opinion.
Proverbs 18:2 (ESV)

In our world today, opinions are abundant and often shared loudly—whether on social media or in everyday conversations. It seems that everyone has something to say about everything, but few take the time to seek understanding before speaking.

This proverb reminds us that a fool doesn't care about understanding; they're only interested in sharing their perspective. This can lead to misunderstandings, conflict and division among friends and family.

In contrast, the wise strive to listen and seek understanding before voicing their opinions. They ask questions and try to understand other people's perspectives. This approach not only fosters better communication but also strengthens relationships.

Are you quick to express your opinion, or do you take the time to listen and understand? Let's strive to be wise by seeking to understand the real matter of things before we speak.

Father, help me to listen more and speak less, seeking understanding in all my conversations.

YF

April 23

A cheerful heart is good medicine, but a crushed spirit dries up the bones.

Proverbs 17:22 (NLT)

Laughter is often referred to as the best medicine. It can lighten our moods and lift our spirits, even during challenging times. The Bible reinforces this idea, teaching us that a cheerful heart is beneficial for our well-being.

When we focus on the good things in life, we cultivate a positive attitude that can impact our health and relationships. In contrast, a crushed spirit leads to despair and can even affect our physical health.

Have you ever noticed how being around cheerful people can brighten your day? Their positive energy can be contagious! On the other hand, negativity can weigh us down, making it hard to find joy.

Let's choose to cultivate a cheerful heart, sharing joy with those around us. Find reasons to laugh, celebrate and be grateful each day.

Lord, help me to maintain a cheerful heart and to spread joy to those around me.

MG

April 24

The heart of the discerning acquires knowledge, and the ears of the wise seek it out.

Proverbs 18:15 (NIV)

In an age of information overload, it's crucial to be discerning about what knowledge we pursue. With so many sources available, we must develop the ability to filter out what is truly valuable and beneficial for our growth.

A discerning heart seeks knowledge and is always eager to learn. Wise individuals don't just accept information at face value; they dig deeper, asking questions and seeking understanding. This habit enriches their lives and helps them make informed decisions.

In contrast, those who are foolish ignore wisdom and remain stagnant in their understanding. They miss out on the growth that comes from seeking knowledge and engaging with different perspectives.

What steps can you take today to cultivate a discerning heart? Make it a priority to seek knowledge, whether through reading, conversations, or prayer.

Father, give me a discerning heart that seeks after knowledge and understanding.

YF

April 25

The wise woman builds her house, but the foolish tears it down with her own hands.

Proverbs 14:1 (NLT)

A wise woman recognizes that her home is more than just a physical structure; it's a place of love, safety and growth. She invests her time and energy in nurturing her family, creating a positive environment where everyone can thrive.

On the other hand, a foolish woman undermines her own home through negative words, actions, or attitudes. She may not realize how her behavior affects her family, but her choices can lead to discord and destruction.

As women, we have the power to build up or tear down our households. Let's strive to be wise in our choices, fostering an atmosphere of love, respect and encouragement.

What can you do today to build up your home? Consider how your words and actions contribute to a positive environment for your family.

Lord, help me to be a wise builder of my home, creating a space filled with love and support.

MG

April 26

The way of the wicked is like darkness; they do not know over what they stumble.

Proverbs 4:19 (NRSVUE)

Darkness can be disorienting, making it hard to see the obstacles in our path. Just like walking in the dark can lead to stumbling and falling, a life lived in wickedness can lead to confusion and missteps.

Wickedness often blinds us to the consequences of our actions. Those who walk in darkness may not recognize the dangers they face or the pain they cause to themselves and others. They may think they're navigating life just fine, but they're unaware of the pitfalls ahead.

In contrast, the wise walk in the light, guided by God's Word. They see clearly and can avoid the traps that lead to destruction. As believers, we are called to shine our light in the world, helping others see the truth and find their way.

Are there areas in your life where you've been walking in darkness? It's never too late to seek the light of God's truth and guidance.

Father, help me to walk in your light and to shine that light for others.

YF

April 27

A soft answer turns away wrath, but a harsh word stirs up anger.
Proverbs 15:1 (ESV)

In moments of conflict, it's easy to respond with harsh words. But the Proverbs teach us that a gentle response can diffuse tension and prevent escalation.

Think back to a time when you responded softly during a heated conversation. How did it change the atmosphere? A soft answer cannot only calm the other person but also help you maintain your composure and avoid saying something you might regret later.

On the other hand, a harsh word can ignite anger and lead to further conflict. It can create a cycle of negativity that's hard to break.

Let's practice giving soft answers, especially in difficult situations. Our words hold power; we can choose to use them to build bridges rather than walls.

Lord, help me to respond gently and wisely, turning away anger with my words.

MG

April 28

He who goes about as a talebearer reveals secrets, but he who is trustworthy in spirit keeps a thing covered.

Proverbs 11:13 (NKJV)

Gossip can spread like wildfire, damaging reputations, and relationships. A "talebearer" is someone who shares secrets or private information, often without considering the consequences.

Trustworthy people, on the other hand, understand the importance of discretion. They know when to keep things confidential and protect the privacy of others. In a world where gossip is prevalent, being a person of integrity is vital.

When someone shares a secret with you, it's a sign of trust. Let's honor that trust by keeping their confidence and not spreading their stories.

Are there areas in your life where you've struggled with gossip? Commit to being a trustworthy person who respects the privacy of others.

Father, help me to be a keeper of secrets and to honor the trust placed in me.

YF

April 29

A joyful heart is good medicine, but a crushed spirit dries up the bones.

Proverbs 17:22 (ESV)

Laughter is often said to be the best medicine. It can uplift our spirits and provide relief during tough times. Today's Proverb reinforces this idea, teaching us that a joyful heart contributes to our overall well-being.

When we focus on the positive aspects of life, we cultivate an attitude that impacts our health and relationships. Conversely, a crushed spirit can lead to despair and affect our physical health.

Have you noticed how being around cheerful people can brighten your day? Their positive energy is contagious! On the flip side, negativity can weigh us down, making it difficult to find joy.

Let's choose to cultivate a joyful heart and share that joy with those around us. Find reasons to laugh, celebrate, and be grateful every day.

Lord, help me to maintain a joyful heart and spread happiness to those around me.

MG

April 30

A wise son hears his father's instruction, but a scoffer does not listen to rebuke.
Proverbs 13:1 (ESV)

As a child, I often heard the phrase, "You'll understand when you're older." At the time, I thought my parents were just being difficult. But now, as an adult, I realize the wisdom behind their words. They were trying to guide me, helping me learn valuable lessons through their experiences.

It's easy to dismiss the advice and corrections of our parents, especially when we think we know better. Yet, Proverbs reminds us that a wise son listens to his father's instruction, recognizing that experience often brings insight.

On the other hand, a scoffer disregards wise counsel, believing they have all the answers. This attitude can lead to mistakes and missed opportunities for growth.

Let's strive to be wise by listening to those who care about us and learning from their experiences.

Father, help me be receptive to instruction and value the wisdom of those around me.

YF

May 1

They may say, "Come and join us. ... Just for fun, let's ambush the innocent!".

Proverbs 1:11 (NLT)

I still remember the horror I felt while reading *The Guest List* by Lucy Foley. This thriller portrays evil in various forms, especially through one character who abuses others throughout his life. What disturbed me most was his ability to deceive everyone with his angelic facade while inviting them to join him in his wicked deeds.

Bullying is a reality in our world. Have you ever been urged to "ambush the innocent" in school hallways? What makes some individuals targets for others? Is it their physical appearance, personality, or socioeconomic status? The parent in this proverb bluntly advises: "Don't give in! Say no!"

Jesus serves as a model against bullying, engaging everyone and defending the weak, like when He intervened on behalf of the woman accused of adultery. He made it clear that He would not break a bruised reed or extinguish a smoldering wick (see Matthew 12:20).

Let's not indulge in harming others "just for fun." Teach your children, nieces, nephews or grandchildren not to engage in bullying. Speak out against it and report those who do it. In the novel I mentioned at the beginning, the greatest tragedy lay in those who remained silent and did not stand up to the bully. If they had, fewer people would have been hurt. Let's take action!

Lord, do not allow me ever to prey on the innocent.

KO

May 2

Search for them as you would for silver; seek them like hidden treasures.
Proverbs 2:4 (NLT)

There are many sayings that speak about "treasure." One states: "Between hidden treasure and hidden wisdom, there's no difference." Could it be that the person who said that had Solomon's proverbs in mind?

Have you ever lost something at home? Sometimes, we make a quick search, and when we don't find it, we feel frustrated. However, if we look more closely, we often discover hidden treasures—items we haven't seen in a long time or items we thought were lost! Could it be that we approach wisdom with a superficial search as well?

As imperfect beings we often need understanding and discernment. This proverb encourages us to seek wisdom as if it were "hidden treasures," for it's not always readily available. Jesus told a parable about a woman who, after losing one of her ten silver coins, lit a lamp and searched her entire house carefully until she found it (Luke 15:8).

God is the source of wisdom and His most regular way of sharing that wisdom with us is His Word. But how diligently do we seek it? Even those who aim to read the Scriptures daily sometimes stop at "what counts for today," feeling they've completed their duty. How often do we meditate on the Word, pray with it in mind and ask God for personal insight? Let's make an effort to "sweep well" and uncover what He wants to teach us.

Father, help me seek You with all my heart and search for Your treasures that may enlighten my daily journey.

MH

May 3

The Lord by wisdom founded the earth, established the heavens by understanding.

Proverbs 3:19 (NABRE)

"Biology is the study of complicated things that appear to be designed with purpose," states scientist Richard Dawkins. From our faith perspective, we might respond, "Perhaps the world appears designed because it was created by God." Beyond biology, fields like cosmology, physics, biochemistry, and astronomy provide evidence of God's design.

Sean McDowell, a professor at Biola University, illustrates this with a simple example: If we wandered into a forest and discovered an abandoned cabin filled with our favorite song, food, and book, we would conclude that someone had prepared all these details for us. Isn't it the same with the universe? Someone knew we were coming and took care of everything.

We are not products of chance. Everything has been created by God and everything He made has a purpose. "The heavens declare the glory of God, and the sky above proclaims his handiwork. Day to day pours out speech, and night to night reveals knowledge" (Psalm 19:1-2, ESV).

How admirable is His greatness and power! If we understand where we come from and our purpose, we will know how to live. No one is an accident; you are a valuable person created in the image of God, designed for a special purpose.

God, help me to appreciate Your creation and to live with the awareness that You have made a world full of details for me.

MG

May 4

Hear, my son, and receive my words, and the years of your life shall be many.
Proverbs 4:10 (NABRE)

Journalist Carolina Benzamat hosted a series called *Los Superhumanos, secretos de longevidad* (Super-humans: Secrets of Longevity), interviewing individuals over 105 to uncover the secrets behind their long lives. Initially focused on Chile, her research extended to regions known for their elderly populations.

The documentary reveals that many people who live long lives have goals and projects they're actively pursuing, even in their advanced age. Others maintain strict diets of fish and leafy vegetables, like *ashitaba*. They also found that people who cultivate spirituality through religion or regularly attend a church live longer.

Isn't this what we all seek? Sometimes, we underestimate God's promises. This proverb teaches that hearing, believing, and obeying His Word is the best way to achieve happiness and peace, regardless of our circumstances. Believers should be the happiest and longest-lived people on earth.

Healthy eating and exercise are essential; but having peace in our souls and loving relationships also contribute to longevity. Let's listen to God's promises.

"How I love your law, Lord! I study it all day long" (Psalm 119:97, NABRE).

YF

May 5

Should your water sources be dispersed abroad, streams of water in the streets?

Proverbs 5:16 (NABRE)

The day the #MeToo hashtag was created it was used over 200,000 times on Twitter. In just one year, it appeared 19 million times—more than 55,000 times each day. This movement, initiated by activist and survivor Tarana Burke, went viral following the Harvey Weinstein lawsuits. While it advocates against sexual abuse and harassment, it also highlights the importance of our sexuality.

Today's proverb cautions us not to waste the water of our spring. Our intimacy is sacred; it encompasses not only the physical but also our emotions and our very essence. God cares about our sexuality and invites us to protect it, ensuring it is not squandered.

God designed us to enjoy intimacy, which is likened to a rippling spring that brings pleasure. Yet, this spring can become muddied. That is not His plan. That was never His plan. Thankfully, He is the expert at making things clean again: "Then I will sprinkle clean water on you, and you will be clean. Your filth will be washed away" (Ezekiel 36:25, NTV).

If our waters have become muddied due to poor choices or abuse, God offers us second chances. Let's approach Him for cleansing and purification, asking Him to help us enjoy the gift of sexuality as He intended it: within marriage.

Lord, cleanse me and purify my understanding of sex.

KO

May 6

Though they have no prince or governor or ruler to make them work, they labor hard all summer, gathering food for the winter.

Proverbs 6:7-8 (NLT)

In some cultures, people address each other by their first name, even their bosses, though in some settings they may use the more formal "sir." In the USA people add their educational credentials to their name to covey respect to themselves for their educational achievements and in some cases to be distinguished from the rest of society (John Smith, M.A., Jane Doe, PhD.).

This proverb marvels at the organization of ants, who work diligently "without prince, governor, or ruler." *A View of Life in an Ant Colony* (a Blog response by Entomologist Chris William, 2012) reveals that ants help each other out and share food with other members of the colony. Although they have queens, their role is not to rule over the colony but to produce more ants.

The New Testament emphasizes that we are all equal before God, co-laborers in building His kingdom. All believers are "kings and priests unto God," each possessing unique spiritual gifts that complement one another. We are part of one body (see 1 Corinthians 12:12) and when we collaborate, everyone is nourished, including new believers.

Do I insist on doing things my way or do I prioritize the unity of my family, my team at work or my church? Will imposing my ideas really lead to better outcomes? Let's strive to be collaborative and egalitarian, like ants.

Father, help me to work as a team for the good of all.

MH

May 7

That they may keep you from a stranger, from the foreign woman with her smooth words.

Proverbs 7:5 (NABRE)

Lucy and René Zapata were a beloved couple in ministry in Latin America. Lucy is now with the Lord, leaving behind an example of how a virtuous woman treats her husband. She affectionately called him by a pet name, yet when speaking to others, she referred to him as "Pastor Zapata." This balance of love and respect conveyed a powerful message.

In my 28 years of marriage, I've observed how other women address my husband. Some are respectful and kind, while others use "smooth words" that come off a bit flirtatious. This has reminded me of the importance of how I speak to him; I want to be the person who meets his needs for love, appreciation, and respect.

I admire Sarah, Abraham's wife, who treated her husband with respect: "Thus Sarah obeyed Abraham and called him lord. You have become her daughters as long as you do what is good and never let fears alarm you" (1 Peter 3:6, NRSVUE).

If we are married, let us learn the art of love and respect, as Sarah and Lucy did. Do you have a special name for your husband? If you're single, consider how to protect your future marriage from outside influences. Thank God for marriages that exemplify these virtues.

Father, bless my marriage. Help me to respect and wisely love my husband.

MG

May 8

Playing over the whole of his earth, having my delight with human beings.
                                        Proverbs 8:31 (NABRE)

I love to imagine God playing with Adam in the Garden of Eden—and so it was! Our God is playful, He loves to laugh, and He has a sense of humor. He delighted in creating man in his image and cherished his time with man in the Garden.

What parent doesn't enjoy seeing their children happy and joining in their games? Can you envision the love on the Lord's face as He watches us and smiles at our creativity? After buying a toy for our little ones, we often sit down to play with them. I believe God smiled at Adam's every idea as he named the animals, surely participating in his joy.

Our Lord desires to enjoy us and longs for our company. This verse is so expressive; it brings joy to know that God delights in us, doesn't it? The English Standard Version puts it beautifully: "rejoicing in his inhabited world and delighting in the children of man."

The Christian life differs significantly from worldly perceptions. Enjoying God far surpasses any pleasure the world can offer. While the world may view God as boring, they have yet to experience His intimacy. May we all embrace the joyful and playful nature of our God, inviting others to know Him too!

Lord, thank You for delighting in creating me.

YF

May 9

"Come in with me," she urges the simple.

Proverbs 9:4 (NLT)

When Alice visits Wonderland, she finds herself in a hall filled with locked doors. She tries door after door after door. She does this because doors lead to new places, and she doesn't want to remain stuck in that hallway. It's only when she discovers a tiny golden key that she can escape into a beautiful garden.

In life we also encounter doors. This chapter of Proverbs presents two: the door of wisdom and the door of foolishness. Both invite us to enter. But what awaits us behind them? If we choose the door of foolishness we find death, for its guests dwell deep in the grave. How tragic! But what lies beyond the door of wisdom?

The most crucial door in our lives isn't a wooden one; it's a person—Wisdom Himself. Jesus said, "Yes, I am the gate. Those who come in through me will be saved. They will come and go freely and will find good pastures" (John 10:9, NLT). By choosing the gate of salvation that Jesus offers, we enter a beautiful garden—one even better than Alice's!

Don't ignore the most important invitation of your life. Jesus is the door. He stands at the door and says, "If you hear my voice and open the door, I will come in, and we will share a meal together as friends" (Revelation 3:20). Open that door today!

Jesus, thank You for being the door. I desire to enter the pastures You have prepared for me.

KO

MAY 10

A wise child brings joy to a father; a foolish child brings grief to a mother.
Proverbs 10:1 (NLT)

Parents often boast about their children's high grades, awards, or lucrative jobs. However, these accomplishments don't necessarily reflect character. We all know of children who have caused great pain to their parents.

King David had many sons, but Solomon was chosen as his successor. Before David died, he charged Solomon: "Keep the mandate of the Lord, your God, walking in his ways" (1 Kings 2:3, NABRE). This was his greatest desire as a father and believer—that his son would be wise and righteous. Unfortunately, another son, Absalom, rebelled against him, seeking to seize the throne, and bringing great sorrow to David. As king David fled his city he wept, accompanied by "all the people" (2 Samuel 15:30, NRSVUE). What foolishness and what sorrow that son caused his father!

"A wise child brings joy to a father." The Hebrew word used here is kjacam, meaning "wise in mind, word and deed." This individual is teachable, sensible, prudent, and God-centered. In contrast, the fool is rebellious, disregarding the wisdom of her elders and God.

If our parents are alive, let's strive to make wise decisions that bring them joy. Remember the valuable advice they gave us as children and pass it on to our children, nieces, nephews, or grandchildren. Let's avoid the path of foolishness, which brings harm and heartache to those we love.

My Father, I want You to rejoice over me. Help me to obey and please You.

MH

MAY 11

Justice leads toward life,
but pursuit of evil leads to death

Proverbs 11:19 (NABRE)

It is well-known that some famous heavy metal and rock singers openly embrace Satanism. Their lyrics often invoke or glorify evil and sometimes even encourage self-harm.

Marilyn Manson, for instance, released an album titled *Antichrist Superstar.* The founder of the Church of Satan called him "Reverend" for promoting satanic themes in his music. Manson and his band have been blamed for influencing the tragic Columbine High School shooting, which resulted in 15 deaths. In the late 1990s, a mother accused Manson of inciting her son to commit suicide, as his song "Antichrist Superstar" was playing when he was found dead.

The troubling aspect of this is that when we consume music, movies or shows that glorify death or satanic themes, we are following those who lead us down a dangerous path, as today's proverb warns. Many lives have been lost due to drug overdoses! One poor choice often leads to another.

Let us choose to follow the righteous paths of obedience and reverence for God, which lead to abundant life—not just in this temporary existence but also in eternity. Who do we follow in our social circles? Who are the "influencers" we admire? Let us prioritize following Jesus above all.

Jesus, I have decided to follow you. I will not turn back. My eyes are set on you.

MG

May 12

The vexation of a fool is known at once, but the prudent ignores an insult.
Proverbs 12:16 (ESV)

I have a jewelry chest that I brought from Spain. It is handmade using an inlay technique where small geometric pieces of wood, mother-of-pearl or metal are arranged to create a beautiful mosaic. The chest stands on four wooden legs shaped like tiny spheres, and I have cherished it for many years.

One day, I came home to find my jewelry box out of place. My sister had accidentally knocked it over, breaking off one of the legs. To hide the damage, she leaned it against the wall. Unfortunately for her, I discovered her ruse and was very upset. I would have preferred if she had simply told me what happened so I could look for the missing leg. I remembered seeing a small wooden ball while sweeping that I had thought was insignificant and had thrown it away. I had been saving my anger for when I would confront my sister.

However, I decided to heed today's proverb and let go of the insult. I reminded myself that my relationship with my sister is far more valuable than a broken leg on a jewelry box. I may not be able to replace the leg, but I believe the Lord is honored when I choose to obey His Word rather than give in to anger.

How do you react when you get angry? If you express your anger immediately, the Bible considers you a fool. Our reactions reveal our hearts. Lift your voice to the Lord; ask for help to respond better in moments of anger.

Deliver me from showing my anger too quickly, Lord! I do not want to be foolish.

YF

MAY 13

Wealth from get-rich-quick schemes quickly disappears;
wealth from hard work grows over time.

Proverbs 13:11 (NLT)

Jocelyn Wildenstein, nicknamed Catwoman due to her many plastic surgeries, gained her wealth after divorcing millionaire Alec Wildenstein in 1999. However, by 2018 she filed for bankruptcy, having spent up to $1 million a month. Today, she has lost it all. Today's proverb reminds us that quickly acquired wealth is fleeting, urging us instead toward hard work.

A perfect example of this is Johann Sebastian Bach. When the Bach-Gesellschaft Society set out to publish all his works, the project took over 46 years and filled six volumes. How did Bach manage to produce such a vast and high-quality body of work while also juggling multiple roles—organist, musical director, private tutor, husband, and father of 20 children? Bach himself said, "I was created to work; if you are as industrious as I am, you will be just as successful."

We are designed to work, following the model set by our Creator. Jesus said, "My Father is always working, and so am I" (John 5:17, NLT). Today's proverb contrasts those who seek quick riches, perhaps through dishonest means, with the "Bachs" of the world who find time to glorify God amidst their responsibilities.

What are you passionate about? Whether it's art, crafts, study or social work, follow Bach's example: Work hard and dedicate your efforts to God.

Father, you are a clear example of hard work. Help me to be like you.

KO

May 14

An honest witness does not lie; a false witness breathes lies.

Proverbs 14:5 (NLT)

Modern technology has proven to be a valuable tool in combating false testimony, with surveillance cameras catching people in the act and witnesses capturing critical moments on their smartphones, providing clear evidence of the truth.

In May 2020, a video of George Floyd, an African-American man detained by police, went viral. An officer knelt on Floyd's neck during the arrest and Floyd's repeated pleas of "I can't breathe!" were captured on film before he died. Despite the officer's attempts to deny the gravity of his actions, the evidence was clear.

"You must not testify falsely against your neighbor" (Exodus 20:16, NIV) is one of the Ten Commandments God gave to Moses, highlighting the seriousness of this sin. What kind of witnesses are we? A true witness does not remain silent about what they know: "And the Good News about the Kingdom will be preached throughout the whole world, so that all nations will hear it" (Matthew 24:14). Every believer in Jesus Christ is called to be this kind of witness!

Our words may seem harmless, but each lie we tell perpetuates falsehood. Lies can spread, convincing others, and causing harm. Let us be cautious before we speak. Above all, let us be bearers of the liberating truth!

Help me, Lord, to be a witness of your truth.

MH

May 15

Better a dish of herbs where love is than a fatted ox and hatred with it.

Proverbs 15:17 (NABRE)

The human mind is remarkable. A certain smell can transport us back to our childhood, triggering cherished memories. I remember the *coyol* sweets my grandmother used to make. The *coyol* is a small, greenish-yellow fruit resembling a miniature coconut, harvested from a tall palm tree. When boiled with piloncillo (a type of brown sugar), it creates a thick, dark candy that is delicious and satisfying.

Some people love the art of cooking, while others see it as a daily chore. One chef in a YouTube tutorial (Kuisine Kreyol) says, "You do it [cook] out of love and not out of emotion." I have tried to adopt this mindset.

A woman can greatly influence the atmosphere of love in her home. Colossians 3:23 encourages us to have a positive attitude: "Whatever you do, do from the heart, as for the Lord and not for others" (NABRE). Whether we are cooking, ironing, or cleaning, let us do it with love, because ultimately, when we do these things, we do them for the Lord.

Regardless of whether we have little or much, let us create strong relationships within our families. Let us strive to make a home like the one described in this beloved hymn: "Where the mother with devotion knows how to show us your compassion; where all live in communion. Where the children resolutely follow Christ from the heart, where your blessing is breathed."

Lord, help me to do everything with love.

MG

May 16

Into the bag the lot is cast, but from the Lord comes every decision.
Proverbs 16:33 (NABRE)

In the Middle East, men and women traditionally wore long tunics called *jalabiya*. When seated, they could throw dice or stones in their lap, using it as a makeshift table. When important decisions needed to be made, these stones were used to determine outcomes. Do we still make decisions this way today?

Many people now turn to horoscopes or other forms of divination for guidance in their decision-making. I remember the Magic 8-Ball toy, which, when shaken, would reveal "yes" or "no" answers—often used by many to navigate the complexities of life.

Today's proverb is straightforward. The writer is saying, "Feel free to cast lots to guide your decisions, but in the end, it is God's plans that prevail." Our reliance on the Lord must be so strong that we remain open to His direction for our lives.

Today, you don't need stones to determine your path. God has given you a mind, people around you for advice and most importantly, the power of prayer. When facing a crucial decision, it is best to pray and seek God's guidance.

Teach me, Lord, which paths to take day by day.

YF

MAY 17

A person with understanding is even-tempered.

Proverbs 17:27 (NLT)

Lakes evoke feelings of peace and beauty, possibly because they lack the dangers of the sea and the turbulence of rivers. Lake Atitlán in Guatemala and Lake Pehoé in Chile are among the world's most beautiful lakes. If you have ever paddled on a calm lake, you know part of its charm is seeing your reflection in its still waters. But is it always like that?

When it rains, the surface becomes disturbed, and the reflection is lost. Our souls resemble lake waters: when we love God and gain wisdom, we move with calmness, reflecting the face of Jesus. However, when we allow foolishness or worries to rain down on our hearts, we lose that reflection.

As children of God, we can "see and reflect the glory of the Lord. And the Lord—who is the Spirit—makes us more and more like him as we are changed into his glorious image" (2 Corinthians 3:18, NLT). Yet, when we lack wisdom and doubt God's help, we become unstable, like waves tossed by the wind and we're unable to reflect Jesus.

Take a moment to breathe deeply and reflect on your soul. Is it like a serene lake or a turbulent storm? What is causing the rain that distorts the image of Jesus in you? Is it anxiety, stubbornness or unforgiveness? Confess this to God and ask for His help. Seek to regain your peace and wisdom.

Father, may others see the reflection of Jesus in my life today.

KO

May 18

The name of the Lord is a strong fortress; the godly run to him and are safe.
Proverbs 18:10 (NLT)

The Twin Towers of the World Trade Center in New York were once the tallest buildings in the world. In 2001, they were destroyed in a terrorist attack that claimed nearly 3,000 lives. Despite their imposing height, these towers were not invincible. Even ancient history's most infamous tower, the Tower of Babel, fell.

In biblical times, towers served as places of protection. In the Book of Judges, we read about the city of Thebes: "There was a strong tower within the city, and all the men and women and all the leaders of the city fled to it and shut themselves in, and they went up to the roof of the tower" (Judges 9:51, ESV).

This proverb compares the name of the Lord to a strong and unyielding tower, a fortress that protects those who seek refuge in it. Unlike the towers that can be destroyed by fire or wayward planes, like the towers in New York. This fortress is eternal.

Like the citizens of Thebes, we have a secure tower to run to when life's challenges threaten to overwhelm us. Unlike theirs, ours cannot fall. Today, amid criticism, external pressures, or internal struggles, let us run to that safe refuge!

Father, thank you for the security and protection I find in you amid this unstable world.

MH

MAY 19

When a man's folly brings his way to ruin, his heart rages against the Lord.

Proverbs 19:3 (ESV)

When applying for a job, candidates typically submit a resume and attend an interview. Their knowledge, skills, attitudes, and motivations are evaluated to determine their competence. Interviewers often ask personal questions about hobbies, relationships, and character, aiming to assess the applicant's decision-making abilities.

The difference between a wise person and a fool lies in their decisions. A decision can be poor, good, or excellent. How can we tell? By the consequences that follow. When God granted us free will, He also gave us the privilege of choice, which means we are responsible for our actions. We cannot blame God or become angry with Him for the outcomes of our poor choices.

Biblical heroes like Moses, David, Joseph, and Daniel faced significant decisions. Daniel served as an advisor to kings, receiving knowledge and wisdom from God. He was found to be ten times better than the magicians and astrologers of the kingdom because he resolved in his heart not to defile himself (see Daniel 1:8).

Those who commit themselves to live with obedience and integrity will make the right choices in every situation they face. They will not have to harbor anger towards God for the repercussions of their mistakes.

May my path be straight. I want to be obedient, Lord.

MG

May 20

Plans made with advice succeed; with wise direction wage your war.
Proverbs 20:18 (NABRE)

Napoleon is regarded as one of history's greatest military strategists. One of his notable battles was at Austerlitz in 1805, where he chose to attack the right flank of the Austro-Russian forces with only part of his army. He knew this tactic would exhaust his enemies. Despite the pressure, he held back his reserves until the decisive moment, leading to victory. Are we effective strategists?

The Bible reminds us that we are engaged in a spiritual battle. We face Satan, his demons, secular philosophies that oppose God and our own sinful nature. A good strategist is said to achieve results, adapt to changing circumstances and employ effective tactics. While we cannot explore all these traits, let's focus on one from today's proverb.

A wise tactic is to seek advice. Others have faced the challenges we are currently encountering and can offer valuable insights. King David, another skilled strategist, surrounded himself with advisors, recognizing that he did not have all the answers. The Bible mentions several trusted individuals, such as Ahithophel the Gilonite, Jonathan and his friend Hushai.

What battle are you facing today? Are you struggling with gossip, discouragement, or a habit you wish you could overcome? Seek counsel from someone who has navigated similar challenges and ask God for a sound strategy. Remember, do not engage in battle without wise guidance.

Lord, show me who I can go to for advice today.

YF

May 21

Whoever loves pleasure will be a poor man.

.Proverbs 21:17 (ESV)

Have you ever heard of hedonism? It is a philosophy that promotes the pursuit of pleasure and enjoyment in all aspects of life. Maintaining satisfaction is essential, and to achieve this, living a life free from pain is considered key.

You may not hear someone at a social gathering proclaim, "I practice hedonism; I follow the teachings of Epicurus the Greek Philosopher." But in practice, many people, young and old, live as though having a good time and avoiding pain is the ultimate purpose of life. They treat pleasure—be it food, dancing, parties, or comfort—as their god, while anything that disrupts their satisfaction, such as financial struggles, illness, hard work or even school, is deemed evil.

However, as today's proverb reminds us, chasing pleasure as a source of happiness will ultimately leave us feeling empty. This is not what we were designed for. The Bible tells us that we were created to praise and glorify God (see Ephesians 1:6, 12, 14). St. Augustine wisely stated, "You made us, Lord, for yourself, and our heart is restless until it rests in you."

The pursuit of pleasure will always leave us wanting more. Proverbs encourages us to find our true satisfaction in God. How can we achieve this? By recognizing that He offers us what we need most: love and acceptance. He is ready with open arms to meet all our needs.

Lord, I do not want to seek pleasure; I want to seek you.

KO

May 22

Just as the rich rule the poor, so the borrower is servant to the lender.

Proverbs 22:7 (NLT)

Today, we are inundated with invitations to buy things that promise happiness and offers for credit cards or loans asking us to consume more and more. In Mexico, 62% of credit cardholders consider their cards to be their biggest financial mistake. In the United States, the average debt per person is around $15,000!

This proverb warns us that going into debt is like entering into slavery. In the Roman Empire, the term *addictus* referred to an insolvent debtor who could be sold into slavery—a practice that persisted in Europe until the 19th century, where debtors were imprisoned and forced to work off their debts.

Connection With Scripture

The New Testament encourages us to be content with what we have. Paul reminds us: "Don't you realize that you become the slave of whatever you choose to obey? You can be a slave to sin, which leads to death, or you can choose to obey God, which leads to righteous living" (Romans 6:16, NLT).

I often receive calls from banks offering new credit cards or loans for various needs. When I decline their offers, they often ask why. I frequently respond that, according to the Bible, it's not wise to owe anything except love (see Romans 13:8). While credit cards can be useful in emergencies, they can also enslave us for life. Let us trust God to provide for our needs.

Lord, you know what I need. I trust that you will provide for me financially and in so much more.

MH

MAY 23

When your eyes light on riches, it is gone, for suddenly it sprouts wings, flying like an eagle toward heaven.

Proverbs 23:5 (ESV)

Shortly before we got married, my husband bought a red car that made me proud when my parents saw him drive it. During our first year of marriage, while on our way to church, another car crashed into us. God protected us, but our car was severely damaged. Two years later, we purchased our first home. We painted it and spent time fixing it up, but then a strong earthquake struck our city, leaving cracks throughout our new home. We learned that material possessions are fleeting; one day they exist and the next day they may not.

These days, with just one click, we can purchase unnecessary things online. We "set our eyes" on the lifestyles of *influencers* who display their beautifully decorated homes and perfect makeovers, igniting a desire in us to want these things.

Jesus gives us a profound perspective on our time on earth: "Do not lay up for yourselves treasures on earth, where moth and rust destroy and where thieves break in and steal, but lay up for yourselves treasures in heaven, where neither moth nor rust destroys and where thieves do not break in and steal. For where your treasure is, there your heart will be also" (Matthew 6:19-21, ESV).

There is nothing wrong with wanting to better yourself, but we must be mindful of our priorities. "Seek first the kingdom of God and His righteousness, and all these things will be given to you as well" (Matthew 6:33, NIV). I assure you, God keeps His promises.

Lord, I do not want to seek pleasure; I want to seek you.

MG

May 24

I walked by the field of a lazy person, the vineyard of one with no common sense. I saw that it was overgrown with nettles.
Proverbs 24:30-31 (NLT)

We used to visit a poor community in the northern highlands of Puebla, Mexico. We would walk a long distance to reach the community where many children and families were waiting for us to begin our praise services. Sometimes the weather was rainy, and our feet would sink into the mud, leaving us tired and wet. Yet, upon arriving at a small wooden house, we were always welcomed with hot soup and coffee.

What struck me was that, despite the dirt floor and wood stove, the house was spotless. The family worked hard growing coffee, and even the children participated in the work. How do you feel when you enter a messy and dirty home? I feel uncomfortable. I don't want to sit down or touch anything. A messy house implies laziness.

Sometimes we have excuses for clutter in our lives, but today's proverb reminds us that neglect leads to disorder. The writer observed a property overrun with nettles and weeds, concluding that the owner lacked common sense.

How do you maintain your home or workplace? Is it disorganized? Now is a great time to place this in God's hands, asking Him to make us diligent and proactive.

Lord, you are a God of order. I want to be like you.

YF

May 25

By patience is a ruler persuaded, and a soft tongue can break a bone.
Proverbs 25:15 (NABRE)

In my first home as a married woman, I faced an ongoing battle with ants invading my kitchen. No matter how hard I tried, even the smallest crumb left out would bring them back the next day. If I blocked one route, they would simply find another. Their patience and determination amazed me. It made me reflect on my own prayer life.

At that time, I was praying for several pressing needs, including financial support and opportunities to publish my books. Yet, I often lacked the persistence of those ants. When obstacles appeared and something seemed to "block" my way, I would give up and fold my arms instead of continuing to seek God's help. Has that ever happened to you?

Jesus told the parable of a persistent widow who wore down an unjust judge until he granted her justice. He explained, "Learn a lesson from this unjust judge. Even he rendered a just decision in the end. So, don't you think God will surely give justice to his chosen people who cry out to him day and night? Will he keep putting them off? I tell you, he will grant justice to them quickly!" (Luke 18:6-8, NLT).

God answered my prayers as a newlywed and He continues to do so, but I have learned to persist with patience and humility, just as this proverb says. What weighs on your heart today? Have you been praying persistently about it? Approach Him with consistency—every day, every hour, every minute. Be like those diligent ants that, despite their small size, can overcome great obstacles.

Father, I want to trust you. Help me pray always and not give up.

KO

May 26

Trusting a fool to convey a message is like cutting off one's feet or drinking poison!

Proverbs 26:6 (NLT)

In biblical times, messages were conveyed through people traveling long distances, which could take days. In the 19th century the *Pony Express* in the United States delivered mail on horseback crossing the plains, rivers, and mountains. It would take ten days for a letter to cross from the Atlantic to the Pacific! Today, thanks to technology, we can communicate instantly via the Internet.

A friend once entrusted letters to someone traveling from Mexico to the United States, believing they would arrive safely. Later, she discovered the courier had forgotten the letters in her suitcase! This proverb highlights the foolishness of trusting an unreliable messenger—messages may not arrive at all, arrive too late or, if it's a verbal message, it can be distorted in transmission.

When leading the Israelites into the Promised Land, Moses sent messengers with words of peace to King Sihon: "So I sent messengers from the wilderness of Kedemoth to Sihon the king of Heshbon, with words of peace" (Deuteronomy 2:26, ESV). While Sihon ignored them, Moses was a faithful messenger and he sent faithful messengers.

God has entrusted me with a message of peace and reconciliation. If I fail to communicate it, or if I do so in an argumentative manner, will I not be a foolish messenger, failing to fulfill my assignment?

Lord, I want to be your faithful messenger. Give me the right words and actions to be one.

MH

MAY 27

*Do not forsake your friend and your father's friend... Better is a
neighbor who is near than a brother who is far away.*

Proverbs 27:10 (ESV)

In my city, rising crime rates led to the establishment
of a "neighborhood watch" system where we look out for
one another. We keep an eye on not just our own homes but on
the entire community. We have group chats to communicate with
each other and there's an increased awareness of the importance of
good neighborly relationships and our need for unity.

I have moved 12 times and have always been blessed with good
neighbors. God has taken care of us by placing a Christian family
nearby each time. We've supported one another in many ways,
such as helping find lost pets or assisting with home repairs. We
grew to love one another and missed them when we moved away.

It's amazing how the Bible serves as a guide for every aspect of
our lives. Today's proverb reminds us of our need for each other. It
encourages us to be available to our friends and family, while also
valuing the closeness of our neighbors.

Do you know your neighbors? Are you available to help them? A
simple greeting, a smile or sharing some cookies can go a long
way. May our lives reflect the love of Jesus.

*Lord, we are where we are for one reason: to be light. May my house bring light
to my neighbors in their dark days.*

MG

May 28

If one is burdened with the blood of another, he will be a fugitive until death.
Proverbs 28:17 (ESV)

The Fugitive was an American television series about Dr. Richard Kimble, played by David Janssen. It was one of the most popular television shows in the world at that time. It told the story of a pediatric doctor wrongfully accused of murdering his wife. Although he was innocent, the jury found him guilty and sentenced him to death. Kimble escaped and was pursued by Lieutenant Gerard while seeking to prove his innocence and find the real murderer.

While Kimble was an innocent fugitive, today's proverb addresses the serious nature of murder. The Bible teaches that taking a life is a grave sin, as it attacks the image of God: "If anyone takes a human life, that person's life will also be taken by human hands. For God made human beings in his own image" (Genesis 9:6, NLT).

The first murderer, Cain, killed his brother Abel and faced severe consequences, becoming a restless wanderer on the earth. The Lord protected him with a promise despite his punishment. You and I may be more like Cain and less like Richard Kimble than we realize, running away from our wrongdoing. What can we do to stop our running?

The reality is that we must face the consequences of our actions. The penalty for sin is death, but someone has already taken our place. "Since we have now been justified by his blood, how much more shall we be saved from God's wrath through him!" (Romans 5:9, NIV). What incredible news!

Lord, thank you for your salvation.

YF

May 29

Fearing people is a dangerous trap, but trusting the Lord means safety.
Proverbs 29:25 (NLT)

The award-winning film Chariots of Fire tells the stories of two runners: Harold Abrahams, who won the 100-meter gold medal, and Eric Liddell.

There is this scene after Abrahams wins the 100-meter race, he has a conversation with his coach and the atmosphere is sad. His coach, Coach Mussabini, asks him, "do you know who you won for today?" Coach replies, "for us, for you and Sam Mussabini."

From the beginning of the film, we're made aware that Eric Liddell did not run for success, wealth or fame. He ran for the love of running and the honor of God, the giver of his athletic abilities. Liddell was scheduled to run the 100-meter race but refused because it was scheduled on a Sunday, instead he determined to run the 400 meters and won gold. It is exciting to see him celebrate in the film. What sets these two stories apart? Why did one of these runners experience only a little satisfaction, even though they both won gold?

The answer lies in their motivations: "Who are you running for?" Today's proverb reminds us that we often act out of fear of pressure, threats, or societal expectations. We want to please others, thinking it will earn us approval. However, humans will always let us down and seeking validation from them will not bring true satisfaction. Instead, when we do things for God we find genuine joy.

Ask yourself today, "For whom do I cook, clean, teach, exercise, study, run a business or write?" If your motivation stems from fear of disappointing loved ones, you may fall into a dangerous trap. Instead, do everything for God and your perspective will shift.

Lord, we are where we are for one reason: to be light. May my house bring light to my neighbors in their dark days.

KO

May 30

I am too stupid to be human, and I lack common sense.

Proverbs 30:2 (NLT)

In today's world, successful models, artists, businesswomen, academics, and athletes vie for our attention. Their stories and images fill magazines and websites, often showcasing the "superwoman" who juggles work and motherhood effortlessly, which can leave us feeling overwhelmed and inadequate.

At one point in my life, I was teaching college courses, pursuing a master's degree, volunteering at church, and managing my responsibilities as a wife and mother. I often felt exhausted and insecure, struggling to excel in every area. Many women share this experience; we tend to compare ourselves to others and lack the ability to set healthy boundaries.

The writer of Proverbs expressed feelings of clumsiness and a lack of common sense. In another translation, he describes himself as "brute" and laments that he doesn't have "human understanding" (NIV). Amid a culture that promotes positive thinking and encourages us to "do it all," it can be comforting to know that we are not alone in our insecurities. The Apostle Paul reminds us that we are not "qualified to do anything on our own. Our qualification comes from God" (2 Corinthians 3:5, NLT).

Our worth before the Father surpasses any comparison to others. We are beloved daughters, rescued by Christ, who strengthens us amid our limitations. He is the source of our wisdom and understanding!

Father, thank you for loving me as your daughter and for overcoming my insecurities with your presence.

MH

May 31

She makes bed coverings for herself; her clothing is fine linen and purple.

Proverbs 31:22 (ESV)

Alvaro Gordoa, a public image consultant, advises us to consider what we project when we dress ourselves: "When we look in the mirror, don't ask ourselves how we look, but what we are conveying." A heavy metal singer will choose a vastly different outfit for a concert than an opera singer would for a recital. Their clothing communicates their identities.

When part of a choir, we wear certain colors and textures. Athletes wear their uniforms with pride and responsibility. When at school, we wear our institution's insignia. We are not only representing ourselves, but the entire institution!

The virtuous woman of Proverbs 31 sought to express dignity and elegance in her attire. She made her own clothing from expensive materials like purple cloth and linen, which reflected her worth and status, as her husband was well-respected in the community. In 1 Timothy 2:9 Paul encourages us to dress decently. Pleasing God should be more important to us than pleasing others.

Today's fashion is diverse, and while some clothes may be provocative, we can always choose clothing that reflects our identity as God's daughters while still being beautiful and dignified. It's essential that our clothing aligns with who we truly are.

Lord, may I be a worthy ambassador of your kingdom.

KO

June 1

But these men lie in wait for their own blood; they set an ambush for their own lives.

Proverbs 1:18 (ESV)

In 2017, Harvard University made headlines when it revoked admission for at least ten incoming students who shared offensive jokes on Facebook. In a private group, they posted memes about serious topics like sexual assault and suicide, along with posting racist and anti-Semitic comments. Even though these students had strong academic records, their digital footprint dashed their dreams of attending this prestigious institution.

Sometimes, it can be tempting to share a meme, a joke, or some image online that we think is "innocent," but it might hurt or demean others. The anonymity of the screen can trick us into believing our words don't have real consequences, but we need to learn from this!

In this chapter of Proverbs, the father warns his son not to give in to the temptations of sin, mockery or to harm others. He warns that those who behave like this are essentially setting traps for themselves, leading to their own downfall. Are you wondering what to post or avoid posting on social media? Try the 1 Corinthians 13 love test. If your post is kind, if it does not boast, if it is not arrogant or rude and if it rejoices with truth rather than wrongdoing, then go ahead and share it! If not, it's best to stay silent. Let's avoid tying a noose around our own souls by participating in what might seem like harmless fun but can lead to serious consequences in your life. Instead, let's share what is good, pure, and kind.

Lord, I want to be wise and guard my soul. Help me think carefully about what I post on social media.

KO

June 2

Speak up for those who cannot speak for themselves; ensure justice for those being crushed.

Proverbs 31:8 (NLT)

Connecting with the Culture

There's a powerful story about a woman who went to an abortion clinic; her baby survived the procedure and weighed only one kilogram. The little girl was later adopted and now, as an adult, Gianna Jessen speaks out against abortion and the laws that permit it. Her life inspired the movie *October Baby*. Those who oppose the legalization of abortion often say they are speaking up "for those who cannot speak for themselves"— those who cannot defend themselves. Others are called by God to advocate for immigrants, refugees and women trapped in trafficking.

Today, it's all about defending rights, but it can go too far when people shout, "My body is mine." Little thought is given to the rights of others or to the values laid out by our Creator.

Both the Old Testament prophets and Jesus in the New Testament call for justice, especially for the vulnerable. God continues to urge us today: "Lift up your voice for the voiceless!" Many Christians heed this call. Jesus invites us to serve "the poor, the crippled, the lame, and the blind" (Luke 14:13, ESV) and we should also consider prisoners, strangers, orphans, and widows.

Maybe you're already involved in a group advocating for the marginalized. I'm part of a social network that prays for trafficked women and those fighting for them. Sometimes, we send supplies to shelters for rescued girls. May the light of Christ shine through us wherever He calls us to serve!

Father, show me how I can defend and support those who cannot speak for themselves.

MH

June 3

In all your ways acknowledge him, and he will make straight your paths.

Proverbs 3:6 (ESV)

Remember Little Red Riding Hood? She ignored her mother's warning not to talk to strangers. In the big forest filled with winding paths and trails, the clever wolf led her astray, taking her down a longer route so he could reach her grandmother's house first. Little Red Riding Hood fell into the wolf's trap, and she nearly lost her life! You more than likely remember how the story unfolds.

Our lives are shaped by the choices we make. Even though the Bible reveals God's instructions for our lives, we often stray—just like Little Red Riding Hood. We take shortcuts, rushing toward what we desire. When we don't know the truth, the enemy's lies can confuse us. We try to control certain areas of our lives and it seems we doubt whether God truly has our best interests at heart.

Today's proverb is a command with a promise. If we acknowledge God in every part of our lives—even in the crooked paths—He has the power to straighten them out. As Psalm 37:5 reminds us, "Commit everything you do to the Lord. Trust him, and he will help you" (NLT).

Is there any area of your life you haven't surrendered to God yet? Avoid the path of disobedience; it only leads to trouble. Be patient and fight the urge to take shortcuts.

Lord, your mercies are new every morning. Please help me walk straight paths today.

MG

JUNE 4

Keep hold of instruction; do not let go; guard her, for she is your life.
Proverbs 4:13 (ESV)

When the pandemic hit in 2020, desperation swept the globe as people tried to stay safe from Covid-19. Some responded in fear and did everything they could to avoid getting infected. Others responded in disbelief, not fully grasping the gravity of the situation.

Some young girls, worried about their mother's getting sick, diligently followed all the government's health guidelines. They only left home to buy food, they wore masks and were careful not to touch their faces. When they returned home, they stripped off their clothes, washed them immediately and took showers. They clung to those instructions because their mother's health depended on it!

In the same way, we should hold tightly to the instructions God gives us in His Word. We need to follow what He expects from us. As the psalmist says, "I cling to your laws. Lord, don't let me be put to shame!" (Psalm 119:31, NLT).

Do we approach the Bible with a sense of urgency? Are we aware that holding onto God's words is vital for us and those around us?

Father, I cling to your Word.

YF

June 5

For a man's ways are before the eyes of the Lord, and he ponders all his paths.
                                                    Proverbs 5:21 (ESV)

Sister Juana Inés de la Cruz's famous poem, *You foolish men*, highlights the inequality and injustice faced by women. Women, she says, never win. If they reject a man's advances, they're ungrateful; if they accept them, they're fickle. However, when we read Proverbs 5, we might feel a sense of injustice because the villain in the story is a woman.

In this chapter, a father advises his son to steer clear of immoral women, describing them as a bitter poison and as dangerous as a two-edged sword. But where's the warning for women about lustful men? Doesn't God care about our rights?

He absolutely does! When Jesus was on earth, He confronted a group of pious Jews, reminding them of the commandment against adultery. Many likely felt self-righteous, thinking, "We don't do that." But then Jesus dropped this bombshell: "But I say, anyone who even looks at a woman with lust has already committed adultery with her in his heart" (Matthew 5:28, NLT). The men must have been shocked. Jesus was making it clear: a woman is not a mere object; she is precious and her integrity matters.

God will not let the guilty go unpunished. While Jesus' words offer us protection, they also serve as a warning. To God, every person—regardless of race, religion, gender, age, or political stance—is sacred. We must treat everyone with honor, even in our thoughts!

> *Lord, thank you for caring about women. Thank you for examining my ways. May they be pleasing in your sight.*

KO

June 6

My son, obey your father's commands, and don't neglect your mother's instruction.

Proverbs 6:20 (NLT)

My husband has a knack for creating beautiful calligraphy and designs on leather. One of his clients, at different moments, commissioned him to create two undergraduate diplomas—one for the degree his parents wanted him to pursue, which he completed, and another for the degree he wanted to pursue. It's surprising how obedient he was to his parents, and even today as an adult.

Families are changing in many ways. Today, an ever-growing number of households are led by women. Many kids grow up without a father present, putting more pressure on mothers to work. Often, children are raised by relatives or caregivers, which limits opportunities for children to learn from mom and dad.

The Bible frequently emphasizes the vital role of parents in a child's education—something often overlooked today. Kids are commanded to obey their parents, and this commandment is linked to a promise: "Honor your father and mother. Then you will live a long, full life in the land the Lord your God is giving you" (Exodus 20:12, NLT).

Whether you live with your parents or are out on your own, try to practice the good advice they've shared. Treat them with respect, recognize the wisdom God has given them and learn from their example while you can.

My Father, thank you for my earthly parents and for the valuable lessons they've taught me.

MH

June 7

For many a victim has she [the adulterous woman] laid low, and all her slain are a mighty throng.

Proverbs 7:28 (ESV)

A couple from India tragically died after falling off a cliff in Yosemite National Park in California while trying to take a *selfie* on the edge. A 20-year-old woman also lost her life at the Malpaso dam in Mexico under similar circumstances, she was also taking a *selfie*. What do these incidents have in common? All of them underestimated the danger of getting too close to the edge, thinking they were safe, only to fall into the abyss.

These examples mirror today's proverb perfectly. Proverbs 7 tells the story of someone who falls into sexual immorality. It's a story of youthful passions and the temptation of fleshly pleasures and it warns us about the serious physical and spiritual consequences of sin. Just like those who died taking selfies, many feeling strong, have fallen. Surely, they got too close to the edge.

"Therefore, let anyone who thinks that he stands take heed lest he fall" (1 Corinthians 10:12, ESV). God knows us well, so let's heed this warning. It's heartbreaking to see marriages torn apart by sin or once-strong leaders stumbling.

Let's commit to purity and holiness. It's not about "not getting too close to the edge"; it's about fleeing temptation and staying vigilant.

Lord, I know I'm weak, but in you, I find strength.

MG

June 8

I was appointed in ages past, at the very first, before the earth began.
Proverbs 8:23 (NLT)

My friend Berna received a pamphlet while visiting an island near Istanbul. As a devout Muslim, she felt uncomfortable reading about Isa, or Jesus. But as she read on, she felt a warmth she'd never known before. Could it be that what it said was true? Was Jesus really God? For her, Jesus couldn't be God; he was just a prophet.

So how do we know that Jesus is indeed God? The Gospels repeatedly show us that Jesus not only acted like God and performed miracles only God could do—like forgiving sins, calming storms, and raising the dead—but He also claimed equality with the Father.

John's Gospel is clear: "In the beginning was the Word, and the Word was with God, and the Word was God" (John 1:1, NRSVUE). Proverbs 8 speaks about God's wisdom and confirms that Jesus is eternal—without beginning or end. When Berna read John 1, she began to reflect. In Islam, the Qur'an is considered the eternal word of Allah, meaning it was revealed but has always existed. For Christians, the Bible contains God's words, but Jesus is the Word of God, co-eternal and uncreated—God Himself! While Muslims honor the words of Allah, Christians worship the Word made flesh.

Today, Berna is a follower of Jesus, not just because He is God, but because He is a personal God who came to save us. How about you? Do you worship Jesus, the Son of God?

Jesus, you have no beginning and no end because you are eternal. You are God.

KO

June 9

Wisdom has built her house; she has carved its seven columns.
Proverbs 9:1 (NLT)

Construction on the Sagrada Familia church in Barcelona began in 1882 and is expected to finish in 2026. It's simply one of the most beautiful churches in the world. It is truly a magnificent structure filled with intricate details that take a whole day to fully appreciate. Though architect Antoni Gaudí died before its completion, he had a clear vision of what he wanted to express.

For him, the church was meant to be a song to the Trinity. Externally, it symbolizes the Holy Family, which is the church and faithful represented by Joseph, Mary, the apostles and the saints. Each of the three facades has a unique theme depicting the birth, passion and resurrection of Jesus. Inside, Gaudí aimed to create a forest-like atmosphere, with light streaming in through the windows. Puig Boada described the church as "a hymn of praise to God uttered by humanity, each stone a stanza sung in a clear, powerful and harmonious voice."

Boada was spot on. In the house that Wisdom built, we are "living stones that God is building into his spiritual temple" (1 Peter 2:5, NLT). We're part of this beautiful, seven-columned structure that Jesus has built and every action we take can be a song of praise for God's goodness and love.

Let's cherish the privilege of being part of such a magnificent structure. May we be those living stones, perfectly placed to bring honor and glory to our Architect.

Heavenly Father, thank you for making me a part of your family. May I be a living stone that adds beauty and honor to your building.

KO

JUNE 10

The wise are glad to be instructed, but babbling fools fall flat on their faces.

Proverbs 10:8 (NLT)

Military parades draw our attention because of the impressive order and precise coordination of everyone involved. In Puebla, Mexico, many tourists admire the famous May 5th civic-military parade where thousands of schoolchildren and teachers march or perform with remarkable discipline after months of practice.

Marchers don't turn around to greet relatives or stop to rest, even if they're feeling exhausted after miles of walking. They must follow each other precisely. And to accomplish this kind of coordination, obeying orders is essential. To "be instructed," as our proverb puts it, means to tolerate, respect, or to agree to something. By obeying orders and following instruction, we're agreeing to do what we're told.

"The wise are glad to be instructed, but babbling fools fall flat on their faces." The opposite of obedience is disobedience. According to this proverb, fools tend to grumble, showing their displeasure through their shouting and rude gestures. Another translation puts it this way, "One with foolish lips will come to ruin" (NRSVUE). Just as a God-fearing person reflects a mix of positive qualities, those who don't fear God exhibit a collection of sinful attitudes, leading to their downfall!

I hope none of us are on the road to disaster, but we all stumble from time to time when we disregard instruction and act disrespectfully. We do this in front of our parents, spouses and even at school and work. Let's be cautious! This behavior doesn't foster good relationships or a hopeful future.

My Father, teach me to act with respect in my words and actions.

MH

JUNE 11

Be assured, an evil person will not go unpunished, but the offspring of the righteous will be delivered.

Proverbs 11:21 (ESV)

Miguel Pita, a genetics doctor at the Autonomous University of Madrid, studies the traits we inherit through our DNA, like metabolism, blood type, eye color and even certain behaviors, including musical talent. He noted in his article *El papel dictador del ADN: 10 cosas que heredamos* (The Dictating Role of DNA: 10 Things We Inherit) that "the propensity for spirituality, for religious beliefs, has a strong genetic component."

This means that in addition to passing down our faith through our actions and words, we also transmit it through our DNA. The Bible emphasizes the importance of inheritance and even tells us that our children and spouse are part of God's inheritance. Righteous, God-fearing parents pass down something special to their children: the blessings of God.

Psalm 112:2 (NRSVUE) reminds us, "Their descendants will be mighty in the land; the generation of the upright will be blessed." A blessed family experiences extraordinary and supernatural blessings. God is faithful to His promises. Many today enjoy these blessings because their grandparents and parents lived righteously.

It's amazing to think that our actions today can shape the future of our descendants. While it's considered a good thing to pass down material wealth, dedicating ourselves to living an irreproachable life for our grandchildren and great-grandchildren is even more valuable.

From everlasting to everlasting, you are God; nothing shall snatch us out of your hand.

MG

JUNE 12

The way of the godly (the just) leads to life; that path does not lead to death.

Proverbs 12:28 (NLT with translator's note)

Justice is often depicted as a blindfolded woman holding a scale, symbolizing that everyone should be treated equally and that judges shouldn't favor anyone.

In law school, they teach that justice has four main qualities: distributive, restorative, procedural and retributive. In the Bible and in the salvation that Jesus offers us, we find all four of these qualities.

Distributive justice seeks equal opportunity for everyone, just as God desires all people to be saved and come to a knowledge of the truth (see 1 Timothy 2:4). Restorative justice requires that the offender acknowledge their wrong and seek to make things right, which we call repentance. Procedural justice establishes the penalties that will be applied to the offender. In the case of sinful man, God gives the verdict: We all deserve death. But Christ paid the penalty for us and by believing in Him we are saved. Finally, retributive justice teaches that all offenders should be treated equally to deter others. Our lives reflect the transformation God is working in us through His gift of salvation.

Are you yearning for true righteousness? Do you know you're on the right path? There's only one way to righteousness and life: Jesus Christ.

Thank you, Jesus, for taking my place.

YF

June 13

Hope deferred makes the heart sick, but a desire fulfilled is a tree of life.
Proverbs 13:12 (ESV)

The baobab tree is more than just a gathering spot for West African communities; it provides shelter, clothing, food, and water for both wildlife and people living in the savanna. Because every part of the tree is useful for survival, it's known as the tree of life.

Imagine walking through the African savanna, thirsty and hungry, with no hope of finding shelter from the heat. And just when you think you can't go on, you spot a tree of life in the distance. Your heart lifts—your dreams have become reality! Life is right in front of you! Isn't this just like our daily lives? We were created for something more, but sometimes we struggle to understand what that is, and that unknown hope torments our hearts. Where can our souls find this "tree of life"?

In the Bible, for years on end, the people of God felt their hope was distant, longing for the Messiah to come and save Israel from sin and sorrow. Then Jesus arrived, fulfilling the dreams of a nation and all of humanity! He is that missing piece we need to find peace. He said, "I am the way, and the truth, and the life" (John 14:6, NLT).

If you feel lost, and hope for meaning in your life seems far away, come to Jesus today. He is the answer to our longings and will fulfill our desires. He is the person we have longed for. And waiting for Him to fulfill all things is to us our tree of life! What are you waiting for?

Father, you are what I need to feel complete. Be my tree of life.

KO

JUNE 14

A scoffer seeks wisdom in vain, but knowledge is easy for a man of understanding.

Proverbs 14:6 (ESV)

In today's world there are many philosophies and belief systems, and for those searching for something to believe in, the choices can be overwhelming. Beyond mainstream religions, people are also exposed to trends like New Age spirituality and Anthroposophy. Many people mix and match their beliefs, claiming to be "seeking the truth," but we must wonder how sincere that search really is.

In high school, I took a comparative religions course and found that while many religions offered appealing teachings, they often contradicted each other. I was left confused. Each religion had demanding ideals, including those from the Sermon on the Mount in the Bible. I thought I was searching for the best path, but it took me a while to truly find Christ.

Today's proverb tells us that the "scoffer seeks wisdom in vain." Perhaps the scoffer isn't looking earnestly; they are arrogant, and they dismiss others. Just like the Pharisees: "You search the Scriptures because you think that in them you have eternal life; and it is they that bear witness about me" (John 5:39, ESV). They thought they were seeking eternal life, but they missed the deeper truths of God's word.

Are we being arrogant or wise? "Knowledge is easy for a man of understanding" because it comes from being rooted in the Word of God! Let's strive to be more diligent than the Pharisees who failed to apply its teachings.

O Lord, help me study the Bible diligently and discover true knowledge.

MH

June 15

A glad heart makes a happy face; a broken heart crushes the spirit.
Proverbs 15:13 (NLT)

Did you know you can spend from $70 up to $1,000 on hair and makeup for a wedding? In the United States, many couples spend an average of $300 on a stylist for the day of their wedding. These costs simply reflect the importance the bride gives to looking "beautiful."

I love looking at photos from my daughter's wedding. Like every bride, she was radiant and resplendent. One of the happiest days in a woman's life is the day of her marriage to the man she loves. She is filled with joy, she looks beautiful and fulfilled as her dreams become reality, surrounded by white flowers and wearing the perfect dress. This proverb is right to say: "a glad heart makes a happy face."

Nevertheless, sometimes the joy is short-lived and when the heart suffers, the spirit is diminished. Eyes lose their sparkle and foreheads crease in frowns. Happiness is fleeting when it comes from external things, but the Bible teaches us that joy as a fruit of the Holy Spirit. Unlike happiness, joy emanates from within. It doesn't depend on circumstances but on the fullness of God within us.

Perhaps you've encountered discouragement and challenges. Life isn't perfect, but it's possible to smile again. Is there something preventing your heart from experiencing joy? Surrender it to the Lord and maintain your heart's union with Him. God listens to our prayers, answers them, and fills us. He fills us with love, joy, peace, patience, goodness, faith, meekness, and gentleness—and when this happens, you radiate beauty!

Lord, change my sadness into joy and make my smile reflect your love.

MG

JUNE 16

The heart of man plans his way, but the Lord establishes his steps.

Proverbs 16:9 (ESV)

Sy Rogers changed cities to avoid being recognized. He was a transgender person. His story to transgenderism is shaped by tragedy and his journey was tumultuous. But God had a different plan.

Sy's friends, who were earlier married, wrote Sy and shared with him that they had separated, abandoned homosexuality and found Christ. They told him about the transformative power of the Gospel. Sy thought that if God could change him, He would have to intervene before the operation. As the date was approaching Sy was having various appointments with psychologists and psychiatrists who were preparing him emotionally for the transition. But, just days before the scheduled surgery, Johns Hopkins Hospital announced it was discontinuing gender reassignment surgeries. Confused and scared, Sy prayed and surrendered his life to the Lord. From that moment on, God began to transform him. He eventually married, had a daughter, and dedicated the rest of his life to serving God.

We often plan our lives as if God doesn't play a role, but in reality, He's always seeking us, drawing us closer to Him to show us His love and purpose. He has plans for us (see Jeremiah 29:11-13).

Father, today I pray for_____. Direct their steps.

YF

June 17

Foolish children bring grief to their father.

Proverbs 17:25 (NLT)

Some animals get a bad reputation—like the mule, often labeled as stubborn or foolish. A fool, in contrast, is someone who ignores what they should know or clings to their misguided ideas. The comparison between mules and fools arose because mules often refused to work the fields. But with patience, kindness and affection, mules can be trained to obey. Are we like mules?

Last Friday, I had a moment of realization: I was as stubborn and foolish as a mule. I found myself arguing with my husband over an issue I thought I had already overcome. I found myself refusing to "plow the ground" of healthy coexistence and forgiveness. It hit me like a bucket of cold water, and I remembered this proverb. I not only caused my husband pain, but I also grieved my heavenly Father, so through tears I asked them both for forgiveness.

Foolishness is sin, and we'll only find peace when we confess it to God. Our eternal Father assures us: "I will guide you along the best pathway for your life. I will advise you and watch over you. Do not be like a senseless horse or mule that needs a bit and bridle to keep it under control" (Psalm 32:8-9, NLT). What joy it is to be forgiven! What relief to be honest about our faults!

Like mules, we might want to do things our own way, but foolishness brings pain to those we love and to God. Let's allow Him to guide us and show us the right path. With His goodness and loving kindness, we'll not only walk the right way but also please Him.

Father, show me the way to walk and deliver me from foolishness.

KO

JUNE 18

Fools have no interest in understanding; they only want to air their own opinions.

Proverbs 18:2 (NLT)

Influencers are everywhere these days—they're people who stand out on social media and express opinions on a variety of topics, like fashion, sports and cooking.

One of the top Instagram *influencers* in 2020 was Billie Eilish, a young singer-songwriter. The British newspaper *The Guardian* described her as "the pop icon who defines 21st-century teenage angst." One of her popular songs, *All the Good Girls Go to Hell*, contains satanic references. *Christianity Today* suggests that parents use her dark messages as a conversation starter with their kids about anxiety, depression, and suicide.

We all know someone who's simply "displaying what they think" (Proverbs 18:2, NABRE) without considering discernment. Job's friends, who came to comfort him during his suffering offered a variety of opinions of why they thought he was experiencing the suffering he was. They criticized him instead of offering genuine support—and their judgments weren't always based on God's revealed Word.

We're constantly bombarded with opinions about how to live and what products we "need" for happiness. Some *influencers* even encourage kids to engage in risky challenges. Let's be cautious and compare those messages with the real message. And let's avoid allowing negative opinions to dominate our lives.

Lord, help me stay centered and discern between your truth and the opinions of others.

MH

June 19

Good sense makes one slow to anger, and it is his glory to overlook an offense.
Proverbs 19:11 (NLT)

Years ago, there was a television campaign against child abuse called *Count to 10*. It showed scenarios where a parent, irritated by their child's behavior, reacted in anger and impulsively. The campaign's message encouraged parents to take a deep breath, to count to ten and to respond with patience and dialogue instead of anger.

It's wonderful to discover that the Bible offers guidance for everyday challenges. Today's proverb teaches us the importance of good sense in managing anger and highlights the honor in forgiving others. When a stranger makes a mistake while driving, it might not hurt us as much because we don't know them. But when someone we love offends us, it can cut deeply.

Consider Joseph's story. His jealous brothers threw him into a pit, took away the beautiful robe their father gave him and sold him into slavery. Years later, he had the chance to get revenge, but he chose forgiveness instead. Genesis tells us, "And he kissed all his brothers and wept upon them. After that his brothers talked with him" (Genesis 45:15, ESV).

Let's take Joseph's example and the wisdom of the Bible to heart. May we learn to be patient with our loved ones and forgive those who hurt us. Forgiveness isn't just a good idea; it's a glorious choice.

Lord, help me to forgive others as you forgive me.

MG

JUNE 20

Even children make themselves known by their acts, by whether what they do is pure and right.

Proverbs 20:11 (NRSVUE)

Katie Davis had dreams of studying nursing in college, but at 18, a short-term trip to Uganda changed everything for her. In December 2006, she worked in Jinja, on the shores of Lake Victoria, and fell in love with the people and their culture. So, she decided to return the following summer after graduating from high school. What did Katie do there?

She taught preschool at an orphanage. And even though she was only 19, she saw the needs of these children and committed her life to serving them. After returning to the U.S. to continue her studies, she soon went back to Uganda, where she founded the Amazima ministry to support children in need. Katie adopted 13 orphaned girls and she's still caring for them to this day. Her actions, despite her young age, clearly show her love for God.

The apostle Paul offers a special encouragement to young people: "Don't let anyone think less of you because you are young. Be an example to all believers in what you say, in the way you live, in your love, your faith, and your purity" (1 Timothy 4:12, NLT).

Someone once asked: "If you lived in a place where believers are persecuted, would anyone have enough evidence to accuse you of being a faithful follower of Jesus Christ?" If you're young, do your actions reflect righteousness? If you're an adult, have you taught the young people around you how to show their faith through their actions?

Lord, may my actions reveal me as a true follower of Jesus.

YF

June 21

It is better to live in a corner of the housetop than in a house shared with a quarrelsome wife.

Proverbs 21:9 (ESV)

Think about all the roots hidden just under the surface and deeper within the soil. When we look at a plant, we often forget that the roots exist, but they're there. And we know they're there because of the fruit they produce. Have you ever heard of the root of bitterness?

We all face tough seasons in life. I remember a particularly stressful season when I took on a job that demanded a lot of my time and it pulled me away from my family. I knew it was wrong to try to juggle between my family world and my work world. But instead of owning my struggle I started blaming others: my boss for piling on the work, my husband for not helping enough and my kids for being too demanding.

What happened next is what the Bible warns us about—a root of bitterness began to grow in me (see Hebrews 12:15). Like those hidden roots, I watered my bitter root with busyness and fed it with the false hope that everything would just work out—until it didn't. Eventually, the bubble burst and I felt sick, alone and frustrated. I was bitter and I poisoned those around me. I had to seek forgiveness and admit my role in the whole thing.

This proverb reminds us that it's better to be alone in a corner than to live with a woman who constantly stirs up conflict or has allowed bitterness to take root. I've been that woman at times. So, what's the solution? Don't let bitterness take root in your life. How? Through humility—being humble enough to ask for forgiveness, acknowledge your role in a problem and seek a solution.

Lord, help me to guard against any roots of bitterness taking hold in my heart.

KO

JUNE 22

Direct your children onto the right path, and when they are older, they will not leave it.

Proverbs 22:6 (NLT)

Three sisters each have their own approach to raising children. One allows her kids to go to bed whenever they want, thinking this promotes independence and freedom. Another sister is strict with her bedtime routines believing that structure and rest will help her children develop well. The third sister is some sort of combination of both philosophies, at times relaxed, at other times rigid. Who's right?

We live in a world filled with parenting books and expert advice. Some suggest giving children total freedom, trusting their "instincts" and individuality to guide them along. But how do we determine the right approach amidst so many opinions?

This proverb doesn't lay out a specific formula for good parenting, but the entire book of Proverbs points us toward true wisdom, which comes from God. In Deuteronomy, God instructs parents to share His law with their children: "You shall teach them diligently to your children, and shall talk of them when you sit in your house, and when you walk by the way, and when you lie down, and when you rise" (Deuteronomy 6:7, ESV). In the New Testament, we're called to make disciples (see Matthew 28:19), which includes teaching and leading by example. Our children should be our primary disciples!

Whether we're mothers, grandmothers, aunts or teachers, God can use us to positively influence the next generation. Let's seize opportunities to guide children and youth in the ways of the Lord so that they'll follow Him into adulthood.

Father, grant me wisdom to make the most of the opportunities you give me to prepare children to walk with you.

MH

June 23

Surely there is a future, and your hope will not be cut off.

Proverbs 23:18 (ESV)

Nelson Mandela spent 27 years in prison for the things he believed. His 50 square foot cell had only a straw mattress for him to sleep on. He endured long days of hammering stones in the sun, which damaged his eyesight. His jailers physically and verbally abused him. And yet, he is remembered for the way he genuinely smiled to anyone who approached him. One of his more famous lines capture this hope, "I never think of the time I have lost. I just carry out a program because it's there. It's mapped out for me."

In difficult times, not everyone reacts with such optimism. When life doesn't go as planned, it can be easy to feel sad or even depressed. But Scripture consistently offers hope for a better future to those who live wisely.

The apostle Paul also faced imprisonment, beatings, and stoning. He endured shipwrecks, robberies, hunger, cold and fatigue, all while worrying about his fellow believers. Yet, in his second letter to the Corinthians, he wrote: "We are afflicted in every way, but not crushed; perplexed, but not driven to despair; persecuted, but not forsaken; struck down, but not destroyed; always carrying in the body the death of Jesus, so that the life of Jesus may also be manifested in our bodies" (2 Corinthians 4:8-10, ESV).

When you find yourself in discouraging situations, remember that in Christ there is always hope for a better tomorrow. Our hope is anchored in God who will fulfill His purpose in you. Trust Him!

God, strengthen me and may your Holy Spirit comfort me.

MG

June 24

Wise words are beyond fools' reach; in the assembly they do not open their mouth.

Proverbs 24:7 (NABRE)

At the Nuremberg trials, Nazi leaders, officials, and collaborators faced justice. Otto Ohlendorf was sentenced to death for the murder of 90,000 people, mainly Jews and Gypsies. In court he defended himself claiming he was just following orders. The court rejected this defense. They argued that individuals who commit illegal acts are responsible for their actions. As this proverb teaches, wisdom was beyond his reach.

Now, let's consider Jesus. Do you remember how He remained silent during His trial? It might seem like He didn't know what to say. But do you think it's possible that the reason He wasn't defending Himself was because He was taking the place of the fool? If He had defended Himself, His display of wisdom would have left His accusers speechless! In other words, Jesus chose to be silent as an act of love for you and me.

In 2 Corinthians, Paul writes, "For our sake he made him to be sin who knew no sin, so that in him we might become the righteousness of God" (2 Corinthians 5:21, ESV). Essentially, our Lord fulfilled the Scriptures and became a fool for us. This realization fills my heart with gratitude and my eyes with tears. The Pure and Holy One took on our foolishness without being foolish.

We may never fully grasp the cost of our salvation! In the most significant trial of all, someone took our place. Our many defenses wouldn't change the verdict of death, but Jesus has already paid that price for us. All that's left is for us to accept His gift.

Lord Jesus, you took my place. Thank you.

YF

June 25

If your enemies are hungry, give them food to eat ... For live coals you will heap on their heads.
Proverbs 25:21-22 (NABRE)

In biblical times people heated their homes and cooked with fire. However, during the night, the fire sometimes went out and people had to leave their homes and search for burning coals from their neighbors. These coals were carried in braziers or containers on their head. So, what does this proverb teach us?

If your enemy or someone who doesn't appreciate you is hungry, feed them. If they are thirsty, give them a drink. In these moments you're responding to hostility with kindness. It's like when that noisy neighbor who throws garbage into your yard comes over asking for some burning coals. You could refuse to give up your precious heat and claim you need it for your own family. Or you can generously fill their container with coals.

Paul referenced this proverb when he encouraged the Romans not to seek revenge. His advice? "Leave that to the righteous anger of God" (Romans 12:19, NLT). The proverb concludes with a promise, "The Lord will repay you." He will ensure that your home remains warm and that your kindness might lead your enemy to wonder why you show them grace, potentially drawing them to Jesus.

There will always be people who don't treat us well and may even wish us harm. But let's not seek revenge or impose our own justice. Hand those people over to God; and if they're hungry or thirsty, be generous. Heap those burning coals on their heads!

Father, I don't want to repay anyone evil for evil. Help me to do all I can to live in peace with everyone.

KO

June 26

As a dog returns to its vomit, so a fool repeats his foolishness.

Proverbs 26:11 (NLT)

In the past, dogs had specific roles—guarding homes, hunting or herding sheep. Nowadays, many of them are considered companions and people affectionately call them "furbabies." However, unlike children, dogs will never learn to clean up after themselves, whether that's vomit or worse.

I once had a friend who battled a severe alcohol addiction. He despised his dependence and recognized how it was destroying his family, yet he felt powerless to stop. There were times when he would find himself passed out on the pavement, spending the night there, only to return to alcohol "like a dog returns to its vomit." It wasn't until he turned to Christ that he finally broke free from that destructive cycle. Just as "a dog returns to its vomit" an addict often returns to the very substance that enslaves them. Similarly, Peter reminds us that a "washed pig returns to the mud" (2 Peter 2:22, NLT). Both Proverbs illustrate the dual nature of sin—its repugnance and its allure. God sees this tendency to return to our wretched ways as unacceptable, but He always offers us a way to break free and be clean.

While we may not be drug addicts, we all have habits we despise. We might gossip, overeat or become hooked on inappropriate shows or novels. Let's turn to God, asking Him to free us from these practices and to satisfy us with what truly nourishes our souls.

Lord, you know me. Free me from those dangerous things that both attract me and harm me.

MH

June 27

For wealth does not last forever, nor even a crown from age to age.
Proverbs 27:24 (NABRE)

In the Egyptian Museum in Cairo lies a mummy known as *The Younger Lady,* discovered in a tomb located in the Valley of the Kings. Her identity remains uncertain, but recent DNA studies suggest she might be Nefertiti, the wife of Pharaoh Akhenaten. There is a bust of Nefertiti in the Berlin Museum that shows her remarkable beauty.

Despite her royal status and even though she ruled as pharaoh for three years after her husband's death, her tomb was looted, and her remains were desecrated with an axe. Her jewelry was taken, and it appears that efforts were made to erase evidence of her royal identity. Her wealth, power, and reign did not last forever.

The Gospel reminds us, "Do not lay up for yourselves treasures on earth, where moth and rust destroy and where thieves break in and steal, but lay up for yourselves treasures in heaven, where neither moth nor rust destroys and where thieves do not break in and steal" (Matthew 6:19-20, ESV). It's painful and devastating to be the victim of thieves and to lose our stuff—our possessions. Today, it's not simply insecurity on the streets, it's also insecurity online as thieves target our online bank accounts.

Worrying about material things is futile. Our time on this earth is temporary. Where our treasure is, there our heart will be. Where do you invest your time, money and energy?

Jesus, thank you for preparing a place for me in heaven.

MG

June 28

A stingy man hastens after wealth and does not know that poverty will come upon him.

Proverbs 28:22 (ESV)

There's a TV show called *Extreme Cheapskates*. Watching some of the episodes, I was shocked by how some people live. Some dig through trash for food and medicine. One man took a date to a drive-through restaurant, ordered one meal for them both and took the glasses and silverware home. Another woman dilutes her children's juice with water to stretch it and even bakes cookies using the heat from her car.

I was particularly struck by a man who had 15 bank accounts, and although each account had over $100,000, he has no furniture in his home, and he feeds his family of six fast-food for each meal.

It's clear that stinginess is sin. God wants us to rely on Him alone. Paul reminds us, "For you may be sure of this, that everyone who is sexually immoral or impure, or who is covetous (that is, an idolater), has no inheritance in the kingdom of Christ and God" (Ephesians 5:5, ESV). This proverb rings true: the miser wants to get rich, but even if he is wealthy, he lives in poverty because he doesn't enjoy what he has.

There's a difference between being a person who saves and being stingy. A saver has a purpose but the stingy person hoards without reason. It's a good moment to reflect on what type of person we are, the saver or the stingy.

Lord, I don't want to be stingy. Help me not idolize material things.

YF

June 29

Discipline your children, and they will give you peace of mind and will make your heart glad.

Proverbs 29:17 (NLT)

I started taking piano lessons at six years old, but I wasn't exactly excited when it was time to go to my teacher's house or when I had to sit down and practice. Today however, I'm grateful to my mother for insisting I stick with it. Now I enjoy playing the piano—praise God. I experience a deep sense of communion with Him when I sing a "new song" in the quiet of my living room. But today as a mother I know that instilling discipline in others is no easy task.

As a teacher, I have my students read the classics—the important books of literature. I knew some of them would chose to watch the movie version and read summaries instead. But others, though they struggled along, would try hard. What's the difference between these two? The ones who read the entire book felt a sense of satisfaction in completing the task, even if it didn't reflect on their grades, it showed up in their hearts.

We can't teach our children discipline if we're not disciplined ourselves. Discipline brings joy and peace of mind. There's nothing quite like the feeling of accomplishing something well and on time. We can hear an echo of this in Jesus' words on the cross when He declared that everything was finished—He had fulfilled His purpose in coming to the world.

Show love to your children by teaching them not to give up or give in. Lead by example and work together to avoid shortcuts. Remember, effort bears fruit.

Father, help me to be disciplined in my life.

KO

JUNE 30

A stingy man hastens after wealth and does not know that poverty will come upon him.

Proverbs 28:22 (ESV)

There's a TV show. called *Extreme Cheapskates.* Watching some of the episodes, I was shocked by how some people live. Some dig through trash for food and medicine. One man took a date to a drive-through restaurant, ordered one meal for them both and took the glasses and silverware home. Another woman dilutes her children's juice with water to stretch it and even bakes cookies using the heat from her car.

I was particularly struck by a man who had 15 bank accounts, and although each account had over $100,000, he has no furniture in his home, and he feeds his family of six fast-food for each meal.

It's clear that stinginess is sin. God wants us to rely on Him alone. Paul reminds us, "For you may be sure of this, that everyone who is sexually immoral or impure, or who is covetous (that is, an idolater), has no inheritance in the kingdom of Christ and God" (Ephesians 5:5, ESV). This proverb rings true: the miser wants to get rich, but even if he is wealthy, he lives in poverty because he doesn't enjoy what he has.

There's a difference between being a person who saves and being stingy. A saver has a purpose but the stingy person hoards without reason. It's a good moment to reflect on what type of person we are, the saver or the stingy.

Lord, I don't want to be stingy. Help me not idolize material things.

YF

July 1

Hear, my son, your father's instruction.

Proverbs 1:8 (ESV)

St. Augustine's book The Teacher is written in the form of a dialogue between him and his son, Adeodatus, who is 15 years old. They both converted to Christianity at the same time. At one point, Augustine viewed his son as a "son of sin" because he conceived him outside the covenant of marriage. However, after trusting in Christ and writing this book, he expresses how much he has learned from his young collaborator. Doesn't this remind you of the wisdom found in Solomon's proverbs?

The first nine chapters of Proverbs contain several talks between a father and his son. Perhaps Solomon is reflecting on his conversations with his father David, or his own talks with his son Rehoboam. What's clear is that both Augustine and Solomon aim to direct their children's attention to the true Master: God Himself.

Augustine's final conclusion is that knowing and loving God is the blessed life; it's the one we all say we're seeking and only a few have the joy of finding. Sadly, Augustine's son Adeodatus passed away shortly after his baptism. Though his time on earth was brief, he experienced "the path of life" (Psalm 16:11, ESV).

Many claim they are searching for a fulfilling life, but true fulfillment only comes from knowing and loving God. If you haven't found that yet, come to Jesus today and be one of the few who have. If you already know this joy, share it with your children, your nieces and nephews, and your grandchildren! Show them the way to the true Master.

Lord, help me to share the blessed life with others.

KO

July 2

She seeks out wool and flax and weaves with skillful hands.

Proverbs 31:13 (NABRE)

Few of us 21st-century women know how to spin wool. But not just that. Most of us don't even make our own clothes anymore since we can so easily buy the clothes we need in the right size. Many of us didn't learn skills like embroidery or knitting in school, unlike the schooling of our mothers and grandmothers where this type of training was common.

In many villages across Latin America, especially in indigenous communities, women still create beautiful hand-woven and hand-embroidered garments. These women work tirelessly for weeks, and sometimes even months, to finish a single piece.

The virtuous woman described in Proverbs contributes to her household's economy. Even with servants, she doesn't look down on manual labor. Another great example is Dorcas (also known as Tabitha) from Acts 9, who was known for her good works and for sewing clothes for widows. When she died, the community mourned her loss deeply. God worked through Peter to raise her back to life, making her the only woman in the Bible referred to as a "disciple." Dorcas' story reminds us how we can use our talents to serve our families and those around us.

While sewing and knitting may not be common today, there are countless ways we can help at home and in our communities. Some of us serve by baking delicious treats or meals, while others use their creativity to decorate homes and offer hospitality. Our gifts in organization, teaching and various other things can have a significant impact in our churches and at our workplaces.

Father, thank you for the abilities you've given me; I want to use them to bless others.

MH

July 3

Let not steadfast love and faithfulness forsake you; bind them around your neck; write them on the tablet of your heart.

Proverbs 3:3 (ESV)

Lying becomes easier when "everyone is doing it." We may think that "little white lies" are harmless. Sometimes lying becomes a habit, and in unexpected moments, we might invent a lie as a way to avoid confronting the truth. Just as many grandmothers used to advise their grandchildren to tie strings around their fingers to remember things, today's proverb encourages us to figuratively tie mercy and truth around our necks.

When I was 23, my parents were blessed with a beautiful baby boy who had an infectious smile. I had always wanted a brother, so I loved him instantly. Jonathan was lively, enthusiastic and a bit mischievous. Though one thing always stood out about him: he always told the truth. While some kids might blame their siblings, pets or other things when caught in mischief, Jonathan faced his consequences bravely and we could always trust his account of how things happened.

For God, lying is serious business. In Acts of the Apostles, when Ananias lied about the money from a property sale, Peter told him, "You have not lied to man but to God" (Acts 5:4, ESV). God took Ananias' life for that lie.

Just as we write reminders on sticky notes and place them on the fridge, the Word suggests we "write them on our hearts" to remember the importance of mercy and truth. Remember, when we lie, we're not just lying to people; we're lying to God.

God, I want to tell the truth always because I know it pleases you. Help me to remember this.

MG

July 4

Ponder the path of your feet; then all your ways will be sure.

Proverbs 4:26 (ESV)

We've all heard the different stories about pastors and various spiritual leaders accused of inappropriate sexual relationships or other types of inappropriate behavior. It's so disheartening! But, despite these sad examples, there are also incredible examples of faithfulness we can follow.

William Franklin Graham, known as Billy Graham, is often regarded as one of the most respected preachers of the 20th century. He preached the Gospel to nearly 215 million people across more than 185 countries. His television programs and internet videos have reached hundreds of millions of people, his books have been translated into many languages. He founded the Billy Graham Evangelistic Association, which broadcasts radio and television programs, produces magazines and articles, children's programs, films and many other ministries.

My admiration for him isn't just based on his education, the organizations he established or the influence he had. He knew he needed to be wise. In order to protect himself and to glorify God with his life he understood the necessity of practicing wisdom.

Perhaps you and I should ponder the path of our own feet to ensure all of our ways will be. Maybe that means dedicating more time to prayer and Bible study. Perhaps we need to confront a particular sin we haven't been able to shake and take decisive action to overcome it. May the Lord grant us the victory through His grace!

Lord, examine my paths and show me where I am falling short.

YF

July 5

In the end, you will groan in anguish when disease consumes your body.
Proverbs 5:11 (NLT)

What does the Wailing Wall in Jerusalem, the Sanctuary of Lourdes in France, the Kashi Vishwanath Temple in India, the Taktsang Monastery in Bhutan and the Nasir al-Mulk Mosque in Iran all have in common? Each of these locations serves as a place of worship, pilgrimage, and cultural heritage for their respective faith communities. How should a person conduct themselves in these sacred spaces?

When the Notre Dame Cathedral in Paris caught fire, the world paused, and millions mourned. It's a reminder of how much we value and respect our places of worship. When visiting a mosque you must wear the appropriate clothes. We don't litter or graffiti the stones of Stonehenge—at least not out of fear of a fine! In a similar way our bodies are temples, sacred places.

Paul reminds us, "Don't you realize that your body is the temple of the Holy Spirit, who lives in you and was given to you by God?" (1 Corinthians 6:19, NLT). Sadly, we often treat our bodies as playthings rather than sacred temples, especially in terms of our sexuality. In today's proverb, a father warns his son about the dangers of relationships outside of marriage. One consequence of infidelity can be the anguish of disease. We must not allow our "temple" to become contaminated in this way!

Your sexual intimacy matters. Your body is a sacred space that needs protection and care. If you don't honor it, why would you expect others to? God has established that intimacy should be reserved for marriage, so let's honor God and respect ourselves by obeying His commands.

Lord, I am a temple of your Holy Spirit. I want to take care of my body and honor your commands.

KO

July 6

Take a lesson from the ants, you lazybones. Learn from their ways and become wise!

Proverbs 6:6 (NLT)

Traditional proverbial sayings are creative and often capture simple truths. For example, "An ant walks farther than an ox lying down." The lesson here is about persistence, how small efforts can lead to great accomplishments. An ox may be strong, but if it's lying down it's not doing anything useful.

I had a dream of writing a book, and although I had some ideas jotted down, the thought of completing a full-length book felt overwhelming. Several writers advised me with a simple piece of advice, "If possible, write a little every day." So, like an ant, I moved forward step by step and eventually succeeded!

Another translation puts our proverb this way, "Go to the ant, you sluggard; consider its ways and be wise!" (NIV). Observing God's creatures can teach us all kinds of valuable lessons. All of nature reflects the handiwork of its Creator. And while the Word of God is our primary source of wisdom, His "works" also speak of Him too: "The heavens proclaim the glory of God. The skies display his craftsmanship" (Psalm 19:1, NLT).

Today, let's take time to observe nature all around us. Listen to the birds, watch the animals, admire the beauty of flowers and notice the rhythms of the stars. Let's learn from these wonders and thank the Creator for the incredible details He provides. And like the ant, let's take small, faithful steps toward achieving our goals.

Lord, help me understand that through small, faithful actions, I can achieve great things with your help.

MH

July 7

Say to wisdom, "You are my sister," and call insight your intimate friend.
Proverbs 7:4 (ESV)

He was born in a humble wooden house and attended school only occasionally. He learned the alphabet at seven and practiced writing with a piece of wood he burned himself to make a pencil, drawing letters on the lid of a box because paper was too expensive. A relative gave him an etymological dictionary—a dictionary that traces the origin and the history of words—which became his treasure. Neighbors lent him books, and although they didn't have many, he read each one multiple times. Despite never completing a full year of formal schooling, Abraham Lincoln had a love for knowledge. He taught himself law and eventually became the President of the United States.

Even when he had little time during the day and limited light at night, he immersed himself in everything he read, which shaped his character and integrity. He earned the nickname "Honest Abe" because of his reputation as a truthful man.

Today's proverb encourages us to build a close relationship with wisdom, treating it as if it were family. It invites us to be intimate with knowledge, just like we are with our best friends. There's no wisdom without knowledge and knowledge without wisdom is vanity.

Let's appreciate the blessing of being able to read. Let's follow Lincoln's example and cultivate a love for reading. A good book is like a friend that shares wisdom, teaches us valuable lessons, and helps us grow as individuals. May God grant us the wisdom to use that knowledge to serve Him and others.

Lord, I want to know You more so that I can serve You better.

MG

July 8

When he set for the sea its limit, so that the waters should not transgress his command.

Proverbs 8:29 (NABRE)

A tidal wave or tsunami is a violent movement of sea water, different from the normal waves caused by wind or the moon's pull. They're much more devastating. They're the results of underwater volcanic eruptions, ice calving, meteorite impacts or earthquakes.

While we know tsunamis have occurred throughout history, documented by ancient cultures and archaeological findings, they seem to be happening more frequently in recent years. Some recent examples include the tsunamis in Indonesia (2004), Chile (2010), Japan (2011) and again two other times in Indonesia (2018)—one of these triggered by the eruption of Krakatoa. Who knows what else might come?

Today's proverb tells us that God has set limits for the sea, determining how far it can go. But it seems—at least in our modern days—that these limits are being tested. Do you think this has anything to do with the behaviors of the world? In our modern world, as wickedness continues to increase, we are seeing the signs that Jesus spoke of in Matthew's Gospel being fulfilled, "Nation will rise against nation, and kingdom against kingdom; there will be famines and earthquakes from place to place" (Matthew 24:7, NABRE).

All of this reminds us that Jesus will return. We shouldn't live our lives in fear. His guidance to be watchful and prayerful is especially relevant for you today.

Lord, teach us to care for your creation and to look forward with eagerness to your coming.

YF

July 9

The fear of the Lord is the beginning of wisdom, and the knowledge of the Holy One is insight.

Proverbs 9:10 (ESV)

Learning is a lifelong journey. Just when we think we know everything about a topic, new facts emerge to remind us that there is always more to discover. This is true whether we're talking about our profession, like education, or a personal interest, like life in the Arctic—new ideas and discoveries are deepening and growing our understanding of these things regularly. But what happens when the subject we're studying is infinite?

How can a person know God? A central theme in the book of Proverbs is the fear of the Lord. Ultimately, the most crucial decision in our lives is: What will we do with God? Will we choose to follow Him or reject Him? There's no neutral ground on this issue, and as today's proverb points out, fear is accompanied by knowledge.

Knowing God is a lifelong exercise, and we will not fully grasp God in this lifetime. He is wholly different from us, and His qualities are often a mystery. God is all-powerful, all-sufficient, holy, just, compassionate and merciful. He is love and light, life and truth. Can we know Him? Absolutely! He desires to be known. That was Jesus' mission; He said, "I have revealed you to the ones you gave me from this world" (John 17:6, NLT).

We can dive into the Bible today and explore its stories. Even those we've heard many times before can teach us new truths about who God is. As we pray, spend time with Jesus and move forward in our journey of faith, God will help us know Him more deeply. When we commit our time and effort to knowing the Holy One, we find true wisdom.

Heavenly Father, I want to know You more.

KO

July 10

People with integrity walk safely, but those who follow crooked paths will be exposed.

Proverbs 10:9 (NLT)

In today's world, shameful hidden acts are becoming harder to hide. People can make secret recordings and security cameras are everywhere capturing more and more of our everyday moments.

In recent years we've been shocked by the revelations of the shameful secrets of powerful politicians and leaders. Their corrupt dealings, their improper words and immoral practices have been exposed. And from one moment to the next we lose all trust in those we once trusted.

Integrity is righteousness, and it encompasses our entire being. "People with integrity walk safely," because their life is transparent; no wrongdoing can be found in them. In contrast, "those who follow crooked paths will be exposed." When that happens, they fall into shame. The Bible assures us, "Whatever you have said in the dark will be heard in the light, and what you have whispered behind closed doors will be shouted from the housetops for all to hear!" (Luke 12:3, NLT).

Let's be cautious about our actions, thinking no one will notice. Most importantly, our heavenly Father sees everything and is grieved by our wrongdoings. With His help, let's strive to walk in integrity and transparency.

Lord, make me a person of integrity so that I may live without fear.

MH

July 11

When the wicked die, hope perishes, and the expectation of strength comes to nothing.

Proverbs 11:7 (NRSVUE)

During the Spanish Civil War, the Museo del Prado stored its valuable art in Geneva at the League of Nations headquarters. Similarly, in 1939, the French hid iconic pieces from the Louvre, like the Mona Lisa and the Venus de Milo, in the countryside, far from the danger of the bombers. Museums safeguard our history and our most beautiful treasures.

In the heart of Vatican Square stands another historic treasure, the Obelisk, brought from Egypt by Caligula. He wanted everybody worship his statue as a god. Yet, his dreams ended with his assassination and his grand illusions perished with him. This proverb rings true, when the wicked die, his hopes and expectations of strength die too.

We can base our dreams and ambitions on something far more enduring than fleeting fame or material wealth. The Bible reminds us, "we look not to the things that are seen but to the things that are unseen. For the things that are seen are transient, but the things that are unseen are eternal" (2 Corinthians 4:18, ESV).

Let's pursue projects that God can use for His glory. Everything we do is significant when we do it for Him. Our hopes stand firm on the eternal foundation of our heavenly Father.

Lord, fulfill your purpose in me.

MG

July 12

A good wife is the crown of her husband, but she who brings shame is like rottenness in his bones.

Proverbs 12:4 (NRSVUE)

When Napoleon elevated Bavaria to the status of an independent kingdom and named Maximilian I as its king, the crown made for him became one of the most expensive in history. Adorned with diamonds, sapphires, rubies, emeralds and pearls, its value today exceeds seventeen million dollars. Why such a high price?

A crown symbolizes authority, honor, leadership and wealth. Throughout history, kings have vied for the most magnificent crowns to showcase their power and earn respect and admiration. After winning a war, a king would often wear the defeated king's crown as a sign of victory.

By understanding how important it is for a ruler to wear the best crown on his head helps us grasp what Scripture is conveying to women: we are the insignia that a man wears. The Lord has given us a remarkable honor; we are our husband's crown. This is not an option we can take or leave. From the moment Eve was created, God elevated us to the role of suitable helper—a crown!

Have you ever wondered why your husband chose you? Do you lift him up publicly as your king? Are you mindful of your words, whether he's around or not? Do you strive to look your best? Can he proudly place you on a pedestal in front of his friends? And if you're single, do you honor Jesus as the King of kings and Lord of lords in your life?

Lord, may I be my husband's beautiful crown.

YF

July 13

A wise son hears his father's instruction, but a scoffer does not listen to rebuke.
                                              Proverbs 13:1 (ESV)

In military movies we often hear the phrase "copy that," meaning "I've heard and understood the message." Sadly, there are times when we hear and even understand a message but fail to act on it—to do the things the message is asking us to do.

My kids are experts at this. When I ask them to pick up their toys, they often just stare at me. So, I ask, "Did you hear me?" They nod, but still don't move. I can be just as guilty! For instance, I know Jesus calls me to love my neighbor, yet I don't always put that into practice. No wonder He said repeatedly, "He who has ears, let him hear" (Matthew 13:9, ESV).

In the Bible, listening means taking in a message with both heart and mind. The apostle James understood this well and wrote, "But don't just listen to God's word. You must do what it says" (James 1:22, NLT). He compared ignoring God's commands to looking in a mirror and then forgetting what you look like!

Let's strive to be good listeners. When we read God's Word or hear His voice, may we respond with a heartfelt "Copy that!"—meaning we've understood and will act on the message.

Heavenly Father, help me to hear and obey your Word.

KO

July 14

Each heart knows its own bitterness, and no one else can fully share its joy.
Proverbs 14:10 (NLT)

In some cultures, especially among men, it is embarrassing to be seen crying. Missionary Bruce Olson, in his book *Bruchko*, tells of the Motilone tribe in Colombia, who never cried, not even at the death of a loved one. After "tying the ropes of their hammocks to Jesus" they eventually experienced the death of the tribe's first believer, a hero to them. Olson noticed that many of them shed tears, and some even fled into the jungle to hide their crying. One of them later joked, "We all caught a cold."

This proverb tells us that "every heart knows its own bitterness, and no one else can fully share its joy." Our emotions are deeply personal. Yet, God's Word encourages us to share these moments: "Rejoice with those who rejoice, weep with those who weep" (Romans 12:15, ESV). Jesus experienced the full range of human emotions—joy, compassion and agony—often more profoundly than we can imagine.

Our feelings are an essential part of who we are. Let's have the courage to open our hearts to God during times of sadness, confusion or joy. And let's strive to be present for those who are hurting, even if we can't say, "I know how you feel." God knows and always understands.

Lord, make me sensitive to the hearts of those you put in my path today.

MH

July 15

The fear of the Lord is training for wisdom, and humility goes before honors.
Proverbs 15:33 (NABRE)

Humility stands in stark contrast to pride. Jesus Christ exemplified humility perfectly. Though He was rich, He chose to become poor; though He was God, He was born in a humble manger. He emptied Himself, taking on the form of a servant and even submitting to His earthly parents. He came not to be served but to serve, and when betrayed, He remained silent, giving His life on the cross in our place.

Jesus' first coming was one of humility and humiliation, coming as a lamb, but at His second coming Jesus returns as a King. God has exalted Him to the highest place, and at His name, every knee will bow, and every tongue confess that He is Lord.

In Peter's first letter, we read that He "has gone into heaven and is at the right hand of God, with angels, authorities, and powers having been subjected to him" (1 Peter 3:22, ESV). After He was humiliated, He was exalted. How can we then take any credit for our work or for the things we do? As His servants, we do only what we should have been doing from the beginning. Yet, in His justice and mercy, God honors His children with crowns.

Our works will be tested by fire. If they endure, we will receive a reward. Those who exalt themselves will be humbled, while those who humble themselves will be exalted. It's human to seek recognition, but it's better to follow Jesus' example. What drives your desire to serve?

Lord, I serve you because I love you.

MG

JULY 16

Everyone who is arrogant in heart is an abomination to the Lord; be assured, he will not go unpunished.

Proverbs 16:5 (ESV)

The movie *Inside Out* features five characters, each the personification of a person's primary emotions. Among the five is Disgust, a little green character who has strong opinions and blunt honesty. Thanks to her, the girl in the story avoids danger. In real life, everyone feels disgust, which encompasses feelings like hostility and contempt. What are the things that disgust us?

Experts say we naturally reject things like vomit, urine and feces to avoid disease. We also turn away from decay and corruption. We despise lying and murder. God also disdains certain things, and in the case of this proverb, He speaks to his disdain of pride.

Pride distorts our sense of self-worth, leading us to believe that we don't need God or others. It convinces us of our superiority, tricking us into thinking we can operate by different rules. This proverb reminds us that pride has consequences. Remember King Nebuchadnezzar? His pride turned him into a wild animal for seven years until he acknowledged that God alone is in control over all things.

Pride can creep into our lives subtly. I've often caught myself bragging about my achievements or thinking I can manage everything on my own without help from God or others. Let's cultivate a sense of "displeasure" when pride rears its head in our lives. Recognize it as a toxic sin that will not go unpunished; so, let us flee from it!

Father, deliver me from pride.

KO

July 17

Whoever mocks the poor insults his Maker.

Proverbs 17:5 (ESV)

Those who have undergone heart transplants form a special tribe of people. These individuals not only receive a new heart but have been found to also acquire new sensory responses and cravings. These people are grateful for the second chance, and they inherit something from the person who gifted them their heart.

When we believe in Christ, we receive a new heart and trigger a powerful spiritual transformation. Not only do we have a new opportunity at life—we're no longer prisoners from sin, but free and saved—we inherit traits from our Father who adopts us and gives us a new will. And there is nothing that characterizes our Father like His compassion.

Jesus lived among the poor and marginalized and "had compassion" on the crowds (see Matthew 14:14). How do we react when we learn that 25,000 people die daily from hunger? What about the millions of orphans worldwide? Or the fact that a child dies from contaminated water every 21 seconds? Does our heart ache for the things that grieve our Creator?

To mock the poor is to offend our Maker. Ignoring those in need is a way of minimizing their struggles. What can we do today to help the poor around us? Let's think of practical ways to make a difference!

Lord, move my heart to compassion and to help the poor of this world.

KO

JULY 18

Haughtiness goes before destruction; humility precedes honor.

Proverbs 18:12 (NLT)

Different sayings and proverbs often hold deep truths. One that resonates with today's topic comes from Saavedra Fajardo, a Spanish statesman and author from the 1700's, "More kingdoms have fallen due to pride than by the sword; more princes have caused their own downfall than been vanquished by others."

One day as I walked down the street, I instinctively checked my reflection in a shop window. As I was attempting to catch a glimpse of myself, I stumbled over some object in the street and nearly fell. Immediately this verse came to my mind; it reminded me that pride and vanity can distract us from what is most important.

Pride—or haughtiness as our proverb puts it—goes before destruction, but humility opens the door to honor. The haughty make foolish decisions rooted in selfishness. But a humble person does not see themselves as superior but seeks the good of others. Our ultimate example is Jesus, who, despite His divine rights, humbled Himself to live and die for us. "He emptied himself, taking the form of a slave, coming in human likeness" (Philippians 2:7, NABRE). And then what happened? "God greatly exalted him" (Philippians 2:9, NABRE).

Paul urges us: "Have among yourselves the same attitude that is also yours in Christ Jesus" (Philippians 2:5, NABRE). Let's move away from self-serving thoughts and follow our Savior's example! In due time, God will honor us.

Father, I want to be more like Christ every day.

MH

July 19

House and wealth are inherited from fathers, but a prudent wife is from the Lord.

Proverbs 19:14 (ESV)

A genealogist is a person who is an expert in family trees and lineages. Some of these genealogists specialize in finding heirs for estates—for those who pass away without a will or an obvious inheritor. They do research to reconstruct a family's ties to help locate these relatives and settle estates.

One morning a man of modest means received a call from a genealogist who informed him he was receiving an inheritance from a cousin he never knew. Initially, he thought it was a joke or even a scam, but once he received the legal documents, he realized how fortunate he was. His life changed overnight and now he lives in gratitude, knowing only God could have orchestrated such a miracle.

Have you considered that you might be God's inheritance to bless the lives of others, especially your husband? Today's proverb assures us that God takes special care in blessing a man by providing him with a prudent wife and the suitable helper he needs.

Whether married or not, if our lives are founded on Christ and we practice His teachings, we become a valuable asset. A gift that God provides to bless those around us.

Let your will be done in me, Lord. Allow me to clearly see your way.

MG

JULY 20

Ears to hear and eyes to see—both are gifts from the Lord.

Proverbs 20:12 (NLT)

Helen Keller lost her sight and hearing due to an illness early in her life. Thankfully, her family was able to provide a governess who helped her connect her inner world with the outside. Helen went on to attend college, write books, lecture and advocate for the rights of the disabled. While we don't know the Gospel's full impact on her life, we do know she was influenced by a minister, her well-worn Bible, and her teacher.

Which would be worse: losing your sight or hearing? Helen Keller wrote, "Between not seeing and not hearing, without a doubt, not hearing is much worse, blindness cuts us off from things, but deafness cuts us off from people." Do you know anyone who is hearing or visually impaired? Do you face a disability yourself?

Sometimes, we question why God allows disabilities. The disciples once asked Jesus about a man born blind; they asked if it was due to his own sins or because of his parents' sin. Jesus replied, "This happened so the power of God could be seen in him" (John 9:3, NLT).

If you or someone you know has a disability, remember that God has great plans for you. Someone once said that the seven wonders of the world are seeing, hearing, touching, tasting, feeling, laughing and loving—and they certainly are. How thankful are you for gifts of hearing and seeing?

Lord, may your power be reflected in me today.

YF

July 21

All day long he craves and craves, but the righteous gives and does not hold back.

Proverbs 21:26 (ESV)

In Les Misérables, Jean Valjean is released from prison after serving time for stealing a loaf of bread. Valjean is then taken in by the kindness and hospitality of Bishop Myriel. However, he repays the bishop's kindness through theft, stealing six pieces of the bishop's silver. When the police catch him, the bishop defends him and, when the gendarmes leave, he gifts Valjean the silver, saying, "Do not forget, never forget, that you have promised to use this money to become an honest man. Jean Valjean, my brother, you no longer belong to evil, but to good. It is your soul I am buying for you. I withdraw it from dark thoughts and from the spirit of perdition and I give it to God!"

Valjean understood he was free when he left prison, yet he chose to commit another crime. Do we not sometimes do the same? We have been set free from the prison of sin and, just like the bishop said, our lives have been given to God. We have a purpose to fulfill.

The Bible reminds us that "Christ has truly set us free" (Galatians 5:1, NLT). Like Valjean, we have emerged from the shackles of sin and death. But Paul advises us, "Now make sure that you stay free." How? By avoiding bad habits, as Valjean did, and by embracing what this proverb teaches: giving generously without holding back.

Lord, teach me to give second chances.

KO

July 22

A prudent person foresees danger and takes precautions. The simpleton goes blindly on and suffers the consequences.

Proverbs 22:3 (NLT)

During the 2020 pandemic I was surprised to learn that a friend of mine didn't see the virus as a threat and refused to wear a mask unless she was forced to. She believed it was all a hoax, even questioning my faith in God's control over life and death. I didn't dare ask her, "Would you stand in the street if a truck were barreling toward you, just because you have faith?"

We live in dangerous times. Crime rates are up, and we hear about robberies, kidnappings and human trafficking. In some countries terrorism is a threat. Many parents worry about their kids falling into online traps. It's vital that we don't let fear control us but instead "take precautions."

"A prudent person foresees danger and takes precautions." This doesn't mean we live in fear. When Nehemiah started rebuilding the walls of Jerusalem, his enemies threatened them. Yet, those who built the wall "carried their loads in such a way that each labored on the work with one hand and with the other held a weapon" (Nehemiah 4:17, NRSVUE). They balanced faith in God with practical action to avoid danger.

Let's not be like "the simpleton [who] goes blindly on and suffers the consequences." God has given us common sense and prudence to make wise decisions. Let's take proactive steps today!

Father, make me wise to face the future.

MH

July 23

Do not ... invade the fields of the fatherless, for their redeemer is strong.
Proverbs 23:10-11 (NABRE)

UNICEF works to ensure the rights and well-being of children and adolescents. Around 170 million children are orphaned worldwide, with Brazil having the highest number due to AIDS-related deaths. Mexico follows, primarily due to organized crime and migration.

In the early Church, believers dedicated themselves to caring for the vulnerable, especially orphans. In those days the growth of the church was impressive. What made God's people so relevant in those days? One key factor was adoption.

James teaches us that true religion involves caring for orphans and widows in their distress, and the early Church put those words to practice (see James 1:27). The Hebrew word "goel" means "defender, redeemer." The "goel" was responsible for defending the rights of orphans and the defenseless. God, the Mighty One, is our protector and redeemer. Today's proverb warns us that if we wrong orphans, the Strong One will judge us.

Perhaps today's Christians need to learn from the early believers. Do we genuinely feel responsible for the welfare of orphans, or do we leave the work to organizations? What can we do practically today? Have you considered adopting a child or supporting children through organizations specifically dedicated to children?

Lord, please bless all the children, and help me find ways to help.

MG

JULY 24

An honest answer is like a kiss of friendship.

Proverbs 24:26 (NLT)

It is said that the word "sincere" describes pure honey without wax. In Latin, it refers to those born without mixing their cultures, thus people of a single or even pure origin. So, a sincere person, in this sense, is someone who behaves in a pure and truthful manner.

Many Old Testament prophets faced mistreatment or even death for their sincerity before evil kings. Remember Jeremiah? He was thrown into a muddy cistern because King Zedekiah refused to heed God's warnings through him, even though those warnings were meant to save his life. Jeremiah's truthfulness brought him problems.

On the other hand, we can remember the sign that Judas had given to the soldiers. He greeted Jesus in the Garden of Gethsemane with a kiss, a sign that Jesus was the one to be arrested. His betrayal was obvious. Yet, God expects sincerity from us. In Hebrews 10:22, we are urged to draw near "with a true heart in full assurance of faith" (ESV).

What kind of kiss will we give today? One of betrayal like Judas', or one that is pure and free from deception? Let's commit to being truthful and straightforward, just like Jeremiah, even if it leads to challenges.

Lord, help me to be sincere.

YF

July 25

A man without self-control is like a city broken into and left without walls.
                                    Proverbs 25:28 (ESV)

In Istanbul you can still see the remnants of the wall that once protected the city. In the past, when it was known as Constantinople, those walls were crucial for defense. If an enemy army breached the walls, they could seize control and cause chaos. Living without walls was unthinkable. What about the walls of our spirit?

Today's proverb teaches us that if we lack boundaries, we're like a defenseless city. Do you feel exhausted, drained or overwhelmed? It might be because you haven't set boundaries or practiced self-control. For instance, a woman without self-control might overeat, under sleep or neglect time for themselves and God. That's why boundaries are essential.

Author Henri Nouwen once said that discipline is "the effort to create some space in which God can act." We need the self-control that comes from the Spirit to carve out time for rest, a place to create and even extra money to save. Jesus Himself didn't heal every sick person, He didn't visit every city and He didn't speak to every person alive in His day. He sought solitude with His Father and quality time with His followers. After intense days, He told His disciples, "Let's go off by ourselves to a quiet place and rest awhile" (Mark 6:31, NLT).

If you're feeling drained and joyless, consider whether your walls have crumbled due to a lack of discipline. Shift your perspective and restore the boundaries that have been neglected or broken.

Father, help me to rebuild the walls of my spirit.

KO

July 26

Do you see a man who is wise in his own eyes? There is more hope for a fool than for him.

Proverbs 26:12 (ESV)

Anne Lamott wrote, "My coming to faith did not start with a leap but rather a series of staggers from what seemed like one safe place to another." This well-known novelist and speaker compared those safe places to lily pads that she landed on, one after the other, as she grew. Each lily pad prepared her for the next step in the swamp of doubt.

Have you ever wrestled with doubts? Today's proverb serves as a reminder that thinking we know it all is foolish. The phrase "wise in his own eyes" signifies someone who doesn't recognize God as the ultimate source of wisdom. Such a person often overlooks the knowledge of others and the possibility that they might be wrong.

The apostle Paul once thought he was wise in his own eyes as a proud Pharisee and persecutor of Christians. It was only by God's grace that he was humbled and later wrote, "Do nothing from selfish ambition or conceit, but in humility count others more significant than yourselves" (Philippians 2:3, ESV). Gideon, too, faced many doubts and sought God's reassurance at every step.

Anne Lamott reminds us that the opposite of faith isn't doubt. Faith helps us confront the chaos and emptiness of this world. Sometimes, we just need to wait for the light to appear. Let's not assume we know everything. When doubts arise, just take a leap to the next lily pad and "grow there," trusting that the next jump will come in time.

Father, forgive me for my vanity; I only desire to be more like Christ.

MH

July 27

Do not boast about tomorrow, for you do not know what a day may bring.
Proverbs 27:1 (ESV)

The New York Times published a 2020 year-in-review titled *A Year Like No Other* featuring a collection of that year's most significant photographs. *Time* magazine declared it "The Worst Year Ever," marked with a bold "X" over the number. The Covid-19 pandemic caught the world off guard, making 2020 a profoundly challenging year.

Yet others remind us that worse events have occurred in history, such as world wars and economic downturns. As the saying goes, "everyone sees things from their own perspective."

This proverb hits home! No one could predict what the future held, and we still can't. The lessons of 2020 taught us humility in facing the unknown. We've learned that we have little control over tomorrow. I remember a song we used to sing at youth camp, "I know nothing of the future; I know not what will be," which also reassured us, "I fear nothing of the future, for Jesus is with me."

Our circumstances might sway us between feeling self-sufficient and fearful. Our true stability lies in hope. May our peace rest on the promise of Jesus, "I am with you to the end of the age."

Lord, I place my life in your hands. You will fulfill your purpose in me.

MG

July 28

Whoever defrauds father or mother and says, 'It is no sin,' is a partner to a brigand.

Proverbs 28:24 (NABRE)

When I lived in a very big city, I rented a small apartment from a couple. On multiple occasions I heard them express concern about their need to lock up their home because of their son, a drug addict who would steal valuable items from them for drugs. In the past, they had lived comfortably and had a big home, but after the husband lost his job, they struggled financially. Then, it was my turn.

I discovered that my apartment had been broken into and my belongings were stolen. While I couldn't prove it, all evidence pointed to the couple's son. The evidence also suggested that multiple people were involved. A group of criminals!

Raising children is incredibly challenging. Adolescence is a particularly tough phase, but it's also a critical time when kids make their own choices and discover who they are. Like young Samuel, this is the season of life when God calls them by name and waits for them to respond: "Speak, Lord, your servant is listening" (1 Samuel 3:9, NLT).

If you're a parent, ask God for wisdom in guiding your children. If your kids are teens or young adults, pray daily for them to be receptive to God's voice. If they've made poor choices, don't lose hope—lead by example and tell God, "Here I am."

Father, give me wisdom to guide my children.

YF

July 29

The bloodthirsty hate blameless people, but the upright seek to help them.
                                                    Proverbs 29:10 (NLT)

Can you imagine being so perfect that no one could find even the slightest fault in you? What if nobody remembered a bad experience when they thought of you. How would you feel to know someone like that? Would you boast about having a blameless friend? What would it be like to be married to someone upright and honorable? Sadly, envy would most likely rear its ugly head.

Think back to your school days. Did we not often resent the smartest, most sociable or funniest people in our classes? Typically, we tend to feel bitter toward those who possess qualities we long for. No story better illustrates this proverb than the life of Jesus.

Few people in the first century recognized that when they encountered Jesus, they were standing face to face with the God of the universe. They thought Jesus was an ordinary man and they misunderstood His words and actions, feeling threatened by His perfect ways. What did they do? They cried out, "Crucify him!" They stained their hands with innocent blood. And although we were not there, we, too, have rejected the Son of God. Yet, He offers us a second chance and salvation today.

When I pray, I often examine my hands, turning my palms upward. This gesture reminds me that my hands wounded Jesus, yet His hands took the nails in my place. Bloodthirsty and murderous men killed Jesus, but He offers us life. Let's accept it!

On the cross, I saw the light and the stains of my soul I washed away. Thank you, Jesus.

KO

July 30

Some people curse their father and do not thank their mother.

Proverbs 30:11 (NLT)

An ancient fable tells of a man walking in his field one cold morning who found a snake nearly frozen to death. Despite knowing how dangerous the snake was, he picked it up and warmed it against his chest to bring it back to life. Once revived the snake bit him. Are we surprised by the snake's ingratitude?

This proverb doesn't give us details about the type of family ungrateful children come. In those days, single-parent families were rare, except in cases of death. Honoring parents is a fundamental principle in Judeo-Christian culture, in fact, it's in the Ten Commandments given to Moses on stone tablets. Disrespecting your parents reflects a lack of gratitude toward them and a lack of gratitude toward God.

When the angel Gabriel announced to Zechariah that his barren wife would give birth to John the Baptist, he revealed that this child would fulfill Malachi's prophecy: "His preaching will turn the hearts of fathers to their children, and the hearts of children to their fathers" (Malachi 4:6, NLT). This restoration of relationships is part of the transformation that God desires for us.

You may be living with resentment toward your parents, have gone through seasons of rebellion against them, or experienced a dysfunctional home. Regardless of what has happened, you can trust that Christ can use you as an instrument of reconciliation. Be grateful and treat your parents with honor.

Lord, teach me to honor and be thankful to my parents, and to forgive them when they fail.

MH

JULY 31

She opens her mouth with wisdom, and the teaching of kindness is on her tongue.
Proverbs 31:26 (ESV)

"The Office" is a popular American television series created by Greg Daniels, based on the British series of the same name. In the show, characters often engage in overlapping conversations, with Michael Scott frequently dominating the dialogue until he is the only one left speaking. He often makes humorous yet inappropriate comments about his coworkers, such as, "That's what she said" or "I am running away from my responsibilities." When he realizes everyone is listening and sees the disapproving looks from his colleagues, he abruptly changes the subject. The group then shares a laugh at his awkward yet funny remarks. Real life is different. If we're not careful with our words, we can offend others and there are consequences. We get in trouble when we speak recklessly.

Queen Esther faced a critical moment when she needed to approach her husband, the king. She wisely waited for the right moment to reveal her Jewish identity and ask for help to save her people. To frame her words, she organized lavish banquets, wore her royal robes and called for prayer and fasting. Every word she chose was deliberate, ensuring her message would be clear and effective.

Proverbs like this and stories like Esther's serve as lessons for us. A virtuous woman opens her mouth with wisdom and is thoughtful when she speaks. Knowing when and how to say the right words is a powerful act of assertiveness.

Lord, help me speak wisely.

MG

August 1

But whoever listens to me will dwell secure and will be at ease,
without dread of disaster.

Proverbs 1:33 (ESV)

Tug-of-war is a game where two teams pull on opposite ends of a rope, trying to drag the other team across a line. Have you ever played it? I remember the scraped knees and blistered hands- and the thrill of winning. But when it comes to our minds, this game isn't fun at all.

When I feel anxious, it's like a tug-of-war in my mind and soul. On one side, worries pull at me, while on the other, God tells me to trust Him. It's no surprise that the Greek word for worry, merimnaó, means to be pulled in two directions, like being fractured.

The antidote to worry is found in Scripture, "Don't worry about anything; instead, pray about everything" (Philippians 4:6, NLT). If we heed this wise advice, as today's proverb suggests, we will live in peace and ease. Is there anything better than living without worries?

If you're feeling anxious today, take a deep breath and sit quietly for a few moments—just five minutes is enough. Close your eyes and share with God what's troubling you. List your worries, describe them and then let go. Stop worrying and trust Him.

Lord, I don't want to worry about anything, but I want to pray about
everything.

KO

August 2

She rises while it is yet night and provides food for her household and portions for her maidens.

Proverbs 31:15 (ESV)

In many parts of the world, having domestic help is seen as a sign of wealth. Yet, not too long ago, it was common for middle-class families in Latin America to have this kind of help, while in first-world countries, it remains a privilege for the few.

Growing up, my mother hired a woman to clean our house once a week. I remember noticing how my mother would hurry to tidy up before the cleaner arrived, eager to make a good impression!

The woman described in Proverbs 31 is far from idle. She rises "while it is yet night" to prepare breakfast for her family, organizing everything. She likely managed a large household with both land and animals to care for. In the New Testament, we see Lydia, "a merchant of expensive purple cloth, who worshiped God" (Acts 16:14, NLT). She opened her heart to God through Paul's preaching, but she also considered her family as a priority, as we see, "she and her household were baptized" (see v. 15).

Whether or not we have help with chores, managing them is a significant responsibility. When life feels overwhelming, especially for those working outside the home, it's wise to delegate tasks. Amidst all this, let's not forget our family's spiritual needs, trusting that God will guide us in that area too.

Lord, help me see that daily chores are part of my service to you and my family.

MH

August 3

So you will find favor and good success in the sight of God and man.
Proverbs 3:4 (ESV)

A few months ago, a warm and faithful believer named Jennie passed away. I had no idea how much she was cherished by her church community until I witnessed their deep sadness at her passing. Many shared photos and memories, highlighting her kindness and how she would hug them tightly. Jennie was a wise and loving woman who earned the respect and admiration of those around her.

It's truly beautiful to be loved and respected by others. This makes me think of Deborah from the Bible. She was a wise woman who became a leader in Israel and was consulted to make judgements about the most critical decisions happening amongst the people. Remarkably, her warriors wouldn't go into battle without her. Her influence was tremendous.

Proverbs 3 speaks about the benefits of obedience and wisdom, assuring us that following mercy and truth will gain us approval from both God and others. Like Deborah, we can set a good example because those who love God are "like the sun as he rises in his might" (Judges 5:31, ESV).

Sometimes, we become overly concerned about how others perceive us, which is only human. Let us love God and we will naturally become examples for others, just as Jennie and Deborah were.

O God, I want to please you. May my life be a fragrant scent for you.

MG

August 4

Do not enter the path of the wicked, and do not walk in the way of the evil. Avoid it; do not go on it; turn away from it and pass on.
Proverbs 4:14-15 (ESV)

Dr. Eduardo Calixto Gonzalez, a Mexican physician with a doctorate in neurophysiology, explains in his lectures the differences between male and female brains and how they complement each other.

It's encouraging to know that while women's brains may be smaller in size, they are often more complex. Women tend to perceive colors more vividly, we recognize sweet flavors in ways men don't and we have a heightened sense of touch. We also absorb information quickly, communicate effectively and experience emotions deeply. Plus, we can engage both hemispheres of our brains simultaneously, enhancing our ability to multitask. However, like all minds, ours are also prone to evil—our flesh tends to stray.

In Ecclesiastes, God's Word says: "See, this alone I found, that God made man upright, but they have sought out many schemes" (Ecclesiastes 7:29, ESV). Even though Adam and Eve were created perfect, their sin tainted our brains. Many people hide behind science to justify this sinful nature, but the truth remains: we are born into sin.

Solomon advises us in today's verse, "Do not enter the path of the wicked." We must not excuse the old nature we inherited from Adam. Only the blood of Christ can transform our flesh when we repent and seek a true change.

Lord, you are faithful and just to forgive us our sins, and to cleanse us from all unrighteousness.

YF

August 5

The iniquities of the wicked ensnare him, and he is held fast in the cords of his sin.

Proverbs 5:22 (ESV)

The fires in Australia during 2019 began in September, intensified in November and were finally controlled by heavy rains in January 2020. Over forty-six million acres burned, nearly 3,500 homes were lost, and 34 lives were taken. At least 80% of the Blue Mountains, a World Heritage Site, suffered severe damage.

In my home, we have a fireplace we use in winter. I enjoy sitting by the fire and watching the flames dance. But if that fire were anywhere else, it could become destructive. If mismanaged, fire could threaten my home and family.

Sex operates similarly. In the right context—marriage—it brings warmth and unity; it "cooks" love. But in the wrong context—outside of marriage, it leads to pain and destruction. Today's proverb warns that a man who engages with a promiscuous woman becomes trapped by his own sins. How different it is for a couple who honors God in their intimacy! As Solomon's young wife put it, "Love flashes like fire, the brightest kind of flame. Many waters cannot quench love, nor can rivers drown it" (Song of Solomon 8:6-7, NLT).

Let's keep the fire contained within the fireplace of marriage, providing warmth and light for our homes. Remember, if we let it spread outside that context, it can only wound. Let's pray for a love that burns brightly and is never extinguished, for it is God who ignites that spark.

Lord, may the fire of my love for my husband be a blessing and light in my home.

KO

August 6

For their command is a lamp and their instruction a light; their corrective discipline is the way to life.

Proverbs 6:23 (NLT)

This proverb highlights the influence of parents. Unfortunately, we are in a war with certain governments that seek to assume primary authority over our children. Parents are fighting for their right to educate their kids according to their own values, including biblical teachings on sexuality.

I once heard a young professional woman express deep admiration for her mother, Anne. She described her mother as "perhaps the best musician in the country," someone capable of teaching at top universities. Yet, Anne chose to answer God's call to raise her children full-time. Her daughter acknowledges that she and her brother have remained faithful to the Lord, largely because of their mother's profound influence.

"For the commandment is a lamp and the teaching a light," says this proverb in a different translation (ESV). According to the Bible, parents are primarily responsible for educating their children. Even though many schools exist today, parents remain a crucial "light" from the moment their children are born. The apostle Paul wrote to Timothy: "I remember your genuine faith, for you share the faith that first filled your grandmother Lois and your mother, Eunice. And I know that same faith continues strong in you" (2 Timothy 1:5, NLT). Here, we see the impact of three generations devoted to God!

Most of us can appreciate our parents' teachings, even if they weren't believers. If they were, we are doubly blessed. Even if we feel insignificant in this world, our influence can shine brightly for future generations!

O heavenly Father, may your light shine in me so that I may be a good influence for my children and grandchildren.

MH

AUGUST 7

So listen to me, my sons, and pay attention to my words.

Proverbs 7:24 (NLT)

In C.S. Lewis' *Prince Caspian*, Aslan doesn't reveal himself to the children right away; he wants them to move forward without seeing him, which requires faith. Susan, the eldest sister, chooses not to believe that Aslan is leading them because she's tired and wants to leave the forest. Aslan tells her, "You have been listening to your fears, child."

Who are we listening to: faith or our fears? Lewis wrote that the real enemy of faith isn't reason, but rather emotion and imagination. Even when we know something to be true, we don't always believe it. For example, when learning to swim, even if we're told the water will support us, our irrational fear can still drag us under.

Faith, according to C.S. Lewis, is "the art of holding on to things your reason has once accepted, in spite of your changing moods." During the 2020 pandemic, fear crept into many homes and impacted the health of countless numbers of people. What's the remedy? We must ground ourselves in God's promises rather than in our imaginations. Remember: "When you go through deep waters, I will be with you. When you go through rivers of difficulty, you will not drown" (Isaiah 43:2, NLT).

The voice of fear can be loud and unsettling, but let's heed today's proverb and listen to God, who is Wisdom itself. As the old hymn says, "And grace my fears relieved."

Lord, I am certainly afraid, but I trust in you.

KO

August 8

I, Wisdom, live together with good judgment. I know where to discover knowledge and discernment.

Proverbs 8:12 (NLT)

A few years back, I had the honor of serving as the administrative director at the Center of Integral Assistance for Women, thanks to a dear friend. My role involved addressing immediate issues and reporting on our material and staffing shortfalls. We provided training in cooking, sewing, literacy, beauty culture and other skills to women in need. Our general director, offered counseling rooted strictly in the Bible.

At one point, the demand for counseling grew so much that our general director couldn't manage it alone. She decided to train some of us in the art of counseling. We attended courses and workshops and conferences. We were inexperienced in the art of counseling, so we spent time in prayer seeking wisdom to help these troubled souls.

Our Lord Jesus, Wisdom personified, invites us to seek Him for the advice we need to guide others. I often think of a few women who never returned to my counseling room. I have sought the Lord's forgiveness for not providing the right support for their struggles. I pray that the Lord has given them comfort through other people.

If you're considering becoming a counselor, what's the best approach? Take refuge in the arms of the Master and spend time with Him to learn His wisdom and guidance.

Thank you, Father, for being the best Counselor. Give me wisdom to counsel others.

YF

August 9

Come, eat of my bread.

Proverbs 9:5 (ESV)

Think of all the different types of bread there are. Bread can be baked, fried or grilled, and when you're hungry, a slice can fill you up for a few hours. Bread is one of the world's oldest and most consumed foods. Did you know it once fell from the sky?

While the Israelites wandered in the wilderness, God provided them with a flake-like substance covering the ground, which they used to make bread. Though they called it "manna" or "what is this," it was a form of heavenly bread. Yet, even with this provision, they still felt empty. Why? Because no amount of food can satisfy the soul's deeper needs for acceptance, forgiveness and peace.

When Jesus walked the earth, He declared, "I am the bread of life. Whoever comes to me will never be hungry again" (John 6:35, NLT). Essentially, He was saying that knowing Him fulfills our deepest longings: eternal life. "I am the true bread that came down from heaven. Anyone who eats this bread will not die as your ancestors did (even though they ate the manna) but will live forever" (John 6:58, NLT).

Wisdom invites us to come and eat the bread of heaven that grants us life beyond this world. Many of us fear the transition from life to death, striving to avoid it and desperate to be remembered. But we hold the key to eternal life: faith in Jesus, the bread from heaven.

Jesus, you are the bread that came down from heaven. Give me eternal life.

KO

August 10

The mouth of the righteous is a fountain of life, but the mouth of the wicked conceals violence.

Proverbs 10:11 (ESV)

What we say can be recorded at any moment, and our words on social media can spread like wildfire. If we speak inappropriately, it often, "conceals violence."

A woman in our church was always very kind to newcomers. She would chat with them and make them feel valued. Many have said, "It was because of her that I came back." Another friend echoed that same sentiment, "I never heard her speak ill of anyone." Her speech truly is "a fountain of life."

According to another translation of today's proverb: "The words of the godly are a life-giving fountain; the words of the wicked conceal violent intentions" (NLT). In biblical times, a fountain symbolized a spring of water, crucial for survival in arid lands—without water, there is no life. Jesus offered the Samaritan woman "living water" that would never run dry (see John 4). When we speak with love and offer that "living water" to others, we help their lives flourish!

Whether spoken or written, our words have the power to heal or hurt, to bring hope or despair. Let's be mindful of the impact we have on others.

Father, may everything I say flow from you, the source of life par excellence!

MH

August 11

Whoever reviles a neighbor lacks sense, but the intelligent keep silent.
Proverbs 11:12 (NABRE)

Educators have discovered that bullying often starts at home, whether from overbearing parents who yell without truly instilling discipline or older siblings who verbally and physically abuse their younger siblings. A study by the University of Bristol found that 28% of the children surveyed experienced name-calling or physical abuse.

When I was nine or ten years old, I began developing unhealthy eating habits, partly due to a young uncle who liked to make jokes about my appearance. He gave me a nickname that was a funny label to some, but deeply hurtful to me. That witty yet cruel nickname was devastating to my self-esteem.

Nicknames among family members are common, yet they often disguise a criticism of a person's characteristics. Another translation of today's proverb states: "Whoever belittles his neighbor lacks sense, but a man of understanding remains silent" (ESV). Highlighting someone's weaknesses with a nickname is a form of belittling. Even if it seems amusing, it's better to be wise and choose silence instead.

Breaking the cycle of teasing and belittling within families can be challenging but making fun of other people's weaknesses is never funny. What can you do? Refuse to participate or laugh. Instead, use the Word to show that's it's better express ideas that reinforce our appreciation for friends and family, especially children.

Lord, please heal my wounds and help me to avoid hurting others with my words.

MG

August 12

No one is established by wickedness, but the root of the righteous will never be moved.

Proverbs 12:3 (ESV)

Caligula was one of the most notorious Roman emperors. Initially, he ruled well—so much so that when he fell ill, some people were willing to offer themselves to the gods for his recovery. However, once healed, he executed those who made those vows and forced suspected conspirators to take their own lives. His excesses led him into debt, prompting him to impose heavy taxes and to seize property by killing property owners.

Caligula claimed himself to be a "god," building three temples in his own honor and demanded worship from the Senate and the people. He was known for his sexual depravity and even named his horse Consul to mock the Senate, claiming his horse was superior. He famously ordered his army to attack the sea, swinging their swords at Neptune, the god of the ocean. It's no surprise that he was the first Roman emperor to be assassinated.

Wickedness cannot establish a position of power. Those who mistreat others under their authority violate divine law. When Caligula died Seneca remarked, "Nature produced it, in my opinion, to show how far unlimited vice can go when combined with unlimited power."

At some point in your life, you may find yourself in a position of authority over others—perhaps you already are. Strive to be a leader your team members remember with gratitude, not with resentment. As Paul reminds us, we all have "a Master in heaven" (see Colossians 4:1).

Father, teach me to treat others with fairness and respect.

YF

August 13

The soul of the sluggard craves and gets nothing, while the soul of the diligent is richly supplied.

Proverbs 13:4 (ESV)

A well-known anecdote tells of a man who approached a virtuoso pianist after a concert and said, "I would give half my life to play the piano like you do." The pianist replied, "That is exactly what I have done." An uncle of mine, an oboe player, shares that he practices for many hours before each concert. What appears effortless on stage requires immense time and dedication.

When I started writing, I thought it would be simple—just sit down and type out a story. However, I soon realized it involved countless revisions, rewriting, negotiating with editors and polishing the text. It's hard work! Diligence is crucial in any endeavor, and the same applies to our spiritual lives.

Ezra, who returned to Jerusalem after the exile, relied not only on God's approval but also on good habits. He was "a scribe, well-versed in the law of Moses ... [and] the king granted him all that he requested, because the hand of the Lord, his God, was over him" (Ezra 7:6, NABRE). Ezra learned from God and taught others what he had learned, and God prospered him, granting him favor with a powerful king.

Let's commit to diligently reading our Bibles. We may desire to know God more deeply, but mere desire won't suffice if we remain lazy. However, if we work diligently, we will thrive!

Lord, help me to be more diligent in your Word, just like Ezra.

KO

August 14

There is a path before each person that seems right, but it ends in death.

Proverbs 14:12 (NLT)

Today's world is filled with motivational messages like Nike's "Just do it" or "You are number one." These sayings encourage people to focus on themselves and their desires. And at the same time, the prevailing philosophy of our day is teaching us that truth is relative—that "your truth" is what really matters.

When I was a young college student, a classmate gave me some advice: "forget what your parents and your religion taught you. Do what feels right." I was suspicious of the wisdom of her words, but her perspective reflected the culture around me and to an extent, I followed that wisdom too. Thankfully, Christ burst into my life and showed me that He is the true path.

If people do not allow God, their Creator, to guide their lives, they will choose the path that "seems right" but ultimately "ends in death." When the kings and people of Israel and Judah went astray, worshipping idols and practicing unrighteousness, they faced defeat and exile. The rich young man in Mark's Gospel, who longed for eternal life, left "disheartened" because he was unwilling to let go of his wealth (see Mark 10:22).

Are we on a path that "seems right" but leads to death? If our priorities are comfort, popularity, or fleeting pleasures, we may have chosen the wrong way. Let's choose the path of life that Jesus Christ offers.

Lord, I want to follow your path, the one that leads to eternal life, rather than my own.

MH

August 15

Plans fail when there is no counsel, but they succeed when advisers are many.

Proverbs 15:22 (NABRE)

Near my town, there's a camp that has been a true oasis for thousands of people of all ages. Every time I attended this camp, a counselor was there to guide us through daily devotionals and offer her advice on any topic we wanted to discuss.

One counselor helped me make the most significant decision of my life: accepting Christ as my personal Savior. Years later, I sought guidance from a missionary regarding my career choice, and when it came to romantic decisions, I sought the advice of one of my seminary professors. I'm grateful for the wise counselors God has placed along my path to guide me through the three most important decisions of my life.

As we grow older, it can become harder to seek advice from others. Yet, the Bible encourages us to seek counsel when making plans. To succeed, it's wise to have a multitude of counselors! We can draw from the wisdom and experience of those God has placed in our lives as leaders and friends. And even if we can't find the right person to turn to, we can always turn to Jesus, our Wonderful Counselor (see Isaiah 9:6).

Let's avoid being overly confident in our own opinions. Are you facing a situation where you could use some advice? Ask God to provide multiple counselors and be open to their guidance, especially for life's most significant decisions.

Lord, grant me the wisdom to solve my problems and the humility to follow the advice I receive.

MG

August 16

The Lord has made everything for its purpose, even the wicked for the day of trouble.

Proverbs 16:4 (ESV)

During the time of the Roman Empire, many of the issues they faced—such as abortion, pedophilia, human trafficking and slavery—we still face today. There were all kinds of human rights violations. Interestingly, early Christians didn't focus on campaigning against specific societal ills. Paul, for example, did not champion one particular cause but instead addressed a broader issue. What was it?

Paul addressed the root of all abuses: the sin that dwells within us. His "anti-sin" campaign is evident in his letter to the Romans, where he repeatedly reminds us that we have all sinned. This sin, which is against God and His law, manifests itself in specific sinful behaviors like lying, adultery and murder.

Today's proverb might be misunderstood, but let's clarify what it means. God created all people with a purpose: to have fellowship with Him. When humanity chose to sin, they turned away from God. Paul explains that the cost of sin is death. And so, "each person is destined to die once and after that comes judgment" (Hebrews 9:27, NLT). The fate of the wicked leads to the day of calamity.

The good news is that God has also established a path to salvation for us all. Sin doesn't have to be the end. "Christ was offered once for all time as a sacrifice to take away the sins of many people" (Hebrews 9:28, NLT). Accept His salvation today.

Lord, I acknowledge that sin is everyone's problem, including mine. Thank you for providing a solution through Jesus.

YF

August 17

A friend is always loyal, and a brother is born to help in time of need.
Proverbs 17:17 (NLT)

My friend Gül, who came from a Muslim background, believed that Allah, being all-powerful, could not have a personal relationship with her. She envisioned God as a sultan residing in a palace, distant and disconnected from ordinary people. Do you think that we sometimes view Jesus in the same way—as a distant king focused solely on our mistakes?

When Gül encountered Jesus, her life was transformed. Although it took her time to understand the carpenter from Nazareth depicted in the Gospels, each step deepened her faith. Today, she is a devoted follower of Christ, even though her faith has cost her a job and created conflicts within her family.

This proverb pictures two images of our relationship with Jesus—which sets Christianity apart from other religions. Jesus said, "Now you are my friends, since I have told you everything the Father told me" (John 15:15, NLT). And He also said, "Anyone who does God's will is my brother and sister and mother" (Mark 3:35, NLT).

Jesus is the most loyal friend we will ever have. He will never fail us. He is also the brother we need during difficult times. If Jesus is not yet your friend or brother, come to Him today. Believe that He came to save you, and like my friend Gül, marvel at the God who became flesh to dwell among us.

Thank you, Jesus, for being my loyal friend and brother.

KO

August 18

The human spirit can endure a sick body, but who can bear a crushed spirit?
Proverbs 18:14 (NLT)

My friend Fatima lives with a chronic illness and posted this encouraging message on Facebook: "Even though I have diabetes, I can do anything I put my mind to. My disease does not define me." It's remarkable—even amongst doctors—what tenacity and hope can achieve in a sick body. Our proverb today addresses two different types of illnesses: those that affect our bodies and those that afflict our souls.

Our bodies can weaken over time and feel the nagging pain of inherited ailments. A hopeful spirit can alleviate pain and even foster healing in the body. The illness in our souls is different and refers to the consequences of sin. Who can mend an anguished or broken spirit?

"The Lord is close to the brokenhearted; he rescues those whose spirits are crushed" (Psalm 34:18, NLT). If you're grappling with the sickness of sin, feeling distant from God and burdened with regret, or if you're struggling to carry on, come to Jesus today. He desires to heal your heart, restore your hope and give you new life.

If you're dealing with a chronic illness, remember that if your spirit has been renewed by Jesus, you have hope. God can grant you the strength to endure physical suffering and can work miracles. Above all, He has already provided the greatest healing of all: the healing of your heart.

Divine Physician, please heal all my ailments, especially those of the heart.

KO

August 19

Whoever cares for the poor lends to the Lord, who will pay back the sum in full.

Proverbs 19:17 (NABRE)

Russian writer Leo Tolstoy was known for his generosity. Despite being the son of a feudal lord with 700 serfs, he made his own shoes and refused to let servants make his bed. He went as far as donating all his possessions to benefit the poor.

In one of his stories, *The Cobbler and His Guest,* he tells of Martin the cobbler, who falls asleep after reading the Bible. He hears Jesus say that He will visit him. In the morning, Martin prepares soup and waits for the visit. He sees an old man tired from shoveling snow and invites him in for tea. Later, he notices a ragged woman and offers her soup and a cloak for warmth. While waiting, he witnesses a young boy stealing an apple from an elderly lady—he intervenes to resolve the conflict and brings peace to the situation.

As the day ends, he hears a voice say, "Martin, Martin, don't you know me? ... It is I." Emerging from the shadows are the old man, the poor woman and the apple thief. Martin feels immense joy and begins to read the Bible on the opened page, "For I was hungry, and you fed me. I was thirsty, and you gave me a drink. I was a stranger, and you invited me into your home... when you did it to one of the least of these my brothers and sisters, you were doing it to me!" (Matthew 25:35-36, 40, NLT).

Are we truly aware of the needs around us? Let's move from mere observation to action, seeking Jesus in every person who lacks sustenance, shelter and care.

Lord, help me to be sensitive to the needs of others.

MG

August 20

The human spirit is the lamp of the Lord, searching every inmost part.
Proverbs 20:27 (NRSVUE)

Did you know there are over 4,300 religions in the world? However, about 75% of the global population practices just five: Buddhism, Christianity, Hinduism, Islam and Judaism. Among these, Christianity and Islam are the most widely followed. Interestingly, if we were to count those with no religious affiliation, they would rank third.

Humans are inherently religious. Throughout history, cultures have worshipped various gods in an attempt to satisfy the spiritual longing of the human heart. God has placed a restlessness within us that prompts us to seek spiritual things. However, this emptiness cannot be filled unless God Himself chooses to do so.

God desires to fill that void, but first He needed to address the problem that separates us from Him: our sin. He did this by becoming a sacrifice for our sins, paving the way for reconciliation. In His Word He promises, "After those days, says the Lord: I will put my laws in their minds and write them on their hearts, and I will be their God, and they shall be my people" (Hebrews 8:10, NRSVUE).

We all have friends, family and acquaintances who have yet trust Christ as their Savior. Our mission is to share the light we possess in our spirits so that it may illuminate their lives as well. Let's pray for God to fill the emptiness they carry in their hearts.

Father, today I lift up _____ who has yet to know you.

YF

August 21

No human wisdom or understanding or plan can stand against the Lord.
Proverbs 21:30 (NLT)

Both telescopes and microscopes serve to help us see what the naked eye cannot. However, they do so in different ways: microscopes reveal the small, while telescopes unveil the vast and distant. For us, we need to learn to see beyond what is obvious and learn to recognize both the individual details of life and the bigger picture.

Our lives are not simply a compilation of all of our small, everyday choices—we are part of a larger, more complex world where our actions and words impact others. As today's proverb reminds us, God has already mapped out our personal journey and His grand plan for humanity. And no one can stand against Him!

Take the story of Joseph, for instance. He wasn't able to grasp the larger picture of his life until after his father's death. His struggles and sufferings did not make sense until he was able to see the complete trajectory of his life—how God used his circumstances to save his family. He later told his brothers, "You intended to harm me, but God intended it all for good" (Genesis 50:20, NLT).

If you find yourself focused solely on your immediate circumstances, try to adopt a broader perspective. Remember that both the good and the bad are part of God's larger plan for you. If you're preoccupied with the big picture, don't forget that today's small decisions shape your future. Let's strive to see as God sees, trusting that He arranges everything for our good.

Lord, help me to view life through your eyes.

KO

August 22

Whoever loves a pure heart and gracious speech will have the king as a friend.
Proverbs 22:11 (NLT)

While there are few kings today, many people long to be close to the influential and famous—presidents, governors or even their favorite celebrities like film stars, athletes and popular singers. In the past, fans sought autographs but now it's more common for people to seek a photo with a celebrity. Yet, true friendship with the famous remains a rarity.

The daughter of some friends of mine had a unique opportunity to meet King Charles of England, not due to wealth or status but by God's grace through a wish-granting organization for children with cancer.

As Christians, we consider Christ to be our King and Lord. We cannot earn His favor through generous offerings, our good works or by gaining vast amounts of knowledge. "Whoever loves a pure heart and gracious speech will have the king as a friend," as our proverb puts it. He Himself has purified our hearts to enter His presence. Consider Abraham's story, "God counted him as righteous because of his faith" and even considered him a friend (see James 2:23).

What a remarkable privilege it is to be friends with our King! We can enter His presence only by grace—through His purifying work and through our faith in Christ, who sacrificed Himself for us. Let's rejoice in this incredible gift of friendship.

My King and Lord, thank you for being my friend!

MH

August 23

Do not look at wine when it is red, when it sparkles in the cup...

Proverbs 23:31 (ESV)

A well-known composition, popularized by Mariano Osorio, offers a striking depiction of alcohol's destructive power, "Do you know me? I am ... the companion of all worldly pleasures, the messenger of death that governs the world. I am present everywhere, in all ceremonies; none takes place without my presence. I fabricate adulteries, I give birth in hearts to criminal thoughts. I destroy the family ... I cause conflicts, crimes, and misfortunes ... I am your king. His majesty: alcohol."

Even though everyone knows the dangers of alcohol, no one ever believes they'd be the person who'd become an alcoholic. Temptation often creeps in subtly. This proverb warns us that it begins with something as simple as looking at a drink.

Did you know that alcohol addiction increased by 250% among young people during the 2020 pandemic? The Bible clearly warns us, "Don't be drunk with wine, because that will ruin your life" (Ephesians 5:18, NLT). If you find yourself lacking self-control, turn to the Holy Spirit for guidance, encouragement and comfort—rather than seeking refuge in a harmful substance.

The widespread abuse of alcohol in our society should compel us to pray, evangelize and engage our young people. We must help our friends recognize that the emptiness they're seeking to fill can only be satisfied by Christ. Do you know someone who struggles with alcohol whom you can pray for today?

Lord, protect us and deliver us from the trap of addiction.

MG

August 24

Do not say, "As they did to me, so will I do to them; I will repay them according to their deeds."
Proverbs 24:29 (NABRE)

"El Chavo del Ocho," a Spanish television character created by Roberto Gómez Bolaños, famously said, "Revenge is never good. It kills and poisons the soul." This catchy phrase relates well with today's proverb. In our world, it's common to see people seeking revenge because of trivial matters.

Corrie Ten Boom and her family were sent to a Nazi concentration camp for sheltering Jews during the Holocaust. They endured humiliation and mistreatment, with her father and sister dying in captivity. After the war, while sharing her experiences, she met one of the guards who had mistreated her. He reached out, confessed his faith in Christ and asked for forgiveness. Corrie felt a surge of hatred.

But then these words of the Bible came to the front of her mind, "If you do not forgive others, neither will your Father forgive your transgressions" (Matthew 6:15, NABRE). Corrie faced a choice: cling to her hatred or forgive. She chose the latter.

Having suffered under Nazism, Corrie's experience reminds us that if she could forgive. Surely, we can too. She wrote extensively about forgiveness, saying, "Those who were able to forgive were the ones who were best able to rebuild their lives." Are we willing to forgive?

Father, I desire to rebuild my life on the foundation of forgiveness

YF

AUGUST 25

To eat too much honey is not good; nor to seek honor after honor.
Proverbs 25:27 (NABRE)

Honey is delicious and nutritious, but if you eat too much raw honey, it can cause an allergic reaction in your body that can lead to heart failure and even death. Honor works in a similar way, if we seek it for ourselves, it's not good. Yet, many of us struggle with this!

Isn't it true that our identities are often shaped by others' opinions? We crave validation, wanting to be seen as "good people," "excellent mothers," or "top-notch professionals." If we don't receive that recognition, we can feel distressed! And so, we often say "yes" when we really want to say "no."

In the Bible, many struggled with this issue. Some Jewish leaders "loved human praise more than the praise of God" (John 12:43, NLT). Peter feared criticism and refused to eat with non-Jews (see Galatians 2:12). So, what's the remedy? Instead of seeking personal glory, let's pursue transformation, because "a person with a changed heart seeks praise from God, not from people" (Romans 2:29, NLT).

We all face this challenge, often without realizing it. The next time you receive an invitation but want to decline it because you're tired or perhaps you have other obligations, be honest. Don't let others' approval sway your decisions. If you fail and then others think less of you, just remember that it's true—you're not perfect!

Lord, fill me with your approval instead of my need for others' validation.

KO

August 26

Without wood the fire dies out; without a tale-bearer strife subsides.
Proverbs 26:20 (NABRE)

What should you do if you're if you're indoors and a fire starts in another room? First, if you see smoke seeping under the door, don't open it! Second, if you don't see smoke seeping under the door, touch the door and see if it's warm, if the door feels warm or hot, don't open it! And third, if the door is cool to touch but the doorknob is hot, still, don't open it! If we are cautious around fire, why are we not cautious around gossip?

Television shows dedicated to celebrity gossip are wildly popular today. Gossip—the spread of rumors, often negative—can sometimes be synonymous with lying. It not only harms others but spreads like a "fire," leaving destruction in its wake.

Just as when there is no firewood, "the fire dies out," gossip fizzles when there are no tales to tell. Although many don't consider gossip a serious sin, it's as harmful as theft and murder, as it seeks to hurt others, "But let no one among you suffer as a murderer, a thief, an evildoer, or as an intriguer" (1 Peter 4:15, NABRE). Gossip defames and dishonors others.

Let's recognize that many fights and conflicts stem from inappropriate words. When gossip starts, how should we respond? Just as we wouldn't open a door to a fire, we should avoid fueling the flames of gossip.

Lord, may my words extinguish fires rather than ignite them.

MH

AUGUST 27

Take good care of your flocks, give careful attention to your herds.
Proverbs 27:23 (NABRE)

New Zealand is famous for having more sheep than people. In 2017, for example, it is estimated that there were about thirty million sheep and four million people. The sheep industry is one of the most important industries on the island. In the 19th century, New Zealand exported wool; today, it primarily produces meat.

Obtaining wool has always been essential for survival, both now and in biblical times. And so, the advice to take good care of our flocks is a broader encouragement toward stewardship—being good stewards of what God provides. As women, we are responsible for managing our households and training our children to care for our homes.

Paul instructed Titus to have the older women teach the younger women "to be self-controlled, chaste, good managers of the household, kind, submissive to their husbands, so that the word of God may not be discredited" (Titus 2:5, NRSVUE). One reason God calls us to live in a clean and orderly way is so our homes can be examples of peace and harmony to others.

In every area of our lives, we need to avoid extremes. Don't let order and cleanliness become an obsession that robs the family of the joy of home life. At the same time, never let your house shine more than you. Caring for yourself should always be a priority.

Lord, help me to prioritize my responsibilities correctly.

MG

August 28

But wise and knowledgeable leaders bring stability.
Proverbs 28:2 (NLT)

We live in complicated times, where courage seems to be a forgotten art. Yet, how desperately we need it! When was the last time you heard of a firefighter risking his life to save a child, or of a student bravely standing up to their professor's questionable ideas?

Martin Luther surely faced fear when he stood before the council of men demanding that he renounce his beliefs. Yet, he remained firm. What kept him from backing down? It wasn't the promise of a better future—he knew he risked death or exile. Instead, he declared, "Unless I am convinced by Scripture or reason ... I cannot in good conscience recant."

Displaying this kind of courage isn't easy. True courage is the relentless pursuit of truth, even when it requires us to reevaluate our own beliefs. Once we discover that truth, we defend our convictions, even when faced with threats or ridicule. Saul of Tarsus embodied this type of courage—first as a zealous Pharisee, convinced he was defending the faith, and later as a devoted follower of Christ, willing to suffer and even die for the Gospel.

Are you brave? It's not easy, especially in a world where the majority prefer falsehoods. But have the courage to speak up, to ask questions when you're unsure and carefully weigh what is presented to discern what is true. As our proverb teaches us, when wise leaders arise, society flourishes.

Father, grant me the courage to stand for the truth.

KO

August 29

Evil people are trapped by sin, but the righteous escape, shouting for joy.
Proverbs 29:6 (NLT)

Theresienstadt was a Nazi concentration camp and ghetto that served as a transit point to different extermination camps. It housed Jews deemed local celebrities, the elderly and disabled before it sent them away. In Nazi propaganda, it was falsely portrayed as a "spa town" where elderly German Jews could "retire" safely. This is how sin works.

Satan, the enemy of God, paints a "resort-like" picture of sin. He tells us that we can do whatever we want and that we have freedom without consequences. Michal Beer, a prisoner in Theresienstadt, wrote about her release in her diary, "After the shots...a woman's voice was heard... 'A red flag!' Cries of joy erupted - and we breathed a sigh of relief. We had managed to survive!"

Today's proverb tells us that the righteous escape sin with shouts of joy. This sounds a lot like a person, wrongly imprisoned, finally tasting freedom. When Jesus liberates us from the bondage of sin, we can rejoice and breathe freely again. Have you felt this type of liberation?

You can free yourself from sin today. A new life is possible if you believe in Jesus' promise: "I tell you the truth, those who listen to my message and believe in God who sent me have eternal life. They will never be condemned for their sins, but they have already passed from death into life" (John 5:24, NLT). Do you believe this?

Lord, thank you for freeing me from sin.

KO

August 30

They are pure in their own eyes, but they are filthy and unwashed.

Proverbs 30:12 (NLT)

Cleaning products have come a long way. We now have a variety of solid and liquid soaps—some of them antibacterial. During the pandemic people scrambled to buy as much soap and disinfectant alcohol as they could, and sales skyrocketed. Even so—regardless of how pungent these soaps may be—none of them can clean us on the inside.

When the conquistadors arrived in Mexico, they found that the indigenous people practiced daily hygiene in lakes, rivers and in steam baths called "temazcales". Their cleanliness contrasted sharply with that of the Spaniards, who often avoided hot baths. In fact, it's said that Louis XIV bathed only twice in his entire life but considered himself very clean because he changed his clothes twice a day.

This proverb refers to those who mistakenly believe they are pure while remaining spiritually unclean. They may regularly practice external religious devotion, but they lack genuine devotion to God. God chastised the church of Laodicea for this very thing, "For you say, 'I am rich and affluent and have no need of anything,' and yet do not realize that you are wretched, pitiable, poor, blind, and naked" (Revelation 3:17, NABRE). They hadn't allowed Jesus to cleanse and heal them from within.

While we can maintain physical cleanliness, our spiritual "daily bath" must include mental and spiritual hygiene. Have you allowed Christ to make you a "new creation"? (see 2 Corinthians 5:17). This is the first step. And then, we confess our sins and draw near to the Lord continually.

Create in me, O Lord, a clean heart.

MH

August 31

The heart of her husband trusts in her, and he will have no lack of gain.
Proverbs 31:11 (ESV)

Samuel Johnson once said, "There can be no friendship without confidence, and no confidence without integrity." This phrase has guided me throughout my life. I've learned that to be trustworthy—both as a friend and a wife—I must embody integrity.

Men today face many pressures that are both demanding and overwhelming. A husband needs to know that his wife stands by him, supports him and is on his team. His heart trusts in her. He trusts that his wife isn't speaking ill of him behind his back. He needs assurance that together they can manage family finances wisely and that she will care for the children even when he's not home.

The virtuous woman in Proverbs does good and not harm to her husband "all the days of her life." She does this even on days when she feels angry, disappointed, sick, and hurt.

A marriage relationship is a relationship of friendship, where trust interweaves itself with integrity. A peaceful husband is a happy husband. God is just, and if you, as a wife, do good, you can expect to reap what you've sown.

Lord, today I commit to bringing goodness to my husband. Please help me to be a trustworthy wife.

MG

September 1

They shall eat the fruit of their way, and have their fill of their own devices.
Proverbs 1:31 (ESV)

The saying "Don't ask for pears from the elm tree" illustrates a fundamental truth: we reap what we sow. We cannot expect apples unless we've planted an apple tree, nor grapes without a vine. This proverb reminds us that in life, we experience the consequences of what we have sown and nurtured.

A life without God leads to a life of lies, conflict, drunkenness, jealousy, envy and anger. When God is absent from our daily lives, we tend towards selfishness. Without God in our lives, we dismiss any thoughts of an afterlife and adopt a "live and let live" mentality. A quick glance at our society reveals the results of this way of thinking: corrupt governments, broken families, grotesque entertainment, abuse and human trafficking.

The apostle Paul wrote that "the one who sows to the Spirit will from the Spirit reap eternal life" (Galatians 6:8, ESV). In Galatians, he emphasizes that when we invite God into our lives, we reap love, joy, peace, patience, kindness, goodness, faithfulness, gentleness and self-control (see Galatians 5:22-23). Isn't this a better list than the one we listed earlier?

Today's proverb reflects the lament of the wise writer that those who reject wisdom will reap the consequences of their choices. What will we cultivate today? Remember, the Word of God is like a seed; if we plant these proverbs in our hearts daily, we will harvest sweet, nourishing fruit.

Lord, help me to sow your Word in my life so I can reap all the goodness that comes from you.

KO

SEPTEMBER 2

She goes to inspect a field and buys it; with her earnings she plants a vineyard.

Proverbs 31:16 (NLT)

It's often said that Latino culture tends to avoid long-term planning, which makes the work of an insurance salesmen challenging. No one saves and no one plans. Most live "day to day" and spend more than they make. They borrow against their future and create large amounts of debt.

A friend of mine, who worked diligently cleaning houses, had limited resources but managed them wisely. She saved up to buy a sewing machine, using it to create clothing for extra income. Over time, she and her husband saved enough to purchase a plot of land and build a modest home, piece by piece. Long before myself or any of our peers (who were older than her by the way) had our own homes, she had hers. And she achieved it through hard work!

The woman described in Proverbs 31 is remarkably forward-thinking. She saves, invests and buys land. Her husband trusts her decisions, knowing she is a competent manager. This looks a lot like the trust Pharaoh placed in Joseph: "Joseph was put in charge of all the king's household; he became ruler over all the king's possessions" (Psalm 105:21, NLT). Stewardship, joined together with responsible living, is truly a beautiful thing.

Are we like this virtuous woman? Are we prudent and forward-looking?

Father, teach me to be a good steward of the resources you provide.

MH

September 3

Be not wise in your own eyes; fear the Lord, and turn away from evil.

Proverbs 3:7 (ESV)

In the film *All About Eve*, Bette Davis portrays Margo, an established actress who loses everything to the cunning "wisdom of Eve Harrington," who is determined to steal Margo's fame and relationships. In the movie, one memorable line captures an important idea: " There comes a time in every woman's life when the world gets a little bit too much for her, and a piano realizes it has not written a concerto."

Adam and Eve lived in paradise where everything was perfect, enjoying a life that looked a lot like a permanent honeymoon. They could have everything except for the fruit of one tree. God provided clear instructions, but Eve craved that fruit. Eve wanted to do things her way and that was her first sin. She did not take God's warning seriously and paradise was lost.

Have we felt "the wisdom of Eve" stirring within us when we're drawn to something forbidden? We often think we know better than God what will lead to a fulfilling life, only to find that this path takes us to despair rather than paradise. God commands us: "You shall walk in all the way that the Lord your God has commanded you, that you may live, and that it may go well with you, and that you may live long in the land that you shall possess" (Deuteronomy 5:33, ESV).

Let's strive for obedience. If we know we're engaging in something that God disapproves of, let's simply turn away. We are like that piano, as one of the actresses in the movie noted, and we didn't write the concerto!

Your statutes are perfect, and your word lights my path. I want to be an obedient daughter.

MG

September 4

For evil people can't sleep until they've done their evil deed for the day.
They can't rest until they've caused someone to stumble.

Proverbs 4:16 (NLT)

Evil is on the rise. We hear about murders, brazen robberies, corrupt politicians, pornography, drug trafficking, kidnappings, disappearances, the sale of children and women and even 21st century slavery. Instead of improving, humanity appears to be declining.

I read the harrowing story of a woman who escaped from a human trafficking gang. They kept her and the other women in a cage with little space and barely enough food, beating them regularly into submission. When one of the guards got drunk and left the keys within her reach, she seized the moment to escape. She urged the other girls to flee with her, but they were too terrified. As she ran, they pursued her, firing shots at her, but she managed to hide amongst the thick vegetation until she could get to a safe place.

Jesus came to "proclaim liberty to the captives" (see Luke 4:18). However, like the women in the story, we often struggle with fear when presented with the opportunity for freedom, hesitating to accept the escape God offers.

Today, let's pray for the liberation of all those suffering at the hands of evil. And let us also reflect, have we accepted the freedom that Jesus offers?

Lord, bring justice to this earth and free those who are suffering from slavery.

YF

September 5

Drink water from your own cistern, flowing water from your own well.

Proverbs 5:15 (ESV)

In Mayan myths, humans were created from corn. The gods endowed them with intelligence and vision that could reach the four corners of the earth. Their vision was so great that the gods began to worry. This gift of sight was too much power. So, they clouded their vision so that they could only see what was near them. While this is merely a legend, it teaches us something true: every day humanity sees less and less! And along with this we've denied an important truth: the importance of marriage!

In every creation myth I've encountered, the union of a man and a woman is depicted as the beginning of humanity. It all began with a marriage. Why is it so difficult for us to grasp this simple truth today?

The Bible clearly teaches us that God created man in His image, making them both male and female. It teaches us that a man will leave his father and mother and be united to his wife, becoming one flesh (see Genesis 2:24). The Hebrew word for "one," *echad*, indicates a complete unity, not just a numerical value. No relationship on earth is as intimate, perfect or fulfilling as a marriage blessed by God. That's why this proverb instructs us to drink only from our own well.

A famous line from the movie Jerry Maguire states, "You complete me." This can also mean "you complement me" or "you make me whole." That's the essence of marriage. God desires us to be one unit, one flesh. Our spouse can fulfill us. Let's cherish our own well and not let outside influences cloud our vision.

Lord, I want to be one flesh with my husband. Please help me.

KO

September 6

For their command is a lamp and their instruction a light; their corrective discipline is the way to life.

Proverbs 6:23 (NLT)

For some, "discipline" is a dirty word. Many prefer what they perceive to be the opposite of discipline, "freedom." In many countries, we're witnessing a resurgence of violence and crime as a form of protest. Do you think this rise in violence has anything to do with our new way of viewing discipline?

One of my children noticed a poorly behaved kid from one of their classes and asked, "Don't his parents love him?" I was amazed that he understood that we discipline our children out of love.

"Corrective discipline...is the way to life." Another verse encourages parents, "Bring them up with the discipline and instruction that comes from the Lord" (Ephesians 6:4, NLT). God's discipline stems from His love for us and aims to instruct, not destroy. It guides us toward life as true disciples. Do you see the connection between discipline and being a disciple?

When we stray from the right path, God's discipline can steer us back toward life. It encourages us to forgive and seek forgiveness, motivating us to abandon harmful habits. He may place obstacles in our way to remind us, "This is not the right path." How has He guided you recently?

Father, as your daughter, I recognize that your corrections are acts of love. Help me to respond in the way you desire.

MH

September 7

"...like an ox going to the slaughter.".

Proverbs 7:22 (NLT)

When we buy meat at the supermarket our minds are not drifting to the realities of a slaughterhouse. There are different children's books and movies that tell the stories of animals—like chickens and pigs—who become aware of their fate on a farm and desperately try to escape. But do real farm animals understand what's happening? This proverb suggests that the ox, perhaps believing it's going to greener pastures, unwittingly marches toward its end.

In context, this proverb refers to a young man succumbing to adultery. But it also invites us to reflect on our own lives. Often, we move toward destruction, acting recklessly and without wisdom—and never realizing it! In the Old Testament, lambs served a purpose beyond providing food; they were sacrificed to atone for sin. And then Jesus came.

Isaiah describes Jesus, "like a lamb that is led to the slaughter" (Isaiah 53:7, ESV). But unlike the lambs, rams and goats, He knew what awaited Him and He went willingly. His sacrifice alone is the only thing that can free us from the penalty, power and oppression of sin. And still, He died willingly.

Before knowing Jesus, we wander the world like animals headed to slaughter—tempted and enslaved to drugs, alcohol, eating disorders and depression. The good news is that Christ came to save us. He sacrificed Himself for our sins and offers us eternal life! Let's turn to Him today and embrace His gift of salvation. If we find ourselves on the wrong path, let's ask Him to rescue us. Let us not be like the ox headed to the slaughter.

Lord, deliver me from the path of destruction.

KO

September 8

I love those who love me, and those who seek me diligently find me.

Proverbs 8:17 (ESV)

Do you remember the women who visited the tomb of Jesus early one Sunday morning? I often imagine myself walking alongside Mary Magdalene, Salome and the other Mary as they brought spices to anoint His body. The Bible tells us that it was very early in the morning.

How much planning went into this visit? Do you think they stayed at one of their homes the night before so they could go together? What discussions do you think they had? It's clear that their love for Jesus united them and they were most certainly emotional at the thought of seeing Him one last time. I doubt they slept much, discussing their plans. They rose before dawn and hurried to the tomb, expecting to find Him dead. They could never imagine the surprise that awaited them. But first, they met the angels who spoke to them.

Can you imagine suddenly finding yourself conversing with an angel? Yet the greatest surprise was discovering the risen Lord Jesus, alive! I can envision Him saying, "Beloved daughters, I love those who love me, and those who seek me diligently find me." Their response must have been one of silent adoration at His feet.

Is our love for the Lord strong enough that we seek Him early in the morning? Like the women in this biblical narrative, we may come with one expectation, only to find ourselves blessed beyond measure in His presence.

Lord, I love you and want to seek you early each morning.

YF

September 9

Do not rebuke a scoffer, lest he hate you; rebuke the wise, and he will love you.
Proverbs 9:8 (NRSVUE)

The book you hold has been carefully reviewed by many—co-authors, editors and proofreaders. Many assume that writers simply draft a text and send it to print, but that's far from the truth! Every publication must go through a thorough process of editing and revision before it's ever printed.

I enjoy teaching others how to write. I've taught several online courses, and my students submit their writing to me for feedback. But I've noticed something along the way: not everyone welcomes correction. Many ignore the feedback and refuse to make changes, even when it's issues with grammar and spelling! The best writers though, those passionate about their craft, crave constructive feedback.

This proverb invites us to embrace humility. The wise love correction. How do you respond when someone points out a mistake or highlights a crummy attitude you might have against others? It requires humility to admit that we all have flaws. But let's be thankful, knowing that in Christ, we always have a second chance. Like Paul, we can also say, "Not that I have already obtained this or am already perfect, but I press on" (Philippians 3:12, ESV).

Since we all have room for growth, let's be open to correction and learn to appreciate those who guide us.

Father, help me to value those who correct me.

KO

SEPTEMBER 10

The earnings of the godly enhance their lives, but evil people squander their money on sin.

Proverbs 10:16 (NLT)

While poverty is a significant issue in Latin America, the mafia and cartels seem to have endless amounts of cash to continue their wrongdoing. Some of them are armed like powerful armies. These "evil people squander their money on sin," causing harm, death and entrapping the innocent along the way.

On the other hand, we are inspired by those who generously use their wealth to create foundations that support health, education, job creation, food security and many other things. Others, though less wealthy, contribute to missionaries, care for orphans and support all kinds of projects that aid those in need.

The Bible has a lot to say about money—as it can be a tool for good or a source of evil, depending on how it's used. This proverb teaches us that "the earnings of the godly enhance their lives," or, as another version puts it, "the wage of the righteous leads to life" (ESV)—because wealth, when used rightly, supports life and families. The apostle Paul commended the Philippians for their generosity toward missionary work, assuring them that "God will supply every need of yours" (Philippians 4:19, ESV). What a contrast to those who squander their earnings on harmful pursuits.

Are we using the wealth that God has given us to enhance our lives in meaningful ways? Does it benefit and bless others? Are we exercising wisdom in our stewardship? Regardless of how much or how little we have, let's remember that everything we have comes from God, who will reward us for our faithfulness.

God, I trust you to show me how to use what you've given me wisely.

MH

September 11

Like a gold ring in a pig's snout is a beautiful woman without discretion.

Proverbs 11:22 (ESV)

Miss Piggy is a well-known character from The Muppet Show. She's a pig who believes she's destined to be a star, but beneath her femininity and charm lies a fierce personality that resorts to karate when she feels insulted or frustrated. And although we laugh, she reminds us that, no matter how much makeup she wears or how fancy her gloves are, she's still a pig.

The modern woman is portrayed in a more balanced way than in the past. She values personal growth beyond a simple focus on external beauty. She pursues a career, learns a foreign language and is more independent. However, personal growth and forward movement is not the same thing as acquiring wisdom. True wisdom begins with the fear of God.

The Bible presents Esther, a woman of beauty and grace. The king of Persia loved her more than all the other ladies in his court and made her his queen. But Esther was not simply attractive, she was courageous, ultimately saving her people by risking her life to intercede for the Jews. Esther showed both discretion and wisdom, and she was rewarded.

Throughout our reflections on the Proverbs, we've been reminded repeatedly of the importance of seeking wisdom. Are we beautiful women who lack understanding?

Lord, may I desire wisdom more than beauty.

MG

September 12

Fools think their own way is right, but the wise listen to others.

Proverbs 12:15 (NLT)

Have you ever heard the phrase "follow your heart"? King Rehoboam, despite being 41 years old, thought like a teenager. It seems that he learned nothing from his father's mistakes during the time he turned away from God. During Solomon's reign, the Israelites felt overburdened by taxes and sought relief when Rehoboam took the throne, they had hoped for a favorable response.

Rehoboam promised to respond in three days. He consulted his father's advisors, who urged him to listen to the people. However, he also sought advice from his friends. Wanting to appear tough, he declared he would be even harsher than his father. This unwise decision led to the dividing of Israel, leaving him to rule over only two of the twelve tribes.

I often wonder if Rehoboam ever read the proverbs his father wrote. Had he done so; he might have avoided his downfall. Not only did he have access to wise counselors, but he also had the Scriptures inspired by God, and yet, he still chose poorly. Rehoboam aimed to establish his kingdom on the right foundation, but his story ended in bitterness.

The Lord desires for us to heed wise advice. He has provided His written Word to guide us, as well as godly individuals who can help us. If you ever feel tempted to "follow your heart," seek counsel.

Father, may I learn to listen to wise advice.

YF

September 13

Some who are poor pretend to be rich; others who are rich pretend to be poor.
Proverbs 13:7 (NLT)

Hetty Green was nicknamed "The Witch of Wall Street." During the Gilded Age (1870-1891), she was America's richest woman, yet she was also stingy and lived like a beggar, dressing in rags despite her wealth. Could something like this happen in other areas of our life? Absolutely!

The Pharisees during Jesus' time believed they were spiritually rich due to their knowledge of the law of Moses. They fasted, prayed lengthy prayers, gave their precise tithes and lived seemingly blameless lives. However, they were spiritually impoverished. When given the opportunity to follow Jesus and love Him, they rejected him.

Jesus said, "God blesses those who are poor and realize their need for him, for the Kingdom of Heaven is theirs" (Matthew 5:3, NLT). To reach God, we must acknowledge our spiritual poverty and our inability to do it alone. When we accept our status as His children, He enriches us: "You know the generous grace of our Lord Jesus Christ. Though he was rich, yet for your sakes he became poor, so that by his poverty he could make you rich" (2 Corinthians 8:9, NLT).

Let's not be like Hetty Green, believing we are rich and self-sufficient. Instead, let's approach God in humility and seek His presence in our lives. And if we already belong to Him and are richly blessed, let's not live like beggars. Instead, let's share God's love with others!

Lord, thank you for the spiritual riches I have in you. Help me to share them with others.

KO

September 14

Only simpletons believe everything they're told! The prudent carefully consider their steps.

Proverbs 14:15 (NLT)

In Hans Christian Andersen's *The Emperor's New Clothes*, an emperor obsessed with fashion hires weavers who promise to weave the most extraordinary fabric—one invisible to the foolish and unworthy. In exchange for a few gold coins, they pretend to weave the non-existent cloth. When the emperor parades through the streets, everyone pretends to admire the new clothes until a child exclaims, "But he is naked!"

In today's online culture, it's easy to believe everything we read on social media without verifying the facts. Many people regularly share posts and articles without questioning their accuracy, assuming that if a friend also shared it, it must be reliable.

Indeed, "simpletons believe everything they're told" and lack discernment. In contrast, "the prudent carefully consider their steps." During Jesus' time, many believed the Jewish leaders who accused Him of being a heretic without investigating what the Scriptures actually teach. Others, like Nicodemus, questioned the legality of convicting Jesus, asking, "Is it legal to convict a man before he is given a hearing?" (John 7:51, NLT).

It's unwise to accept everything at face value. We should evaluate facts from multiple perspectives and align them with Scripture, being willing to admit when we're mistaken.

Lord, guide my thoughts and decisions so that I may seek the truth.

MH

September 15

The heart of the righteous ponders how to answer, but the mouth of the wicked pours out evil things.

Proverbs 15:28 (ESV)

Thomas Edison once gave his mother a note from his teacher that stated, "Your son is a genius. This school is too small for him and doesn't have enough good teachers for training him. Please teach him yourself." Years later, after becoming a great inventor, he found the actual note, which read, "Your son is addled [mentally ill]. We won't let him come to school anymore." Edison was heartbroken but later wrote in his diary, "Thomas Alva Edison was an addled child that, with the help of a heroic mother, became the genius of the century."

What would have happened if his mother had allowed that note to define her son? Words hold immense power. We can either poison someone's soul with our words or uplift and motivate them to realize their potential.

Today's proverb encourages us to think before we speak. When we're angry or upset, we might respond with words we'll later regret. Let's strive to control our tongues. As mothers, we can foster confidence in our children by consistently expressing positivity.

Encouragement is vital. Take a moment today to think of uplifting words you can share with those around you. There's always something positive to highlight, so let's spread love.

Lord, help me to ensure my words encourage and uplift those I care about.

MG

September 16

A just balance and scales are the Lord's; all the weights in the bag are his work.

Proverbs 16:11 (ESV)

As a child, my mother often sent me to the local store, where Don Luis, the owner, would greet me warmly. Since he knew my family, he would sometimes give us credit for things—meaning, he would allow us to take things home and pay for them later. I remember once asking him to weigh something for me, it was something my mother had bought, and I was wanting to make sure the weight was right. I discovered something that day, what do you think it was?

Don Luis placed the item on the scale but discreetly removed a piece of iron he used to manipulate the weight. Initially, I didn't understand why he was doing this, but I later realized he was cheating. Although he wasn't wealthy and may have stolen only small amounts, his actions were inexcusable.

If Don Luis thought he could enrich himself through deceit, he was mistaken. The Bible reminds us, "The blessing of the Lord makes rich, and he adds no sorrow with it" (Proverbs 10:22, ESV). We cannot expect to be blessed while engaging in acts of dishonesty—even if we think they're small.

We don't need physical products to deceive people, we can also defraud people with our lies and our minor omissions. If our purpose is to be truthful in everything, we will find telling the truth becomes easy, and God will bless us for it. Don't you think?

Father, help me to be honest in all my dealings.

YF

SEPTEMBER 17

Sensible people keep their eyes glued on wisdom, but a fool's eyes wander to the ends of the earth.

Proverbs 17:24 (NLT)

Eye contact is crucial for effective communication. Have you ever had a conversation with someone who avoids looking you in the eye? It feels uncomfortable and dismissive—especially if they're distracted by their phone. They are subtly communicating that what's happening in some faraway place is more important than what you're saying right in front of them.

During the pandemic, students used platforms like Zoom for classes. Teachers would require—dare I say beg—their students to keep their cameras on to ensure they were paying attention. But even when they had their cameras on their eyes wandered everywhere but toward the teacher!

Today's proverb compares foolishness with wandering eyes. It encourages us to focus all our attention on wisdom. The writer of Hebrews also advises us to "keep our eyes on Jesus" (see Hebrews 12:2). And remember the story of Peter, who, while walking on water toward Jesus, became distracted by the waves and began to sink (Matthew 14:30-31).

We can navigate life with our eyes darting everywhere and focusing on nothing. We can be foolish and also sink in the midst of troubling moments. We're invited to fix our gaze on Jesus, the embodiment of wisdom. If we do this, we'll not only show good sense, but we'll also be able to face the challenging situations of life.

I keep my eyes on you, Jesus, full of grace and love.

KO

September 18

Giving a gift can open doors; it gives access to important people!
Proverbs 18:16 (NLT)

Cameron Townsend founded the Summer Institute of Linguistics to bring God's Word to people with no access to Bibles in their own language. Over the years, he formed relationships with numerous presidents and influential figures; his generosity and willingness to serve opened many doors. Early in his time in Mexico, the mayor of a small town in Morelos asked him for a Bible as a gift, which led to a transformative moment—he became the first believer in that town.

"Uncle Cam," as he became known, also distributed seeds and taught locals to grow their own vegetables. He even created a primer to help people learn to read Nahuatl. When President Lázaro Cárdenas visited to see his work, he was so impressed that he said, "That is exactly what Mexico needs. Invite all the translators you can find to come."

"Giving a gift can open doors." Generosity shows interest and love, especially toward those who are often approached only when other people need something from them. "It gives access to important people!" In 1 Chronicles, as King David prepared to build the temple, he acknowledged: "Everything comes from you, and we have given you only what comes from your hand" (1 Chronicles 29:14, NIV). As we see, generosity is rooted in grateful hearts.

You don't need to spend a lot to give a gift. A simple card, a Bible verse or a homemade gift can convey love and appreciation, helping you build connections. God can use these gestures of generosity as open doors into the lives of others.

Thank you, Lord, for the gift of your Son. Help me to share your love with others.

MH

September 19

A wrathful person bears the penalty; after one rescue, you will have it to do again.
Proverbs 19:19 (NABRE)

According to the World Health Organization, three out of ten adolescents report experiencing violence in dating relationships, either psychological, physical or even sexual. Many cases go unreported. While each situation is unique, one explanation that sheds light on why these things happen is the explanation of replication. Young people replicate the patterns they see at home. Reacting with violence is often a learned behavior, and when reinforced, it can evolve into a destructive habit.

God has given us the capacity to feel emotions, and each one serves a purpose. However, we must learn to control them. The issue with anger is that if left unchecked, it can take control of a person and lead to violence.

David wrote, "Refrain from anger, and forsake wrath! Fret not yourself; it tends only to evil" (Psalm 37:8, ESV). When we are filled with the Spirit, we can conquer our rage. Anger not only damages personal relationships but it can also make us physically ill.

How do you respond to anger? As a parent, your reactions model behaviors for your children. Let's strive to create a loving and peaceful atmosphere in our homes. Ralph Waldo Emerson wisely said, "For every minute you are angry, you lose sixty seconds of happiness."

Lord, may my home be a sanctuary of peace rather than conflict.

MG

September 20

Don't trap yourself by making a rash promise to God and only later counting the cost.

Proverbs 20:25 (NLT)

I remember after attending a conference that deeply moved me, I made a promise to the Lord that I would wake up early to read the Word and pray. At first, everything was going well; I was reading the Word and spending time in prayer. However, that initial excitement faded, and I fell back into my old habits. Eventually, God reminded me of my promise, and I felt a wave of shame. As humans, we struggle to keep our commitments. I sought the Lord for forgiveness for my failure to keep my promise.

How many times do we make promises to God without counting the cost! Has this also happened to you? Sometimes we believe that we can make deals with God, thinking, "If you do this for me, I'll do that for you." Our emotions can mislead us and cause us to make promises we cannot keep.

Our old nature tends to speak quickly and commit without realizing we may not be able to follow through. The Lord knows how we are. That's why He offers guidance when we make empty promises. The Proverbs also tells us, "If you are snared in the words of your mouth … then do this, my son, and save yourself … go, hasten, and plead urgently with your neighbor" (Proverbs 6:2-3, ESV).

We should remember that promising God, something doesn't benefit Him; He needs nothing from us. Let us not approach God as if we can exchange favors with Him. Instead, by bringing our requests before God, we acknowledge our inability to change our situation and trust in His power.

Lord, I recognize my limitations, yet I thank you for the access I have to you through Jesus.

YF

September 21

Good planning and hard work lead to prosperity, but hasty shortcuts lead to poverty.

Proverbs 21:5 (NLT)

Have you ever participated in a strategy session? In the corporate world, it's common for leaders and managers to gather and plan for the future. It's also beneficial for families to strategize, to create budgets, organize their weeks and plan for future vacations. Today's proverb encourages us to think carefully about our plans and work diligently. In fact, at least the way it seems to me, children of organized mothers tend to be more confident and competent.

John Piper, a well-known preacher, praised his mother, a simple yet hardworking woman who raised the family while her husband traveled to preach. After her passing, John discovered a folder labeled "Unfinished Business" in her home—a place where his mother kept track of her incomplete tasks. To his surprise, the folder was empty!

Ruth Piper, John's mother, didn't attend seminary or consider herself a theologian—she simply read the Bible. Her wisdom and good practices were shaped by the teachings of Proverbs, her favorite book. That's where her wisdom and good practices came from. Perhaps this is where she learned the importance of completing tasks. As we continue to study Proverbs, let's take each lesson on diligence to heart and put it into practice!

If you don't have an "Unfinished Business" folder, create one to help you stay organized and achieve your goals. If you already have one, review it regularly and create time to work on your tasks. What a wonderful legacy it would be if, on our final day, our loved ones discover that our "Unfinished Business" folder was empty!

Lord, help me to become more organized and to learn how to plan effectively.

KO

September 22

The lazy person claims, 'There's a lion out there! If I go outside, I might be killed!'

Proverbs 22:13 (NLT)

Most of us don't face lions on a daily basis, but that doesn't mean that life is without risks—like car accidents, plane crashes, robberies and kidnappings. Yet, we don't let these dangers stop us from living our lives.

We probably all know someone who is terrified of flying, especially because they fear the possibility of a crash. And yet, statistics show that it is more dangerous to travel on foot or by car. Today's "lions" are not as dangerous as we think.

This proverb makes us laugh when we imagine someone so lazy that, to avoid going to work, he makes up the idea that a lion could kill him. However, many people make excuses to avoid fulfilling their responsibilities. Jesus used the parable of a father who asked his two sons to go to work in his vineyard. One refused to go, but he later thought better of it and went. The other said he would go but never did. Jesus was teaching that repenting of a mistake is better than not doing anything (see Matthew 21:28-32).

Have we found excuses for not obeying God? Even the typical, "I'll do it later," generally turns into, "I never got around to it." Let us try to be faithful in the work of the Lord's vineyard.

Father, I want to obey you and serve you today, without excuses.

MG

September 23

Don't eat with people who are stingy... 'Eat and drink,' they say, but they don't mean it.

Proverbs 23:6-7 (NLT)

The word hypocrite comes from the Greek word hypokrisis, meaning "to act" or "to pretend." It carries the connotation of someone wearing a mask, implying a person who lacks sincerity. Today's proverb illustrates a greedy person who offers empty invitations, saying, "Eat and drink," but doesn't genuinely mean it. The wise advice here is to avoid sharing a meal with a person like this.

Delilah in the Bible pretended to love Samson but ultimately betrayed him for money. She asked him three times to reveal the secret of his strength and each time he misled her. Finally, she convinced the strong man to tell her his secret. He told her that if she cut off his long hair, he'd be like any other man. She made him lie on her lap and when he fell asleep a man came and cut his hair. Samson lost his strength. The Philistines gouged out his eyes and took him captive. What a sad story! He put his trust in the wrong person. From the first moment of her dishonesty, he should have just walked away.

The Bible teaches us: "Don't just pretend to love others. Really love them." (Romans 12:9, NLT). We are to love others without a mask—genuine love and not just lip service. The best model of authenticity is Jesus Christ. He genuinely cares for people and continues to do so.

Are we genuinely joyful givers? Eventually, our true nature will show through our actions.

Lord, help me always speak the truth, not just in words but through my actions.

MG

September 24

Rescue those who are being taken away to death; hold back those who are stumbling to the slaughter.

Proverbs 24:11 (ESV)

Hacksaw Ridge tells the story of Private Desmond Thomas Doss, a Seventh-day Adventist who was deeply committed to living in obedience to the Ten Commandments. During World War II, he joined the U.S. Army to serve his country, vowing never to carry a weapon. Because of his convictions he was mocked and faced accusations of cowardice. Undeterred, he served as a medic, bravely saving wounded soldiers in combat.

His greatest act of heroism occurred during the Battle of Okinawa when Japanese forces ambushed American troops. After climbing a cliff to progress against the Japanese forces, the Americans were caught off guard. Doss spent the night lowering his fellow wounded soldiers back down the cliff. While the official count of those he rescued is 75, the actual number may be higher. He even reportedly rescued two wounded Japanese soldiers. His prayer during each rescue was, "Help me save one more."

If saving someone's earthly life is vital, how much more crucial is it to rescue those on the path to eternal death? As daughters of God, our mission is to stop those who are stumbling toward their torment. Jude reminds us: "And you must show mercy to those whose faith is wavering. Rescue others by snatching them from the flames of judgment" (Jude 1:22-23, NLT).

When we consider the suffering of those destined for eternal separation from God, we realize we want no one to endure that fate. Have you prayed for and shared the message of salvation with those around you who do not know the saving work of Christ?

Lord, help me save one more!

YF

September 25

It is the glory of God to conceal a matter, and the glory of kings to fathom a matter.

Proverbs 25:2 (NABRE)

The Bible tells us that Solomon possessed knowledge in various fields, including botany and engineering. His wisdom was so remarkable, when the Queen of Sheba visited him, she was astonished at what she saw. Today, we celebrate scientists who use their gifts to explore and understand our world.

María de los Ángeles, a Peruvian biologist studying the tropical Andes ecosystem and its inhabitants, once explained in an interview, "I have always been amazed by the diversity of colors, the detail of each element, and the majesty that floods our senses. I understand God's infinite love when I see creation."

Many biblical writers, much like María de los Ángeles, have also expressed their immense awe of creation. David, for example, wrote, "When I look at your heavens, the work of your fingers, the moon and the stars, which you have set in place, what is man that you are mindful of him?" (Psalm 8:3-4, ESV).

The world is filled with mysteries. Perhaps God has intentionally left them for us. As the proverb teaches, just as He is too great to be fully understood, so it is His creation. If you find yourself curious about trees, animals, stars, or even how societies and history function, embrace that wonder. Life will always present you with new things to learn. The journey of discovery is truly exciting.

Lord, may I always be curious about how the beautiful world you created works.

KO

September 26

Smooth words may hide a wicked heart, just as a pretty glaze covers a clay pot.

Proverbs 26:23 (NLT)

There are various types of varnishes, each serving a different purpose. Some give furniture an antique look, while others create a glossy or matte finish. Ceramic pieces can have a pearl-like shine or a textured appearance, and jewelry can be plated with precious metals. These finishes enhance the appearance and perceived value of an object.

A woman inherited an elegant necklace from her mother. She was hesitant to travel with it because she believed it was made with an expensive gold. However, when she had it appraised, she discovered it was only gold-plated and held little real value.

As the saying goes, "all that glitters is not gold." A clay pot can appear to be porcelain if it is silver-plated. In the Garden of Eden, Satan deceived Adam and Eve with "smooth words," suggesting that tasting the forbidden fruit would make them wise, making them more like God.

Some individuals are skilled at communicating convincingly, even if they don't speak the truth. Others may use flattery to manipulate. We must be cautious, as attractive words can conceal hidden dangers.

Father, grant me discernment so I may not be deceived by falsehoods.

MH

September 27

Trustworthy are the blows of a friend, dangerous, the kisses of an enemy.
Proverbs 27:6 (NABRE)

It's better to prevent an illness than to work to treat it afterwards. Vaccines protect children from diseases like polio, measles and many others. Immunization has saved countless lives, yet in the moment, when the syringe delivers this good, children may miss the importance of these vaccinations. In a similar way, the corrective actions taken by those who love us can feel painful.

I remember times when my parents or other relatives would point out my mistakes or suggest ways, they thought I could improve. In some of these moments I thought they were being harsh and scolding me. I would cry, be angry or become sad—but deep down, I always knew their correction was for my good.

Today's proverb reminds us that it's better to receive blows from someone who cares than kisses from a hypocrite. The Lord teaches us that "No discipline is enjoyable while it is happening— it's painful! But afterward there will be a peaceful harvest of right living for those who are trained in this way" (Hebrews 12:11, NLT).

It takes courage to confront loved ones with difficult truths. Let's value those who have filled themselves with God and have mustered the courage to speak constructively and honestly with us, even when their words sting. We should be thankful for those who "vaccinate" us against poor choices.

Thank you, God, for the people who sincerely love and care for me.

MG

September 28

Whoever gives to the poor will lack nothing, but those who close their eyes to poverty will be cursed.

Proverbs 28:27 (NLT)

How much wealth does a person need before they're no longer considered poor? Or when is someone deemed poor? One formula suggests that individuals earning 40% or 50% of the average income are to be classified as poor. So, are we poor?

God knew there would always be poor people in the world because of the sin that resides in all our hearts. That's why, in the Law of Moses, He gave specific commandments to care for the poor. For instance, their sacrifices were to reflect their means; during legal trials, they were not to be penalized due to their financial situation; and those who harvested crops were instructed to leave some produce for the needy.

Boaz, a wealthy man, obeyed God's law and instructed his harvesters to leave some harvest behind for those who had no land. Among those in need was Ruth, who would eventually become his wife. When Ruth shared Boaz's kindness with her mother-in-law, Naomi exclaimed, "May the Lord bless him!" (Ruth 2:20, NLT). And indeed, He did!

How can you practice obedience and help others today? The law is summed up in one simple phrase: "Love your neighbor as yourself." (Mark 12:30-31). Consider how you can apply this command in your home or at work today. Perhaps you can encourage someone who's sad, give to someone in need or share food with a struggling family. Your kindness will be rewarded.

Lord, help me to reach out to those in need, even if I feel I only have a little to give.

YF

September 29

So follow the steps of the good, and stay on the paths of the righteous.

Proverbs 2:20 (NLT)

The Yale Babylonian Collection, dating back to 1600 B.C., contains around 30 to 40 recipes that detail what and how the ancient inhabitants of Mesopotamia ate, including broths and stews. If you follow the recipes, they work! That's the purpose of recipes: if you read the recipe and follow it, it works! So, are the Proverbs recipes for life?

Proverbs chapter 2 underscores that wisdom leads to a life characterized by righteousness, justice, and integrity. It contrasts the paths of the wise with those of the wicked, emphasizing the moral implications of one's choices. The wisdom of God leads us to a life of righteousness, justice, and integrity. This also applies to our marriage life and our relationships with our spouses and others. Healthy marriages are built out of God's wisdom. As a special relationship that marriage is, it requires love, and love takes risks, suffers and gives without expecting anything in return. So, what should we do? We should follow in the footsteps of Jesus and, as our proverb suggests, remain on that path. To achieve success in marriage, let's model God's love: constant, faithful, and everlasting. Jesus said, "It is more blessed to give than to receive" (Acts 20:35, NLT).

There's no perfect recipe for a happy marriage, but Proverbs offers plenty of wisdom for us to follow. Let's be attentive and apply it! Love bears all things, believes all things, hopes all things, endures all things—and ultimately, love makes life worth living!

Father, I want to give more than I receive.

KO

September 30

There are three things that amaze me ... how an eagle glides through the sky ... how a man loves a woman.

Proverbs 30:18-19 (NLT)

Have you ever watched an eagle soar effortlessly through the sky, gliding without moving its wings? It circles in place, seemingly suspended in air. While we might think it's hunting for prey below, it's riding thermal currents that allow it to maintain altitude without using energy. Isn't that incredible?

Even more astonishing is the love between a man and a woman. I admire my husband for his persistence, especially when I initially showed little interest. His best friend told him that I wouldn't respond to him. Yet, he traveled to the top of a mountain range to find me in a small town when he learned I was experiencing a difficulty. He offered friendship even when I was clear about my lack of interest in pursuing a romantic relationship with him. And still, seven years after his first proposal, we finally tied the knot!

The tenacity of a man in love can overcome immense barriers to win the woman he desires. In a similar way, God's relentless love for us knows no bounds. He demonstrated the depth of His agape love by giving His life for us. "This is real love—not that we loved God, but that he loved us" (1 John 4:10, NLT). His goodness and unfailing love pursue us every day (see Psalm 23:6).

Have you responded to that incredible love that gave everything for you? If you have, I encourage you to reciprocate by loving those God places in your path and inviting them to join you in the greatest love story of all time.

How wonderful is your love for me, Lord!

MH

October 1

My son, if sinners entice you, do not consent.

Proverbs 1:10 (ESV)

In the card game Monopoly Deal, there's a card that everyone wishes they had. It simply says, "Just say no." If someone tries to take a property or charge you rent, you can play that card, and they can't do anything. In life, we all need a similar card.

This Proverb encourages us to say "no" when we are tempted to do something wrong. An anti-drug campaign famously promoted the same message: "Just say no." Is it easy? Not at all! Saying "no" can be one of the toughest things to do, especially when we want to fit in or be liked. Yet, our emotional well-being often depends on our ability to refuse things that can harm us.

It's important to remember that saying no to one thing means saying yes to something else. For instance, saying no to drugs means saying yes to health and a better life. Saying no to dishonesty means saying yes to truth. Joseph, in the Bible, refused the inappropriate advances of his employer's wife because he valued living a moral life before God more than temporary pleasure.

When you feel pressure from others to go along with harmful behaviors or choices, remember to "just say no." Others might not understand your decision or may even try to make you feel guilty, but if you choose to say yes to God and His ways, you will gain wisdom.

Lord, help me to stand firm and not give in when others encourage me to do wrong.

KO

October 2

She makes sure her dealings are profitable; her lamp burns late into the night.

Proverbs 31:18 (NLT)

Sleep experts recommend that adults get between 7 and 9 hours of sleep to function well. However, many factors in modern life can disrupt this ideal. Stress, excessive caffeine, and the light from screens can all interfere with our natural sleep-wake cycle.

I'm not alone in neglecting my sleep; I have struggled with insomnia at different points in my life, especially during menopause. With a busy job, I often find myself on the computer for long periods. Once I learned that screen light can affect my brain's internal clock, I began to avoid my laptop and phone for an hour before bedtime.

The virtuous woman described in Proverbs kept her lamp burning late at night. She also rose early, likely balancing her need for rest with her responsibilities. We admire her for her hard work and dedication to her family, and in verse 25, we see that she is confident about the future. This suggests that she maintained balance in her life.

Are we finding balance in our own lives, especially between work and home? Are we taking care of our bodies? Let's strive to make wise choices that protect our physical and emotional health.

My Lord, help me find balance in my life so I can give you my best.

MH

October 3

Wicked people are detestable to the Lord, but he offers his friendship to the godly.

Proverbs 3:33 (NLT)

Friendship is incredibly important in our lives. Cicero said, "To live without friends is not to live," and Oscar Wilde reflected, "Love is all very well in its way, but friendship is much higher." Do you have friends? How many of them are truly close to you? Can you imagine being a close friend of God?

The Bible tells us that God considered Abraham a friend because of his righteousness. We can picture them talking, and Abraham likely found comfort in God's presence. The Lord can provide what no human friend can—He fills our hearts in ways that no one else can, not even a spouse!

Jesus said, "No longer do I call you servants, for the servant does not know what his master is doing; but I have called you friends, for all that I have heard from my Father I have made known to you" (John 15:15 ESV). Aristotle described friendship as a single soul inhabiting two bodies, emphasizing the deep connection friends share. Jesus desires that connection with you and me—that's what true friendship is about!

Sometimes, we look to our friends or spouses for what only Jesus can provide. He listens, cares, and sees our hearts, not our appearances. He loves us unconditionally, even to the point of sacrificing Himself on the cross. If we don't experience the joy of His friendship, no one else can fill that void. Remember, you are not alone; He is your friend and is always with you!

Thank you, God, for your friendship.

MG

October 4

Avoid all perverse talk; stay away from corrupt speech.

Proverbs 4:24 (NLT)

In our world, we face many challenges: rejection, harassment, mockery, and scorn. Our homes should be places of peace and respect. God designed families to be safe havens, but unfortunately, many households are filled with hurtful words. Children often grow up thinking this negativity is normal.

I have a neighbor who uses foul language, often insulting her five-year-old granddaughter with words like "dumb" and "stupid." I can't help but wonder if she was subjected to similar treatment in her own childhood, and how those hurtful words may have shaped her life.

God speaks to us in Proverbs with such tenderness: "Listen, my son ... put away corrupt words from your lips." The term "corrupt" means rotten, dishonest, immoral, or depraved. It has long been said that words have the power to create or destroy.

How do you treat your family members? Do you show them respect and love? Let's be so kind and respectful to our loved ones, especially our children, that when they face negativity in the world, they won't accept it as normal.

Lord, may my words bring life to others, not corruption.

YF

October 5

Lest you give your honor to others and your years to the merciless.
                                                    Proverbs 5:9 (ESV)

Honor is highly valued in many cultures, both Eastern and Western. This Proverb reminds us that it is easy to lose our honor, especially in the context of sexual relationships.

Andrew Sullivan defines marriage as "a way in which two adults affirm their emotional commitment to one another." Timothy Keller describes marriage as a commitment where we say to each other, "I belong completely, permanently, and exclusively to you." The first definition highlights feelings, while the second emphasizes commitment, with terms like "permanent" and "exclusive" adding depth.

The Bible teaches that marriage is a commitment, and therefore, sexual relations should occur only within that context. "Let marriage be held in honor among all" (Hebrews 13:4 ESV). Even in films, characters often express this idea. For example, Cameron Diaz's character in Vanilla Sky says, "Don't you know that when you sleep with someone, your body makes a promise whether you do or not?" Every sexual relationship carries a promise, and honor is involved. That's why marriage is the only place where such a commitment can be honored and fulfilled.

Do not give your honor to others or make promises you cannot keep. Strive for an honorable marriage, and be able to say to your spouse: "I belong entirely to you, forever and only to you." This is the greatest gift we can offer.

Father, I want my marriage to be honorable. Help me love my spouse as you love me.

KO

October 6

Take a lesson from the ants, you lazybones ... they labor hard all summer, gathering food for the winter.

Proverbs 6:6-8 (NLT)

Today, we often lack the foresight of our ancestors, who had to store food to survive harsh winters. Nowadays, we can easily access our favorite fruits and vegetables, even out of season, thanks to canning and freezing.

My grandmother embodied the spirit of the "ant." She carefully stored root vegetables in a cool place to keep them fresh through winter. She preserved large amounts of vegetables, pickles, sauces, and jellies, ensuring her family had enough supplies year-round.

King Solomon points us to the ants, who instinctively know the importance of preparing for the future. What about us? We may have more knowledge but sometimes lack the motivation to act on it. A prime example of foresight is Joseph, who, as Pharaoh's steward in Egypt, saved enough grain during seven years of plenty to sustain many during a famine.

Some may mistakenly believe that faith means we don't need to plan for the future because "God will provide." However, that same God has given us wisdom, abilities, and resources to use wisely. Let us plan for the future while trusting in Him.

Lord, thank you for your provision. Help me to invest in my future wisely.

MH

October 7

... like a bird flying into a snare.

Proverbs 7:23 (NLT)

Superhero movies are incredibly popular today, perhaps due to their impressive special effects and our longing for protection from greater forces. In ancient times, the Greeks turned to mythology, creating gods and demigods to control the world. Now, we have superhero teams that save us from impending danger.

In the Justice League movie, everything seems hopeless until Superman is revived by his friends using their extraordinary abilities. With Superman back, the defenders of Earth can once again protect the planet from destruction! Unfortunately, superheroes can't address the real issue we all face: sin. Many of them are flawed, motivated by revenge and anger. So, who can rescue us from the true enemy that destroys marriages, harms the innocent, and leads to misery?

The apostle Paul, who faced constant danger, wrote: "In fact, we expected to die. But as a result, we stopped relying on ourselves and learned to rely only on God, who raises the dead. And he did rescue us from mortal danger, and he will rescue us again. We have placed our confidence in him, and he will continue to rescue us" (2 Corinthians 1:9-10).

Jesus is the hero we truly need. He not only saves us but also offers us eternal life! Like Paul, let us stop depending on ourselves (and fictional superheroes) and place our trust in God alone.

Lord, thank you for rescuing me from sin and the dangers of this world.

KO

October 8

All who fear the Lord will hate evil. Therefore, I hate pride and arrogance.

Proverbs 8:13 (NLT)

Philip Yancey tells the story of Pascal, a man from Madagascar who took pride in his atheism. After being arrested during a student strike, he found himself in a crowded prison with only one book: a Bible, a gift from his family. What happened next was remarkable.

Despite his atheistic beliefs, Pascal began to read the Bible, realizing that science could not help him in prison. Three months later, he started Bible studies with fellow inmates. After his release, he returned to the prison twice a week to distribute Bibles and bring food to those in need.

Pascal's story illustrates the transformative power of Christ when we let go of pride and acknowledge that we cannot do life alone. Remember, pride is the greatest enemy of our souls.

The Lord hates pride and arrogance because they prevent us from approaching Him, the only One who can give us true life. When we draw near to Him, we learn to hate evil.

Lord, deliver me from pride.

YF

October 9

She calls out to men going by who are minding their own business.

Proverbs 9:15 (NLT)

Research shows that those who are heavily focused on materialism often find themselves less happy than others. This observation comes from Marsha Richins, a professor at the University of Missouri, and it echoes the Proverb that states, "the prosperity of fools will spoil them" (Proverbs 1:32).

We all have spaces in our homes—whether a storage room, basement, attic, or garage—where we accumulate both useful and unnecessary items. When someone passes away and we must sort through their belongings, we often find surprising treasures. I remember reading about a woman who had many unopened boxes in her garage filled with products she ordered online but never used. She had amassed things, yet they did not bring her happiness.

In today's Proverb, foolishness places herself in a prominent position, inviting those on the right path to follow her. The subtle trap of materialism whispers, "Just a bit more." One more shirt, another pair of shoes, an extra kitchen gadget, or additional jewelry. Tragically, prosperity can spoil us. Money can become an idol, taking God's rightful place in our hearts. Jesus reminds us, "Life is not measured by how much you own" (Luke 12:15).

If we are on the righteous path of contentment, let us not stray from it. If we find ourselves loving money, it is time to stop hoarding. Upon a careful review of our closets, we might discover clothes we haven't worn or items we bought that are now collecting dust. Let us not allow prosperity to spoil us. Our lives are far more valuable than the possessions we have—or do not have.

Lord, deliver me from materialism.

KO

OCTOBER 10

The words of the godly encourage many, but fools are destroyed by their lack of common sense.

Proverbs 10:21 (NLT)

There has been a noticeable rise in counseling and coaching in recent years. In some places, discussing one's therapist has become commonplace, and people regularly schedule appointments. Coaches aim to help individuals discover their goals and make wise decisions.

According to Wikipedia, coaching involves guiding someone through questions, allowing them to arrive at their own conclusions. Some coaches even focus on helping Christians channel their gifts to serve the Lord.

In today's Proverb, we see that the righteous—those who follow God—"encourage many." The wisdom found in Scripture, combined with the guidance of the Holy Spirit, empowers them to lead others, while also allowing individuals to make their own choices. The Letter to the Romans states, "Do not be conformed to this world, but be transformed by the renewal of your mind, that by testing you may discern what is the will of God, what is good and acceptable and perfect" (Romans 12:2 ESV). A renewed mind helps us avoid suffering from a "lack of common sense."

While professional guidance can be beneficial, we should thank God for His Word and the experienced believers who lead us along the right path. Let us seek out "godly ones" to be our mentors and strive to be wise counselors for others as well.

Father, be my personal coach!

MH

October 11

Kindly [merciful] people benefit themselves [and their souls], but the merciless [and cruel] harm [and torment] themselves.

Proverbs 11:17 (NABRE with translator's note)

Thousands of clay tablets have been discovered that provide insights into the Sumerian, Assyrian, Babylonian, and Persian empires. If these records had been written on different materials, we might know very little about these civilizations. Likewise, the inscriptions on the pyramids have enriched our understanding of Egyptian culture. Benjamin Franklin wisely said, "Write your injuries in dust, your benefits in marble."

You may have experienced words that have hurt you deeply. As our Proverb indicates, forgiveness is a form of mercy. The person who offended you may never seek forgiveness, but it is possible to forgive in your heart. Holding onto resentment only torments us. It is often better to have a short memory about these things.

The Letter to the Colossians advises us: "Make allowance for each other's faults, and forgive anyone who offends you. Remember, the Lord forgave you, so you must forgive others" (Colossians 3:13). Refusing to forgive is exhausting. Even when forgiveness is not requested, it enables us to live in peace.

Show understanding and forgiveness. Treat others as you would like to be treated. As Robert Enright said, "Forgiveness is a quiet gift that you leave on the doorstep of those who have hurt you."

Thank you for your forgiveness. Help me also to forgive those who have offended me.

MG

October 12

Whoever is slothful will not roast his game, but the diligent man will get precious wealth.

Proverbs 12:27 (ESV)

Jackie Pullinger graduated from the Royal College of Music, specializing in the oboe. However, in 1966, she boarded a ship to Hong Kong with only $10 in hand, aspiring to be a missionary. She found work at a school in the walled city of Kowloon, known as a center of darkness due to its opium production. Amidst this place of oppression, Jackie became rich—how?

Jackie encountered several gang members and leaders, and despite the danger, she helped them find purpose and a reason to live drug-free through Jesus. Later, she established a center for addicts and taught music at St. Stephen's Girls' School. By 2007, the St. Stephen's Society housed 200 people.

Today's verse highlights the contrast between a sluggard and a diligent person. The sluggard does not improve his life, not even his own well-being. Diligence, on the other hand, brings wealth—perhaps not monetary—but certainly the wealth of finding purpose in life, as Jackie did. She has never received a salary and relies on donations, but she continues to persevere.

There is no room for negligence and laziness in God's kingdom. Today, I encourage you to be diligent. Do you dream of serving God? Do you want to leave your comfort zone and serve those who are neglected, such as drug addicts, single mothers, the terminally ill, widows, and orphans? Jackie was not deterred by her studies or her lack of money from impacting many lives. You can do the same.

Oh, Lord, send me. I want to be used by You.

YF

October 13

Whoever walks with the wise becomes wise, but the companion of fools will suffer harm.

Proverbs 13:20 (ESV)

Aesop told the fable of a man who wanted to buy a donkey. To test the animal, he brought it home and placed it in the stables. Immediately, the donkey went towards the laziest animal. The next day, the man returned the donkey. The salesman was surprised by the quick decision, but the man explained, "I don't need any more time. I know this donkey will be exactly the same as the one he chose for company." In other words: "Tell me who you spend time with, and I'll tell you who you are."

There are many relationships we do not choose, such as with our parents, siblings, or cousins, but friendship is a choice. C.S. Lewis says that friendship begins when we say to another person, "What? You too? I thought I was the only one." This affinity brings us together. We tend to associate with those who are like-minded.

Who are our friends? Wise people who fear God? Fools who get into trouble? Our friendships reveal much about us. Let's choose friends who "live according to the truth" (2 John 1:4). These wise people will encourage us to seek God.

Another version of today's Proverb says, "He who walks with wise men learns to think." What do your friends teach you? What do you teach them? There is no neutral influence; we all have a positive or negative impact on others. Evaluate the effect others have on you and the effect you have on others.

Father, thank you for my friends. May I be a good influence on them. May they be a good influence on me.

KO

OCTOBER 14

A peaceful heart leads to a healthy body; jealousy is like cancer in the bones.

Proverbs 14:30 (NLT)

The Roman Empire experienced a long period known as Pax Romana, characterized by great internal stability and external security. This time allowed the empire to reach its maximum economic development and territorial expansion.

The Encyclopedia Britannica places this period of relative peace between 27 BC and 180 AD, coinciding with the New Testament era. It facilitated the development of civilization in the Mediterranean area and, along with the well-engineered Roman roads, enabled the spread of Christianity. The apostle Paul, as a Roman citizen, benefited from these privileges.

"A peaceful heart leads to a healthy body; jealousy is like cancer in the bones." Like Roman peace, inner peace contributes to outward health and well-being. Paul wrote, "And let the peace that comes from Christ rule in your hearts" (Colossians 3:15). In such hearts, there is no place for the "cancer" of jealousy and anger. In Hebrew, the word shalom represents peace and well-being, both with man and with God, as well as inner tranquility.

Most of us have experienced the absence of peace due to worry, resentment, or envy. If we have surrendered our lives to Jesus Christ, He is powerful enough to transform us, centering our feelings and thoughts on Him and freeing us from the enemies of peace.

Lord, may Your peace reign in my being!

MH

October 15

A soft answer turns away wrath, but a harsh word stirs up anger.

Proverbs 15:1 (ESV)

In less than 30 seconds, a small flame can turn into a big fire. Sixty percent of December fires are caused by accidents with strings of lights on Christmas trees. Within minutes, a room can be filled with thick black smoke. Some places have smoke detector systems, automatic water sprinklers, and fire alarms to protect occupants and property. Prevention is key to combating these incidents. A fire extinguisher should always be available and on hand.

Anger is like a devastating fire. Sometimes the spark that ignites it can be a single word. In a few minutes, anger can lead a person to make mistakes that they will surely regret later. A soft, soothing, peaceful response is like the water from those sprinklers, able to extinguish the flame, cool the heat, and dissipate the smoke. If only we had an automatic detector to sense the danger and control our words.

Paul advises us: "Let your conversation be gracious and attractive so that you will have the right response for everyone" (Colossians 4:6). Prevention lies in seeking the fullness of the Holy Spirit within us.

We can decide beforehand not to let ourselves be carried away by anger and to be like water rather than gasoline. God helps us to subdue pride, control our moods, and choose the right words for each situation.

Lord, fan the fire of Your Holy Spirit within me.

MG

October 16

Kind words are like honey—sweet to the soul and healthy for the body.
Proverbs 16:24 (NLT)

Dr. Veronica Trochez, who gives conferences on positive language, once needed artwork and prints. She went to a place to have the work done, but the person supposed to assist her was absorbed in his computer. She waited patiently for him to notice her. When he didn't even look up or ask what she needed, she became irritated and considered complaining to the manager. But according to her philosophy, if she wanted respect, kindness, and courtesy, she had to show it first.

The young man, without looking at her, held out his hand for the memory stick with her files. She took his hand and said, "Hello, it's nice to meet you. I am Veronica. What is your name?" Surprised, he replied, "Humberto." The doctor continued, "Nice to meet you, Humberto. How are you today? I can see that you are very committed and responsible with your work." From that moment on, the young man changed his attitude towards her, and when she returned the next day to pick up her order, he treated her with great respect and courtesy.

This way of acting is not new. God's Word, through Proverbs, teaches us that kind words are like honey and sweeten the lives of those who hear them. For others to change their attitude towards us, we need only speak to them with great kindness, respect, and courtesy. People will reciprocate with the same attitude.

Who hasn't experienced the joy when someone smiles at you and greets you kindly? It makes you feel good and leads you to reciprocate with the same kindness. When someone speaks to us with kind words, it sweetens our lives. Let's give it a try.

Father, help me act with respect and courtesy towards everyone today.

YF

October 17

A cheerful heart is good medicine, but a broken spirit saps a person's strength.
Proverbs 17:22 (NLT)

Endorphins are chemicals produced by the body that stimulate areas of the brain where we experience pleasure and joy. Known as happiness hormones, we can generate them through exercise, a good night's sleep, and using our imagination. But one of the easiest ways to release them is by laughing!

Today's Proverb tells us about a joyful heart. Try it right now and smile. The simple physical reflex makes us feel better, right? How much more so a good laugh! But what if you have no reason to laugh? During the day, we may find more opportunities to cry or feel fear and anxiety.

But Paul recommends the same as this Proverb: "Always be full of joy in the Lord. I say it again—rejoice!" (Philippians 4:4). Interestingly, he does not ask us to be joyful "in the circumstances" we are in, or "in our strength," but "in the Lord." What does this mean? Our joy comes from who Jesus is. Think about it: Jesus is good, kind, holy, and perfect. Moreover, He is all-powerful, all-knowing, and all-seeing. Above all, He loves you, chooses you, forgives you, cleanses you, heals you, embraces you, seeks you, saves you, and welcomes you. Doesn't this make you rejoice?

Rejoice today. Regardless of what may go wrong or the feelings that dominate you, rejoice. Take a deep breath, draw a smile on your face, and think of Jesus. Your joyful heart will be a good remedy for any ailment.

Lord Jesus, I rejoice in You.

KO

October 18

Rumors are dainty morsels that sink deep into one's heart.
Proverbs 18:8 (NLT with translator's note)

A "bocadito" is a tiny cake or pie, often filled with cream or custard in various flavors. The term can also refer to small portions of food that can be picked up with a toothpick. In some places, bocaditos or bocadillos are an art form; you can't visit Madrid without trying a squid bocadito in the Plaza Mayor. However, in this Proverb, the bocaditos represent something different.

Have you ever met up with friends for coffee? Along with our hot drinks, we might order some appetizers. But, as our Proverb suggests, perhaps the most tempting "morsels" are the rumors we hear about others. What is the problem with indulging in these seemingly delicious morsels?

The issue is that these rumors penetrate deeply into our hearts, creating problems. Gossip distorts our perception of others. Since we don't know if the rumors are true, they paint a potentially false picture. Furthermore, such comments can feed our pride, making us feel momentarily superior to the person being discussed.

What should you do if you find yourself in a conversation where these "morsels" are being served? The best course is to steer the conversation away from gossip and refuse to listen. I learned to ask myself these questions before speaking about someone who isn't present: Is it true? Is it helpful? Is it inspiring? Is it necessary? Is it kind? If the answer to any of these questions is "no," it's best to remain silent.

Father, give me the strength to avoid gossip and rumors.

KO

October 19

To acquire wisdom is to love yourself; people who cherish understanding will prosper.

Proverbs 19:8 (NLT)

Robert O'Connor holds the Guinness World Record for collecting 1,221 items related to the Ghostbusters movies. Since his fourth birthday, when the first film of the series was released, he has been acquiring collectibles—though they probably don't make him any wiser. However, today's Proverb tells us that we do well if we acquire wisdom.

When we make an effort to gain understanding, we show love for ourselves. Living wisely protects us and helps us to prosper. When we make wise decisions by obeying God's commands and living in fear of God, we love our soul.

To live with prudence, wisdom, and purpose, we need God to reveal His will to us and grant us divine wisdom. God continues to tell us what He told Joshua: "Study this Book of Instruction continually. Meditate on it day and night so you will be sure to obey everything written in it. Only then will you prosper and succeed in all you do" (Joshua 1:8).

Do you collect anything? It's enjoyable to collect stamps, mugs from different countries, miniatures, or postcards. However, there is something even better: treasuring the advice our Father has left us in His Word.

Lord, thank You because You always want the best for me.

MG

OCTOBER 20

Unfailing love and faithfulness [mercy and truth] protect the king; his throne is made secure through love [and mercy].

Proverbs 20:28 (NLT with translator's note)

When an actor passes away, their successes are often highlighted more than their failures: the number of films they made, the years they spent in the industry, the titles they earned, and the awards they won. Rarely are their acts of devotion or pious works mentioned.

Consider this: "The rest of the events in Hezekiah's reign and his acts of devotion are recorded in the Vision of the Prophet Isaiah Son of Amoz, which is included in the Book of the Kings of Judah and Israel" (2 Chronicles 32:32). If you read about Hezekiah's life, you will see that he was a good king, faithful to God from the heart. God granted many of his requests when he prayed. He also accomplished great things. If you visit Jerusalem, you can see an aqueduct he built through a mountain to bring water to the city.

How many of his people did King Hezekiah show mercy to? Surely many, and God upheld him and affirmed his throne. We can be certain that God is pleased when we show mercy. Today's Proverb confirms this.

Showing mercy is something within our reach. We show mercy when we bring food to someone who is sick. We show mercy when we care for the children of someone in need. We show mercy when we share what we have with someone who asks or is in need. Our God is pleased with such acts and will sustain us!

Father of mercies, I want to be like You.

YF

October 21

A secret gift calms anger; a bribe under the table pacifies fury.
Proverbs 21:14 (NLT)

The word "bribe" often brings to mind giving money to a public servant to expedite paperwork or accept incomplete documentation. We might also think of a traffic cop who accepts something for his "break" instead of writing a ticket, or a boss who receives gifts at Christmas as encouragement to give a promotion or stay on good terms. But bribery can also happen at home.

A couple argues, and the next day the husband brings flowers while the wife cooks an excellent meal. A mother feels guilty about working outside the home and neglecting her children, so she buys them toys to alleviate her guilt. According to today's Proverb, these secret gifts and bribes can soften the ground and placate anger. Sadly, they don't solve the underlying problem! This also applies to our spiritual lives.

We might donate a lot to feel less guilty about not reading the Bible or praying. We attend all the services but don't give up the sins of gossip and envy that consume us. And you know what? Neither God nor anyone else wants our bribes. God said, "I want you to show love, not offer sacrifices. I want you to know me more than I want burnt offerings" (Hosea 6:6).

More than flowers and dinner, we should ask for forgiveness from our partner. More than toys, we should take the little time we have with our children to do something meaningful, like playing or talking. Let us not fall into the bribery game but do things in the right order and let God work miracles. Let's go to Him with an empty heart, and He will fill it with love.

Lord, keep me from bribing others. Give me an upright heart.

KO

OCTOBER 22

Don't befriend angry people or associate with hot-tempered people, or you will learn to be like them and endanger your soul.

Proverbs 22:24-25 (NLT)

In our digital world, we make "friends" with hundreds of contacts, often without knowing them in person. Even from a distance, we can see from their comments that some are irritable and irritate others. If we reply in the same style, we "learn to be like them." In the long run, the best decision might be to unfriend or unfollow them.

A friend's husband began to get angry with her over a simple detail immediately after arriving home. She asked him, "What happened to you today?" It turned out he had an accident on the road, became annoyed with the other driver, and took it out on her. Losing our temper can lead to unnecessary harm to others.

In this passage, Solomon exhorts us to avoid friendships with angry people who lose their temper easily because we may follow their bad example. Knowing how to respond appropriately requires great self-control. Let us practice the following: "You must all be quick to listen, slow to speak, and slow to get angry. Human anger does not produce the righteousness God desires" (James 1:19-20).

Do we hang out with irritable people? Watch out! We can become like them. Worse yet, are we irritable and lose our temper easily? Let's ask God for help today.

Father, help me to practice self-control so that I do not react in anger.

MH

OCTOBER 23

Commit yourself to instruction; listen carefully to words of knowledge.

Proverbs 23:12 (NLT)

In nature, we find great examples of mothers. For instance, sea otters give birth in the water. The pup is born with its eyes open, 10 teeth, and thick fur that prevents it from sinking. The mother keeps the pup on her belly to nurse it. When she goes for food, she ties him up with seaweed so that the current does not carry him away. When he grows a little, his mother teaches him to swim, dive, and search for food. Some females have even been known to adopt an orphaned pup.

We, too, set an example with our lives, communicating a message in each of our actions and words. Mothers are full-time teachers for their children, their families, and all who observe them. Every instance of our behavior offers a lesson, both voluntarily and involuntarily.

In the letter to Titus, the apostle Paul clearly wrote that older women should be teachers of good and should instruct the young. Every mature woman is called to share her life experience with the next generations. What is the subject matter? Topics such as "how to love one's husband and children" or "how to take care of the house."

We are full-time teachers, so let's apply ourselves wholeheartedly. If you are a young woman, listen to the words of wisdom from mature women. When they teach you, they do so because God has entrusted them with this task. There are times when it falls to us to be pupils and other times when it is our turn to be teachers. Let us learn in order to teach; we are blessed by blessing the lives of others.

Help me, Lord, to keep my heart willing to learn.

MG

OCTOBER 24

Do not rejoice when your enemy falls, and let not your heart be glad when he stumbles.

Proverbs 24:17 (ESV)

"It backfired" is an expression used to say that someone's plan went wrong, and not just that it didn't work out as hoped, but that the results were negative. The Bible tells us about someone who was overjoyed at his enemy's misfortune, but it all backfired on him.

Shimei, son of Gera, a relative of Saul, considered King David his enemy. He probably thought that David had stolen the throne from his kinsman, so he was overjoyed when David was betrayed by his own son, Absalom. As David passed through Bahurim, Shimei met him, throwing stones and cursing him, even in the name of God. He reveled in David's apparent defeat. But imagine his disappointment when the Lord restored David's kingdom! Shimei had to swallow his words and went out to meet David to ask for forgiveness. When Solomon became king, he restricted Shimei, but Shimei did not adhere to the restriction and had to face the consequences.

I don't know if Solomon was thinking of Shimei when he wrote this passage, but the following verse explains why we should not rejoice in the misfortune of our enemies: "For the Lord will be displeased with you and will turn his anger away from them" (Proverbs 24:18).

How hard it is not to rejoice at the misfortunes of our enemies! Many times I have wanted to see those who wronged me face difficulties. Surely the same thing happens to you. But the Lord notices everything. He asks us to forgive.

Lord, may I not rejoice in the misfortune of others.

YF

October 25

With patience a ruler may be persuaded, and a soft tongue will break a bone.
Proverbs 25:15 (NLT)

Roman Cassiodorus said, "Mankind can live without gold, but not without salt." Salt not only enhances the flavor of food but also relaxes the proteins in meat and tenderizes it. Salt is important even in the world of fantasy; Samwise Gamgee, a hobbit in The Lord of the Rings, says you never know when you'll need salt, so it's best to have it close at hand and ready for an unexpected journey. According to the Bible, salt is also necessary for conversation.

Soft words, like a tenderizer, can break bones and soften the hardest heart. Have you ever experienced someone exploding at you in frustration, and you responded calmly? What happens? The person lowers their voice, regularizes their breathing, and converses with you more patiently.

Paul said, "Let your conversation be gracious and attractive so that you will have the right response for everyone" (Colossians 4:6). What kind of seasoning can we use? Grace, prudence, and holiness in our words act like salt.

Perhaps today you have something important to say, whether verbally or in writing. Maybe you want to discuss an essential topic. Your words may be "meat" or "vegetables," essential and nourishing elements; however, if they are not accompanied by salt, if they are not seasoned with grace, they will not be well received. Seek to say everything with love, patience, and gentleness, and like Samwise, have salt always ready and close at hand for your conversations today.

Lord, may my words today be seasoned with the salt of Your love and Your Word.

KO

October 26

Whoever digs a pit will fall into it, and a stone will come back on the one who starts it rolling.

Proverbs 26:27 (NRSVUE)

In times past, it was common to dig a pit and cover it with earth and leaves to trap animals. According to this Proverb, the hunter could fall into his own trap. Similarly, huge stones used as weapons of war could roll back onto the person who set them in motion and crush them.

In the Persian Empire under King Ahasuerus, the vizier Haman devised a plot to kill all the Jews in the kingdom. He also ordered a gallows to hang Mordecai, cousin and adoptive father of Queen Esther, who were also Jews. In the end, the king had Haman hanged on the instrument of his own creation.

This verse and many others teach that sin brings consequences. Specifically, those who desire to harm others will fall into their own "pit." The Lord reminds us that it is not our place to seek revenge: "I will take revenge; I will pay them back, says the Lord" (Romans 12:19).

Have we been wounded by hurtful words? Have we had valuables stolen? Have we been treated unfairly? Let us not hold grudges or seek revenge. Let us recognize that the eternal judge is God, and He will do justice.

Lord, I recognize that it is in Your hands, not mine, to bring justice.

MH

OCTOBER 27

As iron sharpens iron, so a friend sharpens a friend.

Proverbs 27:17 (NLT)

When I was a child, I would accompany my mother to the market. There was a large butcher shop where several workers, dressed in white coats and hats, tirelessly served the customers. They would flatten the meat by placing it on a huge log and beating it with a heavy metal tenderizer. To make a good cut, they would sharpen their large knives with a rounded, sword-like device called a steel. When two iron blades are filed together, each becomes sharper and more effective.

When we share friendship, interests, experiences, and ministry with other believers, the result is mutual edification. Together, we become better, polishing our character and talents. In my Christian life, I have had mentors who have helped me learn. Accepting recommendations requires humility and a willingness to improve. Sometimes, like two machetes rubbing together, we may make "sparks," but the result is positive.

Our best achievements in life are those we accomplish with the help of others. The wise preacher said, "Two people are better off than one, for they can help each other succeed. If one person falls, the other can reach out and help. But someone who falls alone is in real trouble" (Ecclesiastes 4:9-10, NLT). Beautiful friendships arise when we take care of reciprocity, that is, mutual help.

Do you team up to achieve your goals? Do you take a genuine interest in your spouse or your friends achieving their goals? Reach out to people who can be a good influence in your life and with whom you can synergize. Pray for the Lord's guidance; He has placed them close to you for a reason.

Enable me, Lord, to work as a team for Your glory.

MG

October 28

The rich are wise in their own eyes, but the poor who are intelligent see through them.

Proverbs 28:11 (NABRE)

Have you ever come across a person who, because of their money, thinks that everyone should cater to them and show them preference? Generally, such people, because of their influence, buy powerful positions and engage in fraudulent business. They humiliate and despise those who do not have the money they possess.

On one occasion, when he should have gone off to war, King David stayed in his palace. It was then that he met Bathsheba and sinned against the Lord. Nathan the prophet visited him and told him the story of a rich man with much livestock who took advantage of a poor man by stealing his only lamb, which he loved like family. Hearing this story, David was enraged and judged the rich man worthy of death, saying that he should pay four times the value of the little lamb. Nathan then told David that he was that wicked man, for he had taken advantage of his superiority as king to seize the wife of a poor man like Uriah.

It seems that during this time, David had become conceited and arrogant. He did not consider it necessary to go to war with his army or to respect his neighbor's wife, as God's Word commands. He thought he was very wise, but it took a poor man to see through him, for Uriah showed more faithfulness than David.

We will encounter people who think they are very wise and who may humiliate us. The best we can do in such cases is to pray for them, so that they find a poor person who will see through them and help them realize their lack of wisdom.

Lord, give me wisdom and defend me.

YF

October 29

The poor and the oppressor have this in common—the Lord gives sight to the eyes of both.

Proverbs 29:13 (NLT)

Many people visit the Louvre to see the famous Mona Lisa. Some only give it a passing glance to say they've seen it; others admire it for hours if the museum is not too crowded. Its creator, Leonardo da Vinci, wrote that the average person "looks without seeing, hears without listening, touches without feeling, eats without tasting, inhales without perceiving the fragrances, and speaks without thinking."

Our Proverb today reminds us that we all have something in common, regardless of our lifestyle: God has given us five senses. But many of us go through life without truly using them. Loving God with our soul involves having a heart full of awe that is silent before the greatness of the Creator.

The Bible says that when God looked upon His creation, "God saw that it was good" (Genesis 1:25). Do we do the same? When we see billowing storm clouds, do we tremble as we recognize our smallness and raise our hands in worship of the One who made the lightning?

When was the last time our eyes drank in a captivating landscape, when we ate slowly and enjoyed every burst of flavor, when we listened to music and savored the sound of every instrument, when we touched the skin of a loved one's hand and let ourselves be overwhelmed with love, when we inhaled and let the scent of wet earth take our breath away?

We have a great gift in our senses. Let us allow ourselves to be amazed by God today as we contemplate His creation.

Lord, I want to be still and acknowledge that You are God. All that You have done, I see it, and it is good.

KO

October 30

Never slander a worker to the employer.

Proverbs 30:10 (NLT)

When a British newspaper defamed Keira Knightley by claiming she suffered from an eating disorder, she sued them and won. The money she received was donated to charity. What is defamation? It means publicly saying or writing negative things against a person's good name, fame, and honor. Synonyms include slander, calumniate, disparage, discredit, and malign, all of which express the idea of damaging a person's reputation.

An acquaintance lost his job at a well-known institution because he was defamed. He had a very good reputation and expected to continue there for many years. There is no way to prove the false accusations, so the lawyers believe that in a few years he may be able to return. In the meantime, financially and especially emotionally, it has been a heavy blow for my friend. It will be difficult to restore his prestige.

This Proverb advises against defaming "the worker before his employer." Doing so can lead to mistrust, reprimands, and even the loss of a job. The New Testament offers similar guidance, inviting us not to accuse a brother or sister in the faith before speaking personally with them. "If another believer sins against you, go privately and point out the offense" (Matthew 18:15). Slander, in fact, is a weapon frequently used by Satan. Remember how he spoke evil of Job before God?

Despite what our main enemy tries to do, we can shield ourselves under the protection of our Advocate. "Who shall bring any charge against God's elect? It is God who justifies" (Romans 8:33 ESV). Let us be careful and avoid unjustly accusing others.

Father, thank You for covering my mistakes. Help me to stay away from defaming others.

MH

October 31

Her children rise up and call her blessed; her husband also, and he praises her: "Many women have done excellently, but you surpass them all."
                                                    Proverbs 31:28-29 (ESV)

"To you who gave me your life, your love, and your space," says the song "Señora, Señora" by Brazilian singer-songwriter Denise de Kalafe. This song, which has become an anthem, is heard in many versions on Mother's Day in Mexico. Denise sat down at the piano one day, and feeling nostalgic for her mother, began to write a song of admiration and recognition on a brown paper bag. This is the song that thousands of us make our own at least one day a year.

My mom died suddenly when she was still young. I told her "I love you," but not enough. I didn't give her enough recognition, gratitude, and praise that she deserved.

Fortunately, the children of the "virtuous woman" in Proverbs 31 did. Perhaps they learned from her example. She was so kind that she surely tried to and did honor her own mother. To praise is to express in words how good a person is and the good she does.

If you are blessed to have your mother, honor her with your best words and most heartfelt verses. Most of us children think our mom is the best of all. Make sure you tell her that enough.

Lord, I thank You for the mother You gave me.

MG

November 1

Then they will call upon me, but I will not answer; they will seek me diligently but will not find me.

Proverbs 1:28 (ESV)

Industrialized foods have expiration dates because they spoil after a certain time. Appliance warranties also expire after a certain period. Computer software stops working properly when it is not updated. We understand that few things "last forever." Today's Proverb gives us an expiration date as well. The time will come when wisdom will no longer be available.

Many enemies of the Bible argue that if God is love, He must forgive everyone. Yet they themselves call for justice and punishment for those who trample on the rights of others. God is love, but He is also just. His love and justice go hand in hand. There is a time for everything, and just as today is the time to seek wisdom, there may come a day when we cannot find it, and this is just.

In Matthew 25, Jesus tells the story of ten bridesmaids at a wedding. Five of them listened to wisdom and prepared themselves with oil for their lamps. The other five, who acted foolishly, did not have enough oil and had to go buy some when their lamps ran out. While they were away, the bridegroom arrived and locked the door. It was too late!

Today is the day to seek God. Today is the time to listen to wisdom. Today is the opportunity to prepare and be ready for when Jesus comes again. Tomorrow may be too late. One day, even if men seek her, wisdom will not answer. Let us not be foolish!

Lord, I want to be prepared. Today I want to listen to You and invite You to be part of my life.

KO

November 2

She opens her hand to the poor and reaches out her hands to the needy.

Proverbs 31:20 (ESV)

There is poverty in Mexico. Every day we see beggars stretching out their hands in the streets, or children standing at intersections asking for a handout. We have seen shacks in deplorable conditions and people shivering in the cold for lack of adequate clothing.

Maggie Gobran was head of a department at the American University in Cairo. When she saw the dire situation of the slums where people lived off garbage, she gave up her career and her comfortable life to minister to the poor and alleviate their suffering. She founded Stephen's Children, which has provided clothing, food, and education for some 33,000 children. Maggie is a Coptic Christian and was nominated for the Nobel Peace Prize in 2020.

The woman of Proverbs 31 "opens her hand to the poor and reaches out her hands to the needy." She is not only concerned about her own family; she is generous with others. The website of Maggie Gobran's organization highlights this verse: "If you pour yourself out for the hungry and satisfy the desire of the afflicted, then shall your light rise in the darkness and your gloom be as the noonday" (Isaiah 58:10 ESV). Jesus Christ himself especially served the poor, the sick, and the despised of society. God invites us to bring hope to those who suffer in this world.

How can we help the needy around us? Let us ask God for ways to "reach out" to the poor with more than just "alms."

Lord, grant that I may have a heart sensitive to those who suffer and be able to give them hope.

MH

November 3

Her ways are ways of pleasantness, and all her paths are peace.
Proverbs 3:17 (ESV)

A trend in garden design in ancient times was the labyrinth. There are still magnificent castles with beautiful gardens in front. Walking through their tangled paths is like a fantasy adventure. The single-path, or classic design, has just one path that, although twisted, always leads to the center. The multi-path mazes have more than one entrance and more than one path to choose from; these can even lead to a dead end.

Life is like these gardens. Sometimes we have no choice but to continue along a tangled path to reach the end. At other times, we have to choose between several options. This journey can be stressful since, from our earthly perspective, we don't know where the path is leading us. To walk the paths with delight and peace, we need an aerial view of the route. That heavenly view is provided by divine wisdom.

When we acknowledge God in our ways, He leads us on the right path. Let our petition be the words of the psalmist: "Teach me, O Lord, the way of Your statutes; and I will keep it to the end. Give me understanding, that I may keep Your law and observe it with my whole heart" (Psalm 119:33-34 ESV).

A peaceful and delightful life is directly related to the kind of decisions we make. Be wise and filter everything you do with the light of God's Word. When His light illuminates the path of life, the journey is smooth and you can enjoy it to the fullest.

Lord, I want to obey You with each of my decisions.

MG

November 4

For I give you good precepts; do not forsake my teaching.

Proverbs 4:2 (ESV)

What does it mean not to forsake God's law? Is that possible? Many people accept that the Bible is the Word of God but never read it or follow its teachings. Others are Christians only on weekends or when with other Christians, but their lives leave much to be desired.

Flor's father inherited the Christian religion from his parents, who were Sunday believers. For him, it was not important to follow God's Word, so in Flor's family, there were bad words, fights, hatred between relatives, and other issues. It seemed normal to her to live a Christian life without reading the Bible or obeying it. She married a boy because she got pregnant, but he did not believe in God. Her life became hell: she endured beatings, infidelities, divorce, and many fleeting and bad relationships. She developed a nervous illness, was unable to sleep, and her health collapsed. Seeing herself plunged into depression and illness, she asked for God's help and understood that she had to give her life to Christ. Her problems have not been completely resolved, but she has peace. She knows that the Lord is on her side.

How important it is not to abandon the law of the Lord! What would Flor's life have been like if her family had loved and followed the Word of the Lord? The Bible is not a book that should be left on a shelf or merely carried in a purse on Sunday. It should be a text that we love, read, and obey.

If you love the Bible, if you follow it with all your heart, if you have respect and love for those closest to you, they will follow your example, especially your children. Don't you think this beautiful Proverb is worth heeding?

Father, I do not want to forsake Your law. Help me to follow You with all my heart.

YF

NOVEMBER 5

Get wisdom; get insight; do not forget, and do not turn away from the words of my mouth.

Proverbs 4:5 (ESV)

When I was in school, I had a teacher who emphasized the importance of continuous learning. She often said, "Education doesn't stop at graduation; it's a lifelong journey." This wisdom has stayed with me, reminding me always to seek knowledge and understanding.

Today's Proverb encourages us to pursue wisdom and insight actively. These are not just abstract concepts but practical tools for navigating life's complexities. We are urged not to forget or turn away from the wisdom we receive, whether from Scripture, mentors, or personal experiences.

In my Christian walk, I've found that wisdom often comes through the guidance of others and the lessons learned from my own mistakes. It's essential to remain teachable and open to correction. As iron sharpens iron, so we can sharpen one another, growing in wisdom together.

Do you make it a priority to seek wisdom and insight in your daily life? Do you listen to the counsel of trusted friends and mentors? Remember, wisdom is more valuable than gold, and understanding more precious than silver.

Lord, help me to seek wisdom and insight daily. Keep me from turning away from Your words and guide me in the path of understanding.

MG

November 6

The righteous who walks in his integrity—blessed are his children after him!
Proverbs 20:7 (ESV)

Integrity is a rare and valuable trait in today's world. It means being honest and having strong moral principles, even when no one is watching. Walking in integrity is not just about personal righteousness but also about the legacy we leave for our children.

I remember a story about a man who always insisted on paying his taxes accurately, even when he could have easily evaded some of them. His friends mocked him, but he stood firm in his integrity. Years later, his children spoke of him with deep respect and admiration, recognizing the importance of honesty and integrity in their own lives.

This Proverb reminds us that the righteous who walk in integrity leave a blessed legacy for their children. Our actions and decisions today will impact future generations. When we live with integrity, we set a powerful example for our children to follow.

Are you walking in integrity in your daily life? Do your actions reflect honesty and strong moral principles? Remember, your integrity will bless your children and those who come after you.

Lord, help me to walk in integrity and righteousness. May my actions leave a legacy of blessing for my children and future generations.

YF

November 7

Whoever gives to the poor will not want, but he who hides his eyes will get many a curse.

Proverbs 28:27 (ESV)

Generosity is a fundamental aspect of the Christian life. It reflects God's character and His love for humanity. When we give to the poor, we are participating in God's work of justice and compassion.

I once met a woman who dedicated her life to serving the homeless. She shared how, despite her modest income, she never lacked anything because God always provided for her needs. Her generosity was a testament to God's faithfulness and provision.

Today's Proverb teaches that those who give to the poor will not want, but those who ignore the needy will receive many curses. It is a reminder that our actions have consequences, and generosity brings blessings while neglect brings repercussions.

Are you generous with what you have? Do you look for opportunities to help those in need? Remember, giving to the poor is not just an act of charity; it is a reflection of God's love and justice.

Lord, help me to be generous and compassionate. Open my eyes to the needs around me and give me the courage to act with kindness and love.

KO

November 8

The name of the Lord is a strong tower; the righteous man runs into it and is safe.

Proverbs 18:10 (ESV)

In times of trouble, where do you seek refuge? Many people turn to wealth, relationships, or their own abilities for security. However, today's Proverb reminds us that the name of the Lord is a strong tower, offering true safety and protection.

I recall a period in my life when I faced significant challenges. I was overwhelmed and uncertain about the future. During this time, I clung to this verse, finding comfort and strength in the Lord's name. It became a fortress of peace and assurance.

The righteous run to the Lord because they know He is their ultimate refuge. His name represents His character, power, and faithfulness. When we trust in Him, we find safety and security that the world cannot provide.

Do you run to the Lord in times of trouble? Do you trust in His name as your strong tower? Remember, He is always there, ready to offer protection and peace.

Lord, I run to You, my strong tower. Thank You for being my refuge and strength. Help me to trust in Your name and find safety in Your presence.

MG

November 9

A friend loves at all times, and a brother is born for adversity.
Proverbs 17:17 (ESV)

True friendship is a rare and precious gift. It means being there for someone, not just in good times but also in times of adversity. Today's Proverb highlights the unwavering love of a friend and the steadfast support of a brother.

I have a friend who has been with me through thick and thin. Whether I was celebrating a victory or facing a crisis, he was always there, offering support, encouragement, and love. His friendship has been a source of strength and comfort in my life.

This Proverb reminds us that a true friend loves at all times, and a brother is born for adversity. It challenges us to be that kind of friend and brother to others, offering unwavering support and love.

Are you a true friend to those around you? Do you stand by your friends and family in times of adversity? Remember, your presence and love can make a significant difference in someone's life.

Lord, help me to be a true friend and a loving brother. Give me the strength to support and love others, especially in times of adversity.

YF

November 10

The fear of the Lord is the beginning of wisdom, and the knowledge of the Holy One is insight.
Proverbs 9:10 (ESV)

Wisdom begins with the fear of the Lord. This fear is not about being afraid but about having reverence and awe for God's majesty and holiness. It is the foundation of true understanding and insight.

I remember reading about a scientist who, despite his vast knowledge, acknowledged that his wisdom began with a reverence for God. He understood that all his learning and discoveries were grounded in the awe of the Creator.

Today's Proverb teaches us that the fear of the Lord is the beginning of wisdom, and knowing the Holy One brings insight. It is a reminder that true wisdom and understanding come from a deep relationship with God.

Do you have a reverent fear of the Lord? Do you seek to know Him more deeply? Remember, wisdom and insight flow from a heart that honors and reveres God.

Lord, help me to fear You with reverence and awe. Grant me wisdom and insight as I seek to know You more deeply.

KO

November 11

The fruit of the righteous is a tree of life, and whoever captures souls is wise.

Proverbs 11:30 (ESV)

On Instagram, you can find the account De Meal Prepper, created by Jolanda Stokkermans. Jolanda began by sharing cooking tips and recipes, but, prompted by her children, she decided to take it to another level: her dishes are now presented with portraits of animals and pop culture characters. The food she prepares offers nutrition and art, but life? Jolanda has gained fame and recognition, but souls? Today's Proverb reminds us of the importance of winning people for Jesus.

Pluvia is a woman who has a special gift for talking to people about God's love. One day she came to visit me, but I was a few minutes late in getting home. While she was waiting, she chatted with the lady who was helping me with housework. When I arrived, we spent some time together. As she said goodbye, she mentioned simply, "Ah, the woman helping you is already saved; she made her decision with me to accept Christ."

We are all called to share the good news of salvation. At the beginning of our Christian life, it may have been easy to talk about faith with a schoolmate or childhood friend, even with the person sitting next to us on public transportation. But we must continue to do this. Today's Proverb says that the believer bears fruit and that this fruit is eternal life for the soul that we can win for Christ.

We are wise when we proclaim the good news of salvation. Let us thank our Father for the interest and love He placed in the person who showed us how to reach the feet of Christ. Let us do the same for others! Jesus is the only hope for a world in such need.

"Lord, put a soul in my heart ... may I happily do my duty to win it for You."

MG

November 12

Truthful words stand the test of time, but lies are soon exposed.

Proverbs 12:19 (NLT)

In Romania, when someone is about to lie to you, they use an expression that translates as "you sell donuts." Donuts are a favorite treat of many, but this is the expression Romanians use to warn that someone is not telling the truth.

Our Proverb reminds us of one of the most important tests to know whether something is true or not: the test of time. We can list many proposals that, in their time, were novelties but have since been forgotten because they were not true. However, a book that has withstood the test of time, criticism, and persecution still stands today, bringing us peace.

"People are like grass; their beauty is like a flower in the field. The grass withers and the flower fades. But the word of the Lord remains forever" (1 Peter 1:24-25). The Bible is unique in that, despite being written by more than 40 different authors over many years, it has one common thread: Jesus himself. He is the central theme of the Bible, and He has not gone out of fashion.

Lies are discovered sooner or later. People can often guess when we are trying to "sell them donuts," but the truth stands the test of time. Believe the truth. Stand firm in the truth. Hold fast to the truth. You will not regret it.

Your Word is truth, Lord.

KO

November 13

The godly hate lies.

Proverbs 13:5 (NLT)

When Pilate was judging Jesus, he asked what the truth was. Should he trust the word of Jesus? Pilate, sadly, was not interested in knowing what or who was the truth. Rather, he evaluated the consequences of what he believed. He thought of the rebellion that might arise from the Jews if he angered them and what his superiors would demand of him. The truth was set aside.

We do the same today. We don't care about the facts: that the fetus is already a human being; that God created men and women and did not make a mistake; that the excessive use of plastic affects the planet. Many times, what matters to us is the consequences of what we believe. If following the truth may affect our reputation, cause us to lose money, or force us to give up our sinful lifestyle, we will choose to ignore it.

Truth is a complex issue in the modern world. No one seems to care about "the truth." Instead, we look at how something affects our comfort and, accordingly, we accept it as a truth or label it as a lie. Do we hate lies? Do we tolerate them out of convenience? Those of us who belong to God have heard the truth from God and His Word. So we must answer Jesus' question, "And if I tell you the truth, why then do you not believe me?" (John 8:46).

Our commitment must be to the truth regardless of the consequences. In other words, we must believe and do what is right, even if it means ridicule, scorn, or problems.

Lord, I want to hate lies. Help me to love the truth.

KO

November 14

Those who oppress the poor insult their Maker, but helping the poor honors him.

Proverbs 14:31 (NLT)

We often bargain to reduce the price of handmade crafts, not realizing that the indigenous creator does not receive what is fair for their work. We might not pay vacations or Christmas bonuses to domestic employees. We might run a small business that barely pays minimum wage and does not offer health insurance. There are many ways to discriminate against the poor.

A couple started a children's ministry for the disadvantaged in my city. One day, they noticed a man walking slowly and wearily, with difficulty breathing. They befriended him and learned that he suffers from pulmonary fibrosis. As a result, he is unable to hold steady employment. His home lacked a good roof to protect him from the cold, and winter was approaching. The couple and other Christians pooled materials and labor to put in a sturdy floor and a roof with shingles.

This Proverb says that by oppressing the poor, we insult the Creator! And in helping the poor, we honor God. Jesus himself asserted that He came to fulfill Isaiah's prophecy, for His Father "anointed [Him] to bring Good News to the poor" (Luke 4:18). He also indicated that by showing compassion to the poor, we minister to Him: "For I was hungry, and you fed me" (Matthew 25:35).

It is not only up to us to minister to the needy with some specific help. We can go beyond that and provide opportunities to improve their way of life. We must see to it that they are treated justly and with respect for their rights.

Lord, open my eyes to ways to alleviate the suffering of the poor.

MH

November 15

The Lord is far from the wicked, but He hears the prayers of the righteous.

Proverbs 15:29 (NLT)

Have you ever been in the middle of a thunderstorm? The first time I heard the rumbling of thunder, I was six years old. It sounded like the sky was angry and was sending its lightning to vent its anger. Then, to make it worse, the power went out. Fortunately, my mom was there with her comforting hug. "We're going to say a prayer. You ask God for the light to come back and for the rain to stop." My mom always told me that God listened to all prayers. I began to pray. Just as I said "Amen" and opened my eyes, the light came back! We were so surprised that we began to laugh with delight.

Today, I am grateful that my mother instilled in me the certainty that God listens to me. Although at times it may seem that our prayer is too insignificant to change what is predestined, let us pray anyway, for He is attentive. Let us pray for those suffering from cancer, for those without work and food. Let us pray for those trapped in addiction, for the children who have to work. For refugees, politicians, victims of human trafficking, insecurity, and crime ... there is so much to pray for!

Today's Proverb is clear. The Lord hears our prayers. The New Testament confirms this: "So let us come boldly to the throne of our gracious God. There we will receive His mercy, and we will find grace to help us when we need it most" (Hebrews 4:16). What a precious invitation!

"Lord, before You are all my desires and my sighs are not hidden from You."

MG

November 16

Pride goes before destruction, and a haughty spirit before a fall.

Proverbs 16:18 (ESV)

Can you imagine breaking the nose of a famous statue? That's what the book "Breaking Stalin's Nose" is about. It follows a 10-year-old boy who, in addition to becoming disenchanted with communism, fears reprisals for the accident he has caused to the bust of the Soviet hero. Stalin wanted to be venerated and believed himself to be the savior of the Russian people until the fall came. And that is what our Proverb is about.

King Uzziah followed the example of his father Amaziah in wanting to honor the Lord. He sought the Lord with all his heart, and God allowed him to prosper. He helped him defeat the Philistines, the Arabs, and the Ammonites, and the biblical story recounts that he became so powerful that his fame spread far and wide. Sadly, there is a "but." The Bible says that when he was already strong, his heart became boastful. He thought he deserved everything. His pride grew so great that he thought he no longer needed a priest to mediate between him and God, so he entered the temple to offer incense in place of the priests. When the priest Azariah rebuked him, he was furious, and in his anger, leprosy broke out on his forehead.

The great King Uzziah was humiliated before his subjects. He could no longer be king. He had to live separated from his people and his family because he was a leper for the rest of his life. For a reason, Peter says that "God opposes the proud but gives grace to the humble" (1 Peter 5:5).

We all want to win the hearts of others. Isn't that what many politicians like Stalin crave? We like to be the "saviors" of others, but this only leads to pride. Beware! Let us recognize our place in this world and give God the place He deserves.

Father, deliver me from pride.

YF

November 17

Love prospers when a fault is forgiven, but dwelling on it separates close friends.

Proverbs 17:9 (NLT)

After her bachelorette party, a friend playfully pushed Rachelle Friedman Chapman into the pool where they'd been swimming. Sadly, Rachelle fell badly and became a quadriplegic. Can you imagine the tragedy? Obviously, the wedding was postponed, although a year later, Rachelle married her fiancé. Even more incredible is the pact Rachelle made with the four friends who were present that day by the pool. They would not name the one who had pushed her, and since 2010 they have kept their promise.

Has a friend betrayed or offended you? Have you been hurt by someone you care about? I know friends who, because of a less dramatic situation, stopped speaking to each other and can't even hear each other's name without shuddering. I don't know if Rachelle and her friends will keep their covenant forever, but in the Bible, we have powerful examples of forgiveness, mainly from God himself.

The apostle Peter echoed this Proverb in his epistle when he wrote: "Most important of all, continue to show deep love for each other, for love covers a multitude of sins" (1 Peter 4:8). Forgiveness, as Peter himself experienced, is the greatest proof of friendship. Remember how Peter denied knowing Jesus before He was killed? And yet Jesus remained his friend and gave him the mission to share the good news of His resurrection. He forgave him!

Forgiveness does not imply ignoring the wrong done or minimizing the harm. Rather, love chooses to try to unite the fraternal bonds with the other. It is certainly not easy, but it is the best way. What shall we do in this regard?

Father, help me to forgive those who offend or hurt me, just as You have forgiven me.

November 18

To find a wife is to find happiness, a favor granted by the Lord.

Proverbs 18:22 (NABRE)

There are many myths about marriage. Supposedly, girls dream of their Prince Charming .... and what about men? Maybe their Princess Pleasantness! There is also talk of finding "a soul mate." But those images of perfection soon collapse in the light of reality.

Shortly before I got married, a little niece asked me: "Why are you marrying my uncle?" I told her we loved each other and wanted to serve God together. She gave her own interpretation: "I think he doesn't want to get old and be alone." She probably wasn't entirely wrong, for he was already in his 40s.

Although this Proverb mentions "happiness" as one of the benefits of marriage, it never says that there will be a perfect couple. Of the husband, it is said: The Lord has given him a favor. We receive a blessing when we choose within God's will for us. To make a team is an advantage of the couple: "Two are better than one, because they have a good reward for their toil" (Ecclesiastes 4:9 ESV). At the same time, maintaining a strong union requires personal effort and faith in the Lord.

If you are single, trust that God will show you in due time the person with whom you can form a team. If you are married, remember that the Lord wants to use you to make your home happy.

Father, thank You for the gift of giving happiness!

MH

November 19

The false witness will not go unpunished, and whoever utters lies will not escape.

Proverbs 19:5 (NABRE)

One morning, Armando met a friend on the bus, who greeted him by saying, "Hi, Arturo, it's good to see you!" Perhaps because of his fear of correcting another or his need to look good, Armando said nothing. The joy of the person greeting him was enough for him. But six months later, Armando realized something. Every morning, between 7 and 7:30, his name was Arturo.

Situations like this are common. If we do not tell the truth immediately, we may unintentionally become wrapped up in a lie. There is no such thing as a "white" lie. When we make something appear as what it is not, even if we do not utter words, we create a deceptive situation — such as pretending we have not seen a message on our cell phone or not answering the phone at home so they think we are not there.

Sadly, "There is nothing concealed that will not be revealed, nor secret that will not be known. Therefore whatever you have said in the darkness will be heard in the light, and what you have whispered behind closed doors will be proclaimed on the housetops" (Luke 12:2-3). It is necessary to resolve with the heart to always act in truth.

Do you consider this aspect as something you can improve in your life? If you had to evaluate how often you have resorted to a lie, how would you answer: never, sometimes, or often?

God, help me to remember that I will give an account of all my words.

MG

November 20

An inheritance obtained too early in life is not a blessing in the end.

Proverbs 20:21 (NLT)

The great painter Rembrandt identified himself with the prodigal son from Jesus' parable, for, in his youth, he acted in a profligate and arrogant manner. As today's Proverb suggests, the prodigal son received his inheritance early, but it became a stumbling block. In his midlife, Rembrandt painted a powerful scene where the father receives the son and lays his hands on the son's shoulders in forgiveness. Many years later, this painting profoundly impacted Henri Nouwen, a Christian thinker and writer. Nouwen spoke of the second son in this story.

Rembrandt and Nouwen could also identify with the older son, resentful of the father's forgiveness and reluctant to forgive the younger son and give a second chance. The two sons in this story, portrayed by Rembrandt, could be you and me. But Nouwen goes a step further and tells us about the compassionate father.

The compassionate parent represents God, who will "wait for you to come to Him so He can show you His love and compassion" (Isaiah 30:18). Even though we are more like both sons, we can eventually become that compassionate parent and help others.

Let us be like the father who "stretches himself out to all who suffer, gives his shoulders to all who come to him to rest, and offers the blessing that comes from the immensity of God's love." Look for Rembrandt's painting of the prodigal son and reflect further on this story as you interact with the main characters. Are we like the younger son, the older son, or the father?

Lord, give me compassion for others.

KO

November 21

The violence of the wicked sweeps them away, because they refuse to do what is just.

Proverbs 21:7 (NLT)

The Dutch monopolized not only the cinnamon trade in the 16th century but also the trade in nutmeg. Nutmeg grew on a few islands in what is now Indonesia. The Dutch did their best to make it grow only on the islands of Banda and Ambonia: they cut down the trees in other locations. But, they did not consider the birds. The birds did not care about the laws and rules of the Dutch and spread the seeds on the surrounding islands. Despite man's efforts, nature showed generosity. Yet, thieving, plunder, and the violence of hoarding are not limited to the past.

Have you seen adults and children competing for the prizes of a piñata? Don't we always seek to win and get the biggest piece of the pie or the best raffle gift? Don't we try to destroy the competition? Win. Have. Stockpile. Monopolize. In our culture, these verbs have become synonymous with "self-improvement," yet they reveal something dark within us.

Jesus told the story of a rich man who foolishly hoarded riches but in the end lost everything. He concluded the story by saying, "A person is a fool to store up earthly wealth but not have a rich relationship with God" (Luke 12:21).

Are we foolish? Do we resemble those Dutch of the past who wanted the profits of the spice trade for themselves instead of sharing what nature so generously gives? Amassing, hoarding, and monopolizing are words that should not describe our actions and attitudes. Rather, let us be generous and "rich" in our relationship with God.

Lord, I don't want to be foolish and think that life is measured by how much I have. Deliver me from greed.

KO

November 22

Don't cheat your neighbor by moving the ancient boundary markers set up by previous generations.

Proverbs 22:28 (NLT)

You may have seen some thick concrete or stone posts in the countryside, seemingly in the middle of nowhere. I once learned that they are called mojoneras in Spanish, and that some are very old. The term is still used to refer to property boundaries that are marked on the plans of a building or plot of land.

In centuries past, there was no way to measure latitude and longitude to determine the exact location of a piece of land, let alone a system such as GPS. Therefore, these markers were extremely important to indicate the boundaries of a property. Moving them was terribly dishonest, as it was obviously done for one's own benefit.

This Proverb teaches that one should not deceive one's neighbor by changing the place of the boundary markers. Other biblical passages prohibit another type of deception: "Do not use dishonest standards when measuring length, weight, or volume" (Leviticus 19:35). Being honest has to do not only with words but also with actions; we must live with justice.

Be careful not to engage in actions that harm your fellow man. If you have a business, treat your customers and employees fairly. Give exact change to those who pay you. See to it that your actions and your life are transparent so that God may be glorified.

Lord, make not only my words but also my actions pleasing to You.

MH

November 23

Do not withhold discipline from a child; if you strike him with a rod, he will not die.

Proverbs 23:13 (ESV)

Incredibly, a child dies every five days from choking on something. This is one of the leading causes of death among children under the age of 14. For example, the marshmallows that little ones love so much can get stuck in their throat if they don't chew properly. What if a two-year-old throws a tantrum over wanting a food that you know can kill him? Would you give it to him?

Our Proverb today invites us to reflect that there are things that children want, but that we must deny them. And in doing so, trust that they will not die. In fact, we can save them from an accident! We can think of examples like what to eat, how many hours of screen time a day, or who to go out and play with. A teacher said to me one day, "Do you want your daughter to read? Let her get bored! As far as I know, no one has ever died because they had nothing to do. On the contrary, it has been the gateway to creativity."

Let us not be afraid to say "no" to our children. The Lord does the same with us, motivated by love. He knows that many times we don't get what we want because we don't ask for it. At other times, we do not receive it because when we ask, the "motives are all wrong" (James 4:3). We desire only what will give us pleasure.

Maybe your children, grandchildren, or nieces and nephews want what will bring them pleasure, from junk food that doesn't nourish them to video games or excessive screen time, but this will affect their development. Let's learn to say "no." As the Proverb concludes, discipline "may well save them from death" (Proverbs 23:14).

Lord, You desire to find us blameless. Help us to live in obedience and teach our children to have discipline.

November 24

Don't excuse yourself by saying, "Look, we didn't know." For God understands all hearts, and He sees you.

> Proverbs 24:12 (NLT)

When Andrea graduated as a nurse, she got a job in a clinic under a doctor who specialized in obstetrics. As a surgical nurse, she was there for deliveries and was amazed at the wonder of God's miracles. However, she began to notice that her boss did not invite her to certain procedures and attributed it to her lack of experience. But then her illusions were shattered.

Another colleague told her that the doctor did not invite her to perform the many abortions that made him rich. He knew that Andrea was a Christian and that she did not approve of this practice. Now she was in a dilemma. Although at first she had been unaware of what was being done in the clinic, she could not now excuse herself and say she did not know. She decided to resign.

In life, we will have many opportunities to show where our loyalty lies. We may work in places where workers are abused or dishonest things are done. Accountants and administrators may find themselves in a dilemma, even teachers who are required to lie or teach falsehoods. The Proverb adds: "He who guards your soul knows you knew" (Proverbs 24:12).

God took care of Andrea's soul by giving her the courage to look for a new job. Likewise, when we know that something wrong is taking place around us, let us not feign ignorance. Let us remember that God sees us, knows us, and cares for us. And if injustice in the world makes us feel helpless, the proverb concludes: "He will repay all people as their actions deserve."

Father, You know my soul. Weigh my heart and watch over my soul.

KO

November 25

Trustworthy messengers refresh like snow in summer.

Proverbs 25:13 (NLT)

The conquest of Mexico is a part of history that causes controversy. Many religious who set foot in our country, moved by greed and avarice, added to the violent attitude of the first conquerors. They were bad messengers of the Gospel of Jesus. However, there were others who were faithful.

Fray Bartolomé de las Casas is still remembered as a defender of indigenous rights. For example, he renounced the encomienda he had been granted to show that this type of institution was slavery in disguise. He insisted on evangelization as the only justification for Spain's presence in America and proposed reforming the laws to give more opportunities to the natives of these lands.

What kind of messengers are we? Do we go around proclaiming what the Bible says, but without being personally convinced or living what we preach? Or are we faithful messengers who don't just stand for what Jesus says, but embody His love and goodness? The Scriptures say, "How beautiful are the feet of messengers who bring good news!" (Romans 10:15).

If we have believed in Jesus, we have a message to share with others, a message of love and hope: that Jesus died to forgive our sins and offers us eternal life. Let us be faithful messengers with beautiful feet that bring life to others.

Lord, I want to be a reliable messenger. May I live what I preach.

KO

November 26

A lying tongue hates its victims, and a flattering mouth works ruin.
                                         Proverbs 26:28 (ESV)

The huapango is a type of Mexican song that translates as "on the stage," in reference to the place where it is danced. Its main characteristic is the falsetto used by the troubadour to reach the high tones and link the verses, which are often improvised. A famous huapango is that of Elpidio Ramírez, who says: "What beautiful eyes you have, under those two eyebrows!" We are referring to La Malagueña, and what woman doesn't want to hear it in a serenade?

Compliments, adulation, and sweet talk flatter us on occasion. Women are prone to believe such words and be swayed by their charm. In Mexico, traditional serenades combine romance and music to tug at the emotions of sensitive hearts. Unfortunately, the flattery is not always true.

Once again, the Bible speaks of the power of the tongue. When words are born of selfishness and hatred, they are destructive and bring ruin. Those who lie may pursue dishonest gain: Some "brag loudly about themselves, and they flatter others to get what they want" (Jude 1:16).

People can speak words of flattery that are not sincere. Let us beware of people who pay us compliments, because such sweet talk may be born of a desire to receive some favor or to lead us away from the Lord. How can we know if a love song is sincere? Let us follow the advice of our grandmothers: let their words be accompanied by their deeds.

Make me sensitive, Lord, to Your voice, and not to those voices that want to deceive me.

MH

November 27

A person who strays from home is like a bird that strays from its nest.
Proverbs 27:8 (NLT)

He lost his wealth overnight. In one day, his ten children died. To make matters worse, he was afflicted with a disease that caused him intense pain and itching, as well as the repudiation of those who saw him. We refer to Job who, in a moment of anguish, recalled his happy days and exclaimed: "Then I thought, 'I shall die in my nest, and I shall multiply my days as the sand'" (Job 29:18 ESV). Who would not want to die in his nest, in his place of comfort and consolation?

Our Proverb, however, reminds us that some of us leave the nest, perhaps driven by exile, circumstance, or personal choice. We are left at the mercy of predators.

The Book of Job gives us a clear picture of suffering and how often there is no earthly explanation for life's tragedies, only a heavenly one. Job was not suffering because he had done something particularly wrong or because he had turned away from God. His pain stemmed from a "cosmic gamble." Satan wanted to know if Job's faith was true or if he was only seeking God for convenience.

Perhaps today you feel like a bird far from its nest. Are you suffering like Job? Instead of asking why me or what for, hold on to your faith. Perhaps Satan has also made a bet: that you will turn away from God in the midst of your tears. Like Job, remember that faith is not something you hold in your hand but something that holds you in the storms. "Your nest is set in the rocks" (Numbers 24:21).

May your home be God, and may you, like Job, be able to say, "The Lord gave and the Lord has taken away; blessed be the name of the Lord!" (Job 1:21 NABRE).

Lord, life is not just, but You are just. Although I do not understand many things, I trust in You.

KO

November 28

When the righteous triumph, there is great glory, but when the wicked rise, people hide themselves.

Proverbs 28:12 (ESV)

In Mexican wrestling, there are two sides, representing good and evil. On one side, there are the "técnicos," who respect the rules and fight with honor. On the other side are the "rudos," who cheat and try to win no matter what. In a match, when the técnicos win, everyone shouts with joy, but when the rudos win, there are whistles and howls of disapproval.

In Numbers 22, God, as the star wrestler, is on the side of Israel. Balak, on the side of the Moabites—the rudos—is seeking the destruction of God's people. The referee is Balaam. So Balak, by trickery, tries to destroy Israel and buy off Balaam so he will curse them. But they do not count on the fact that God is the one who protects Israel; He brings Balaam to bless Israel instead.

For as long as sin has existed in the world, this has been the story: the wicked against the righteous. But we also have the promise that "the righteous shall inherit the land and dwell upon it forever" (Psalm 37:29 ESV). Certainly, on many occasions, it will seem that evil is winning, but the end is already assured when Jesus will be the King of kings forever.

The wicked may be winning the battle for now, but we have the omnipotent God on our side, who, in the end, will give the wicked what they earned, and we will celebrate! Which team are you on?

Lord, thank You that You are on my side. I will not fear.

YF

November 29

He guards the paths of the just and protects those who are faithful to Him.

Proverbs 2:8 (NLT)

I heard the song "Not While I'm Around" in Barbra Streisand's voice and imagined it as a tender song from a mother to her son. It was composed by Stephen Sondheim for the musical Sweeney Todd, where the orphan Toby sings it to Mrs. Lovett, who turns out to be up to no good, despite taking him in. However, the song reminds us of what we all long for.

"Nothin's gonna harm you, not while I'm around... No one's gonna hurt you, no one's gonna dare ... not while I'm around." The reality is, although we sing this to our children, deep down we know that it is not possible to take care of them all the time. However, there is someone who can promise us this and much more.

Today's Proverb says that the Lord protects us, and this promise is repeated again and again in the Bible. Listen to this promise that God made to His people Israel, but that He makes today to all who are part of His family: "I have cared for you since you were born. Yes, I carried you before you were born. I will be your God throughout your lifetime— until your hair is white with age. I made you, and I will care for you. I will carry you along and save you" (Isaiah 46:3-4).

Perhaps you have felt God's care since you were a child. Or maybe you say, "I had a terrible childhood. I've been through some very bad things. Where was God?" Our most difficult circumstances are meant to bring us back to the Father's protective arms. Our decisions often take us away from Him, and it is possible that bad things happened in our family when He was not taken into account. But that does not mean that He cannot change your past into something new and beautiful.

Lord, only You can take care of me and protect me. Thank You because You have, You are, and You will.

November 30

Rock rabbits—they aren't powerful, but they make their homes among the rocks.

Proverbs 30:26 (NLT)

Rock rabbits, or hyraxes, are mammals abundant in Africa and the Middle East. They are often confused with rabbits. Hyraxes are known to live in groups and communicate by means of various cries. The terrestrial species are diurnal and inhabit burrows and crevices in rocks. But they are not the only ones.

Men have also learned to use natural rock formations to live there. Cappadocia, in central Turkey, is characterized by a geological formation unique in the world. Due to erosion, there are many caves, natural and artificial, that have been inhabited for centuries. In fact, today you can visit the area and find many churches from the Byzantine era, with frescoes and paintings that testify to the Christian heritage of the inhabitants.

What are the advantages of living in the crags? Protection and permanence. From the time of Moses, God used the figure of a rock to speak of Himself. Yet even when He cared for His people in their wilderness wanderings and provided water for them from a rock, the people "forsook God who made him and scoffed at the Rock of his salvation" (Deuteronomy 32:15 ESV). We also read that they neglected the Rock that begot them. They forgot the God who gave them life.

On the one hand, Moses reminds the Israelites that the rock of their enemies is not like their Rock. Even the enemies realized this. What about us? On the other hand, he warns that we are all in danger of taking refuge among the wrong rocks. Let us be wise as the rock rabbits and make God our Rock.

Rock of eternity, be my faithful hiding place.

KO

DECEMBER 1

Fear of the Lord is the foundation of true knowledge, but fools despise wisdom and discipline.

Proverbs 1:7 (NLT)

The Russian scientist Ivan Pavlov conducted conditioned reflex experiments with dogs. He rang a bell to feed them, and they came to associate the bell with food. At one point, the mere sound triggered the dogs' digestive systems. Pavlov proposed that humans could also be trained to change their behavior through the stimulus-behavior relationship. Perhaps we have thought that the purpose of Proverbs is to modify our behavior. "If I do this, that happens." But that's not how it is!

We have talked a lot about the tongue. We may think, "If I don't open my mouth, I will be wise." In a way, this is true. But wisdom asks a little more of us. Wisdom teaches us that, "God has created you and your neighbor. Care for your neighbor as God cares for you." Notice the difference?

The basis of Proverbs is in the fear of the Lord. In other words, true wisdom looks at who God is and how He governs the world and acts according to those truths. The fear of God invites us to respond not to a stimulus or reward but to the very person of God. We do not do things to score points but because we want to please a supreme being, God Himself!

Pavlov's experiments work to threaten and provoke responses, but scholars have concluded that human beings are more than just animals. God agrees. Wisdom is not about outward behaviors but about changed hearts. May the glory of God be more than a reward.

Lord, I want to know more about You and respond by giving You glory.

KO

December 2

Charm is deceitful, and beauty is vain, but a woman who fears the Lord is to be praised.

Proverbs 31:30 (ESV)

First magazines, then television, and now digital media practically shout at us: You can be more beautiful! Use this makeup, this anti-wrinkle cream, these clothes, and this perfume to be attractive and popular. This product will take off the pounds that disfigure you ... and so on and so forth.

I fell for it once. I had a product applied to one side of my face and was amazed to see how much smoother it looked than the other side. Yes, it cost too much, but I liked the idea of looking younger. Then, long before it was supposed to run out, the product dried up. I wasn't interested in wasting my money like that again.

"Charm is deceptive, and beauty does not last; but a woman who fears the Lord will be greatly praised," says the New Living Translation. The beauty of women has been the subject of thousands of poems and songs. Just as women often dream of their powerful Prince Charming, men long to conquer the beautiful, curvaceous princess. The Bible warns us that this is deceptive because it is superficial and vain; it ends with time. Scripture offers us many examples of women who stand out, not so much for their physical attributes but for their faith in God. They will be the ones who are praised.

We take care of our appearance, and there is nothing wrong with that. We beautify ourselves to feel good and to please others, but if we do not take care of our relationship with God, we do not "beautify" our spirit and our inner beauty. With the presence of Christ, "though our bodies are dying, our spirits are being renewed every day" (2 Corinthians 4:16).

Father, I want the beauty of Christ to be reflected in me.

MH

December 3

Long life is in her right hand; in her left hand are riches and honor.
Proverbs 3:16 (ESV)

If I could make three wishes to the genie with the marvelous lamp, my first urge would be to ask for a chocolate cake, to be thin, and to have Max Lucado's complete book collection. However, the list in today's Proverb offers something more interesting: long life, riches, and honor. Do all wise people get these three things?

A look at the Bible and the history of the Church will tell you no. Some died young, like the martyr Stephen or the missionary David Brainerd. Not all had riches, dying in poverty. Others, like the prophet Jeremiah, were despised by their contemporaries. So, what does our Proverb refer to?

As we have learned, if you are prudent, you will avoid life-threatening accidents. If you are thrifty and a good steward, you will not lack resources. If you watch your words, you will be honored. But remember that Proverbs are pieces of a puzzle. Proverbs are not amulets to carry in your purse. That is a big mistake made by many people who follow Christianity and sooner or later become disillusioned.

God is not a genie in a marvelous lamp. His purpose is not to fulfill our whims or give us a formula for success. He seeks to be our Father, our Friend, our God. Therefore, the journey of faith does not imply a path without obstacles, but a pilgrimage to know Him more. I congratulate you for having come this far in reading this devotional. What new things have you learned from the Lord Almighty? That is the real treasure! To be able to say every day that we know a little more about Him and that we love Him a little more than yesterday.

You know that I love You, Lord.

MG

December 4

Do not swerve to the right or to the left; turn your foot away from evil.
Proverbs 4:27 (ESV)

John Bunyan, a 17th-century English preacher, wrote a book called "The Pilgrim's Progress," in which he tells the story of a man called Christian on his way to the Celestial City. The book is a beautiful story about the Christian life and, after the Bible, is one of the most translated texts of all time.

In one of their adventures, Christian and his friend Evangelist have to walk along the narrow and straight road, which has many stones, as well as hills and dips. Tired and weary, they see a meadow with a path that runs alongside the narrow one. It is full of flowers and green grass, so they decide to walk along it. Further on, they meet Vain-Confidence, another walker who assures them that the second path does not lead to the Heavenly Gate. As night falls, Vain-Confidence falls into a well, and it begins to rain torrentially. They realize that this is not the right path and decide to turn back. When they take a detour, Giant Despair, who owns those lands, makes them his prisoners in Doubting Castle.

This story exemplifies what our Proverb says: "Turn neither to the right nor to the left." How often we have to decide to do good! Sometimes we think it's better to tell a little white lie or borrow something we plan to give back. We move onto the other road thinking that what we are doing is not such a big deal. As a Christian, we must depend on the promises that the King of the Celestial City has made to us and trust in Him to endure the hard road ahead.

Lord, teach me to make the right decisions.

YF

December 5

Her paths ramble, you know not where, lest you see before you the road to life.

Proverbs 5:6 (NABRE)

What do Ludwig van Beethoven, Claude Debussy, and George Gershwin have in common? Or Bono, Jimi Hendrix, and Keith Moon? They are all considered musical virtuosos. However, in the Bible, the word "virtuoso" is broader. In fact, there is a whole poem in the last chapter of the Book of Proverbs dedicated to the virtuous woman. But, when we look at our lives, we can only come to one conclusion: we are not exemplary.

Our paths are rather like those described in this Proverb: unstable. Perhaps we are not interested in the path of life. Maybe we are staggering along a crooked path and we don't even realize it! Rather than resembling the virtuous woman of Proverbs 31, we resemble the women described in other Proverbs.

Solomon wrote: "God created people to be virtuous, but they have each turned to follow their own downward path" (Ecclesiastes 7:29). Isn't it amazing? God made us to be capable and noble in character. We have made bad decisions, preferring to do what we like rather than what God commands, or seeking the approval of others rather than God's. What is our hope?

Jesus came to straighten the crooked. He came to give us peace with God. If we want to be virtuous women who return to God's original plan, there is only one way: come to Jesus and let Him transform our character. Let us choose today an upward path and let God be part of our life.

Lord, I no longer want to walk on unstable paths, but to be the virtuous woman You created.

KO

December 6

What are worthless and wicked people like? They are constant liars.

Proverbs 6:12 (NLT)

The term "little white lie," also called "pious lies," is well known. These are supposedly less harmful and more acceptable than other falsehoods. They are told to protect a person or not to offend. This does not excuse the perpetrator, but "black" lies definitely have a selfish motivation, such as to gain a benefit or to avoid blame.

A woman visited our church shortly after an earthquake in the area. With great sadness, she told us that she came from a village, her house had collapsed, and she had lost everything. After the meeting, several people spoke with her personally and gave her a donation. Later we learned that the stories she told varied from person to person. We had fallen into a trap!

"A worthless person, a wicked man, goes about with crooked speech," says the English Standard Version. Other translations refer to the liar as "villain," "scoundrel," "vagabond," and "depraved." In this case, his lies are not an occasional fault, but a constant habit, the proof of a corrupt character.

In Revelation, we read a terrible sentence. Along with murderers and other sinners, the lot of "idol worshipers, and deceivers of every sort" is in "the burning pool of fire and sulfur" (Revelation 21:8). Whatever our culture and friends may say, lying is serious.

"But I only tell little lies," we tend to say. Unfortunately, when we start with one lie, it becomes a habit, and we may keep going with bigger ones. We do harm not only to other people but to our own selves, as we become accustomed to this sin. If this has happened to us, let us be brave enough to confess it before God.

God, You know my heart and my tongue. Cleanse me from the sin of lying.

MH

December 7

So she seduced him with her pretty speech.

Proverbs 7:21 (NLT)

On one occasion, a client of the famous painter Rembrandt refused to pay, saying that the portrait the artist had made was too ugly. Rembrandt had a "realistic" style. In other words, he painted what he saw. Sadly, many of us do not like to see things as they are.

In today's Proverb, a young man was walking down the street when a woman came up to him and said she was looking for him. Her husband had gone on a trip, so she was inviting him to come into her house and be her lover. She cajoled him with her wiles, promising a bed with beautiful linens and the finest of wines. This young man was not looking at a realistic painting, but one that concealed the truth. The woman forgot to mention to him the dangers of adultery and unprotected sex.

Going back to Rembrandt: When the buyer returned to visit the artist, who was demanding payment, he saw a gold coin on the floor and decided to pick it up. What do you think happened? It wasn't real! Rembrandt had painted it! In the same way, when we become accustomed to the lies of a world that only pretends in order to keep us from seeing the reality of sin, we will be taken up by disillusion. That which is truly worthwhile will be an illusion. And what is that? It could be the true love of a couple.

When you see a realistic picture that does not please you, remember that it is better to see what is true and not to live in deception. The Bible paints a realistic picture when it describes the hearts of men as "deceitful" and "wicked" (Jeremiah 17:9), but it also reminds us that God can give us a "new heart" (Ezekiel 36:26). What do you see around you today?

Give me, O God, a new heart, a tender and receptive heart.

KO

December 8

O simple ones, learn prudence.

Proverbs 8:5 (ESV)

A young man had sent his resume to a well-known company. When he went to the job interview, from the moment he walked in, the interviewer was looking at him keenly, making him uncomfortable. After a while, the person asked the young man if it was true what he had put on the resume and if he could verify all his experience.

"Experience?" the young man asked a bit confused. "But I just finished my degree!" The interviewer showed the young man the resume he had sent in. In disbelief, the youth burst out laughing. The interviewer, puzzled, looked at him in annoyance until the young man explained that somehow, he had sent his father's resume and not his own. For this young man, accepting that he had made a mistake and that he did not have the necessary experience for the job was a sign of courage and humility.

Our verse calls us "simple," inexperienced in the way of knowing God. We need the humility necessary to accept that we do not know, not even a little bit, the infinite God before whom we stand. We need the courage and humility to recognize that we are unwise, that everything goes wrong for us because of our inexperience.

If you have ever felt that you already know the Bible, if you have felt that you don't need to pray, if you no longer want to attend services because you think you already know it all, then you better stop and remember: Before the Lord, we are inexperienced. Go to Him and learn!

Lord, I don't know everything, but thank You for teaching me.

YF

DECEMBER 9

If you are wise, you are wise for yourself; if you scoff, you alone will bear it.

Proverbs 9:12 (ESV)

Modern phones and social networks are designed to be addictive. They cause certain of our behaviors to be reinforced by stimuli or rewards. For example, when you post something on Facebook, you receive the stimulus of a like. The more likes, the better you feel, so you become addicted to receiving attention.

There comes a time when the quality of a photo doesn't matter anymore, only how many people follow you on Instagram or how many people react to what you post. Sadly, this becomes a game of acceptance. We place our value and our identity in that virtual recognition we've been caught up in. But the reality is that neither phones nor social media are going away.

What can we do then? Be wise. Wisdom is a personal decision. We can decide not to fall into the game of social media likes, and find acceptance in Jesus. At the end of the day, Paul recommends to us: "And whatever you do or say, do it as a representative of the Lord Jesus" (Colossians 3:17).

The only "like" that counts is the one Jesus gives to what we do, say, or post on social media. And what does He look at? The heart. It's not about what we post but why. If we only seek acceptance, recognition, and adulation, we will not find satisfaction. If we seek to share something useful, encourage others in their walk with God, or be thankful for what God has given us, our motivation is not in the reward of a "like," but in helping others and being faithful representatives of the Lord Jesus.

Lord, I want to hear from Your lips: "Good and faithful servant." This is the most important "like" in the universe.

KO

December 10

The hope of the righteous brings joy, but the expectation of the wicked will perish.

Proverbs 10:28 (ESV)

Author Jim Rohn said, "There are two ways to face the future. One way is with apprehension; the other is with anticipation." If our gaze into the future is based on what we see, the future is not very promising, although one version of this Proverb uses the word "prospects" in the sense that something gives an indication of success or satisfaction (NIV). Violence, crime, human trafficking, divorce, and other sad situations are on the rise.

In the midst of the 2020 pandemic, the future was especially unpredictable. On the one hand, there were those who said the virus would never go away and painted a very dark picture. On the other hand, those with positive expectations planned to "make the most of every day," knowing more than ever how fragile this life is.

"The hopes of the righteous bring joy," for they are based on faith in what God can do. "Faith is the assurance of things hoped for, the conviction of things not seen" (Hebrews 11:1 ESV). It is trusting that God is in control. In contrast, "the expectations of the wicked will perish." They arise from selfishness, pride, or fear.

The New Year is approaching. What are your expectations? If they are based on what God wants to do in your life, in your family, and in your community, they will undoubtedly bring great happiness.

Oh, Lord, I long for a future filled with growth and opportunities to live!

MH

December 11

One gives freely, yet grows all the richer; another withholds what he should give, and only suffers want.

Proverbs 11:24 (ESV)

The largest transnational chocolate companies obtain cacao through exploitation and child labor. Many of these children do not see their parents for years, subsisting precariously. There are adults whose livelihood is to "get" these children for work. They earn more than is fair, but they also live in misery. The miserliness produces more scarcity. He who is generous and unselfish generates abundance.

Rick Warren, author of the best-selling "The Purpose Driven Life," made it a point at an early age to commit to tithing, and God miraculously provided for his needs. Then he decided to give more than the tithe. Over time, he has managed to live very well on 10% of his earnings, giving the remaining 90% to God.

In the Bible, we have an incredible example: Jesus was in the temple one day and observed the rich people depositing their offerings. Then a poor widow passed by and dropped two coins into the box. Jesus remarked, "I tell you the truth, this poor widow has given more than all the rest ... she, poor as she is, has given everything she has" (Luke 21:3-4).

Meditate on these three examples: Are you like the cocoa traders who exploit others or withhold what belongs to others? Do you give like Rick Warren and offer God more than 10 percent? Are you like the poor widow who has given all she has? Your handling of your money speaks volumes about what is in your heart.

Lord, examine me and tell me how to live.

MG

December 12

Worry weighs a person down; an encouraging word cheers a person up.

Proverbs 12:25 (NLT)

Many Christmas songs revolve around the young girl from Israel who suddenly found herself pregnant, probably rejected by her family, and afraid. An angel had told her that the Holy Spirit would come upon her and she would have a baby. But how? Why her? Would she have felt fear, worry, and anxiety? I suppose so. Fortunately, she received a word of encouragement.

In her moment of greatest fear, she went to the only person who could help her. She visited her cousin Elizabeth who, by the way, was also pregnant and had conceived in her old age. She, too, was experiencing a miracle and said to her when she saw her, "You are blessed because you believed that the Lord would do what He said" (Luke 1:45). What a beautiful gift she received from her cousin!

Whether we have sad news or joyful news, we need companions along the way, people who offer encouragement. Our burdens can be lightened or shared when someone wise and trusted acknowledges them. Do we have wise friends?

And where can we find them? Ask God to open your eyes and show you wise, obedient women who fear the Lord. When worries overwhelm you, turn to a good friend who will encourage you with the Word of the Lord. I imagine how sweet those weeks were for Mary in the company of Elizabeth. Together they prayed, sang, and dreamed of their babies. May God grant you the blessing of an encouraging friend today!

Give me, O God, words of encouragement today.

KO

December 13

Good people leave an inheritance to their grandchildren, but the sinner's wealth passes to the godly.

Proverbs 13:22 (NLT)

Did you know that we receive 50% of our DNA from our paternal grandparents? But that 50% is not homogeneous. We may have 19% from grandma and the rest from grandpa. I knew a grandmother who left something for each grandchild in her will - what a touching gesture! Yet, today's Proverb may not be talking about genetic or monetary inheritance. Think about this: What do grandparents have that parents don't have?

If I had to describe what there was at my grandparents' house that there wasn't at my home, besides books, pictures, and food, it would be time. At my grandparents' house, time seemed to stand still and move more slowly than at my parents' house. Of course, this is only an impression, since the same twenty-four hours governed both places. However, in my mind I felt that my grandmothers were not in a hurry as they cooked, and perhaps that is why there was more abundance and a long time to visit after the meal.

The apostle Paul knew young Timothy's grandmother well, and was so impressed by her faith that he said of her, "I remember your genuine faith, for you share the faith that first filled your grandmother Lois and your mother, Eunice. And I know that same faith continues strong in you" (2 Timothy 1:5, NTV). What a beautiful inheritance from Lois! A sincere, firm faith that she surely sowed with hours of listening and talking.

If you are a grandmother, use the gift that God has given you: time. Invite your grandchildren home and, besides spoiling them with a good meal, listen to them. They want to talk, be heard, and have a captive audience. You can offer them that, along with prayers and advice.

Father, I want to leave my grandchildren a spiritual inheritance.

KO

December 14

Godliness makes a nation great, but sin is a disgrace to any people.
Proverbs 14:34 (NLT)

The fall of the great Roman Empire was due to various factors, but the author Edward Gibbon attributed it mainly to internal causes in his book "History of the Decline and Fall of the Roman Empire." Among them, "the victorious legions ... acquired the vices of strangers and mercenaries."

Another author, the Spaniard César Vidal, has made an analysis of the countries that historically were based on biblical principles, comparing them to others. Values, laws, education, and art, among other aspects, were different. We could say that justice and morality prevailed among the former - and we continue to see marked differences today.

Righteousness aggrandizes a nation and makes its citizens prosper so that the nation gains the admiration of other countries. When the opposite prevails, "sin is a disgrace to any people." Inequality, corruption, and lack of respect for human rights are some of the characteristics of countries without justice. In the time of King Solomon, many marveled at the wisdom God granted him to administer justice. But then the sin of consorting with pagan women and building altars for their gods caused the division of the kingdom.

What prevails in my country: righteousness or sin? How can I contribute to the growth of my nation? How can I pray for my country?

Lord Almighty, I pray for my nation. May You raise up leaders who love righteousness.

MH

December 15

The Lord detests the way of the wicked, but He loves those who pursue godliness.

Proverbs 15:9 (NLT)

The Greek myth tells of the nymph Echo falling madly in love with Narcissus, but he despised her heart. Desolate and offended, she locked herself in a solitary place and stopped eating and taking care of herself. She was consumed little by little, and the pain made her disintegrate into the air. Only her voice remained, repeating everyone's last words. Today we call her "echo." This is one of the most emblematic stories of unrequited love. Have you experienced it?

Giving our heart to someone who rejects it leaves us wounded. We are hurt by relatives who should have loved us and did not, or friends who did not visit us in times of illness. The truth is that human love can fail.

Only God's love is perfect. Only our Father has loved us with a love whose flame is never extinguished. He says to us, "I have loved you, my people, with an everlasting love. With unfailing love I have drawn you to myself" (Jeremiah 31:3). Our heart thirsts for this kind of love. Do not seek to satisfy it with human love because no person can surpass it. Your heart has an emptiness in the form of God, and only He can fill it.

But I invite you to think about something else. Is it not God who suffers most from unrequited love? He is constantly searching for the human being, through nature and His Word. He gave His own Son! Remember that He loved us first. How do we reciprocate His love? Let us listen today to the echo of His voice.

"I want to hear the divine echo of Your voice ... let it tell my ears that You will not leave me" (from the Himnario de Suprema Alabanza).

MG

December 16

Those who listen to instruction will prosper; those who trust the Lord will be joyful.

Proverbs 16:20 (NLT)

The quest for prosperity has made human beings capable of many things, from working without rest to offering human sacrifices. Perhaps we think that the life of faith is similar.

We have the idea that if we pray more, read more, or go to more services, God will reward us. Certainly, if we heed biblical principles we will find blessings, but they may not be as we imagine them. Obeying God, for example, does not imply financial security or being free of illnesses.

Ruth belonged to the people of Moab who had been cursed. She married a young Israelite who died young. When her mother-in-law decided to return to her homeland, Ruth decided to give up a secure future, close to her own family and people, and took the risk of following her mother-in-law. How did Ruth decide to heed the Word of that God who was strange to her? Have you ever wondered what conversations these two women would have about the God of Israel? Ruth was willing to do anything. And the God of the Hebrews, the God of the Bible, saw the decision of her heart and wanted to make her happy by giving her a husband and a son.

However, let us not view her story as one of prosperity in human terms. Although Ruth married and had a son, she probably continued to shed tears for many reasons. Her joy stemmed from something deeper and more lasting: being accepted into God's family. Like Ruth, we did not have the remotest chance of being part of the divine people, but now, we belong to that people, and what remains for us is to worship the wonderful God who accepted us through His Son Jesus Christ.

Thank you, Lord, for making me part of Your people.

YF

December 17

Starting a quarrel is like opening a floodgate, so stop before a dispute breaks out.

Proverbs 17:14 (NLT)

Much of the territory of the Netherlands is below sea level. The Dutch have built large dams or dikes that are under constant maintenance to hold back the water. On the night of January 31, 1953, the sea overcame the dikes, which collapsed at 200 different points. The flood affected 133 towns and villages. More than 1,500 people died, and many livestock and other animals were lost. The sea was a cruel enemy.

This Proverb reminds us of the great tragedy that can arise from starting a fight—as bad as a flood! Many times we speak without thinking twice, sure that nothing will happen, and when we realize it, we are already fighting with someone else! It's like an overflowing river impossible to control.

What causes quarrels among human beings? James tells us that they "come from the evil desires at war" within us (James 4:1 NLT). Envy makes us strive to take from others what they have and what we desire; pride makes us want to look better than others; anger makes us explode and speak out of turn. And what is the antidote? "Yet you don't have what you want because you don't ask God for it" (James 4:2 NLT). Let us ask God for the wisdom to stop and not fight.

Let us follow the advice of this Proverb: Let us stop before we start a fight or an argument! Let us curb our lips, otherwise, we must abide by the consequences.

Father, don't let me be the one to start an argument. Help me to stop before I open my mouth.

KO

December 18

There are "friends" who destroy each other, but a real friend sticks closer than a brother.

Proverbs 18:24 (NLT)

The expression "toxic people" is popular today to refer to those who always talk about their problems, criticize others, and cover up the truth. They are jealous and manipulative; they resist change. Above all, they are called toxic because their poison can influence us for the worse.

Undoubtedly, any of us can mention at least one person who appeared to be a friend, but who in reality destroyed us. The one who wanted to take advantage of you; the one who only sought you out to tell you gossip; the ones who wanted to convince your daughter that "one more drink" would not affect her, and then uploaded photos of her on social networks with comments that embarrassed her ...

The most famous example of "a true friend ... more loyal than a brother" is that of Jonathan with David, especially since the father of the former wanted to kill the latter! Jonathan saved his friend's life in one of King Saul's outbursts of anger. In contrast, the apostle Paul mentions "danger from men who claim to be believers but are not" (2 Corinthians 11:26, NIV). It is a sad reality that some people appear to be friends and Christians when they are not, and their influence can be dangerous.

Do we destroy or are we loyal? I hope the latter. May we know how to avoid close contact with toxic people. Above all, let us be "true friends."

Lord, with Your help I want to be a loyal friend.

MH

DECEMBER 19

The fear of the Lord leads to life, and he who has it will sleep well, and will not be touched by sin.

Proverbs 19:23 (NLT)

When I was a dental student, we used to make medical trips to rural villages as part of our internships. On one occasion we went to a village where we were offered the facilities of a school to spend the night. At bedtime, my colleagues turned on a portable tape recorder to listen to music. To my surprise, it was a method that many of them used, as they were uncomfortable with silence, remorse, memories, and terror.

Bedtime is the close of the day. Our thoughts tend to make an evaluation of our actions, and the conscience that God has placed in us summons us. The enemy of our souls and king of darkness begins his activity in the middle of the night. Spiritual struggles between principalities and powers are waged in the dives and streets where immorality and delinquency have their dominion.

Believers are not perfect, but we have the fear of God. We are privileged because we can sleep with the peace of a baby. We know that "the angel of the Lord is a guard; he surrounds and defends all who fear him" (Psalm 34:7). When we cannot sleep, perhaps it is time to get right with God, or to practice our trust in His care.

We have no need to be afraid. Our Father covers us under His wings, and just as the chicks sleep warm and safe under their mother's wings, we can rest in a deep sleep full of peace.

I will lie down and sleep in peace. O Lord, You alone keep me safe.

MG

December 20

The king's fury is like a lion's roar; to rouse his anger is to risk your life.
                                             Proverbs 20:2 (NLT)

When the Pevensie siblings heard about Aslan in C.S. Lewis' kingdom of Narnia, they were afraid. Could they trust a lion? But they were assured, "'Course he isn't safe. But he's good." As our Proverb says, the roar of a lion makes us tremble. Lions are dangerous. If we encounter one, we risk our lives. We humans also respect the Creator, the omnipotent God. The Israelites who saw His manifestation on Mount Sinai were so afraid that they asked Moses to intercede for them. They would die if they tried to approach this powerful and unknown God!

But as C.S. Lewis wrote, God is dangerous, yes, but also good. In the Psalms we find over and over again that the psalmists sing, repeat, and whisper to themselves that God is good. What an extraordinary quality! While we can respect the roar of the Lord, who is the Almighty, we can also rest in the fact that He loves us and that His essence is goodness.

What should we do before the Lion of Judah? The same thing one of the characters in the Chronicles of Narnia did. He discovered he could look "into the piercing eyes of the Great Lion." Why? Because in doing so he forgot his worries and felt totally at peace. Let us go to God. He is good.

Thank you, Lord, for You are good.

KO

DECEMBER 21

The Righteous One knows what is going on in the homes of the wicked; He will bring disaster on them.

Proverbs 21:12 (NLT)

Have you ever been curious about what life is like for the most terrible criminals behind closed doors? Was Hitler a happy man? Did Stalin sleep peacefully? What is the family relationship like for the many men and women who are immoral and do wrong? What's sadder is to discover that, behind many people's appearance of uprightness, inside their homes they are tyrants, abusers, and bullies. Many are even involved in pornography, human trafficking, and violence. However, this Proverb reminds us that God knows all about them.

Immanuel Kant, an agnostic, thought that people should live as if there were a God. Why did he come to that conclusion? Because seeing that many bad people did not receive their punishment here on earth - or at least not visibly - there should be justice in eternity.

Have you ever thought of it this way? Don't we often feel frustrated because the wicked don't seem to receive punishment? Yet we trust in a just God. He sees all things and will not treat the guilty as innocent. On the other hand, perhaps this Proverb should also be a warning for us. How do we behave at home? What would others think if they saw how we treat our spouse, our children, our parents, or our siblings?

When others think of us, may they be able to tell their neighbors: "Jesus went back to Capernaum (put the name of your city here) and the news spread quickly that He was back home" (Mark 2:1 NLT), and may that "home" be yours and mine.

Lord, You look upon the house of the wicked and the upright. Come into my house and cleanse what needs to be cleansed. Let it be a place where You feel comfortable and You are always welcome.

KO

December 22

Do you see any truly competent workers? They will serve kings rather than working for ordinary people.
Proverbs 22:29 (NLT)

We have seen in the news several cases of important people who "bought" their academic degrees or cheated to get them. Surely there were those who realized that, no matter how much some document stated it, those fake professionals lacked the real skills of their profession.

A great linguist and biblical translator was a genius and creator of a linguistic theory. Someone once lamented that he was wasting his talents in missionary work. His response: "God deserves the best we can give Him!"

Today's Proverb stresses that someone "truly competent" will one day "serve kings." Another version describes someone "attentive." King Solomon sought out the best craftsmen for the construction of the temple, which included gold work and textile design. David himself became king after being faithful and skillful as a shepherd and valiant defender of sheep.

God does not want the leftovers of our life, but the best. He has given us abilities that we can develop in order to be faithful. With His guidance, we will serve the King of kings.

Lord, You deserve the best. Make me skillful and faithful in serving You.

MH

December 23

My child, if your heart is wise, my own heart will rejoice!

Proverbs 23:15 (NLT)

Just as the most precious jewels are kept in a jewelry box, Mary, the mother of Jesus, kept many things in her heart. Surely she treasured moments, memories, and experiences with her Son, one who was always obedient, wise, and kind, and who filled her life with joy and happiness. The Bible says that Jesus lived subject to His earthly parents. He was also obedient to His heavenly Father, obedient unto death, even death on a cross.

When Jesus was baptized, God was so pleased with His Son that His voice could be heard from the heavens expressing His predilection. Just as earthly children gladden the hearts of their parents, Jesus made our Father God feel very proud.

When we do wrong, God, in the person of the Holy Spirit who dwells in us, is grieved. Those of us who are parents can understand what the heart feels when a child acts foolishly. It hurts us deeply because we know that the consequences will cause him to suffer. The great love of a parent desires the best for his child.

Consider that not to grieve the Spirit is a commandment. Would you like to draw a smile on God's face? Serve Him with faithfulness, holiness, and love and one day you will hear: "Well done, good and faithful servant; you have been faithful over a little, I will make you ruler over much; enter into the joy of your Lord."

Lord, how I would love to see You smile! One day my eyes will be able to contemplate You.

MG

December 24

The wise are mightier than the strong, and those with knowledge grow stronger and stronger.

Proverbs 24:5 (NLT)

In many countries around the world, children often write a letter to Santa Claus or the Three Wise Men to ask for their end-of-the-year toys. Some lists make us chuckle, like when they ask for something to eat, such as a ham sandwich. Other times they wish for more serious things, such as for their parents not to argue or for a war to stop.

When the Lord says to Solomon: "Ask for whatever you want me to give you," the young king had the opportunity to ask for anything he wanted. He could have asked for dominion over the whole world, or never to die, or perhaps to travel to outer space. But he asks for wisdom! And the Lord gives him wisdom and adds other things to it: wealth, peace, dominion, and influence. Remember that the Bible says he was one of the greatest kings of Israel and, at that time, of the whole world.

We can reflect on how much power Solomon had just from seeking divine wisdom. As today's Proverb says, Solomon grew stronger and stronger. Fearing the Lord not only gives us wisdom, but also power and strength.

We can be like Solomon: with great power, with great strength, and thus we can influence others and command respect. All we have to do is ask for wisdom, just as Solomon did. Then wisdom "is shown to be right by the lives of those who follow it" (Luke 7:35 NLT).

Lord, give me more wisdom.

YF

December 25

Like cold water to a thirsty soul, so is good news from a far country.
Proverbs 25:25 (ESV)

Christianity came to the American continent by means of the Spanish Conquest. From Mexico to Argentina, the Catholic Church was established as the one in charge of evangelizing the indigenous peoples, but corruption and internal jealousies made it become in many countries a political and social influence rather than a spiritual one. Then, in 1818, a man named James Thomson arrived in Buenos Aires.

Thomson, better known as Diego Thomson, was a Scottish Baptist pastor who, moved by God, traveled to Argentina commissioned by the British and Foreign Bible Society to establish an educational system. As he helped bring about literacy, he distributed Bibles in various countries. In 1827, he arrived in independent Mexico with 300 Bibles and 1,000 New Testaments. His friend, the priest José María Luis Mora, encouraged the people to read the Bible and study it.

For a society thirsty for good news, Thomson's arrival was like fresh water. In his time, Paul also considered himself a man of good news, and when he wrote to the Corinthians, he reminded them of something with which Diego Thomson would surely agree: "It's not important who does the planting, or who does the watering. What's important is that God makes the seed grow" (1 Corinthians 3:7 NLT).

Let us give away Bibles and New Testaments when we have the opportunity. There is nothing better than spreading the Word of God. We can also sow it in our social networks by posting verses and words of encouragement.

Lord, how can I bring the good news to others today? Show me a way today.

KO

December 26

As a door swings back and forth on its hinges, so the lazy person turns over in bed.

Proverbs 26:14 (NLT)

This Proverb is actually comical. We know that snuggling into bed doesn't give the majority of us any trouble. Just like that, "the door swings back and forth on its hinges." It is all too easy to be lazy, but in the long run, it bears no fruit.

One characteristic of the modern era is seeking to make life easier. For example, household appliances save us time and work. GPS helps us not to get lost, although now we fail to learn how to get places. Alarms and digital calendars remind us of commitments, but if the battery dies, we may miss an important meeting.

In one of Jesus' parables, a master entrusts his goods to his three servants. He gives a certain number of coins to each of them. Two of them invest what they receive and double its value. The other chooses the less difficult path and buries his bag of silver. Of course, it does not multiply and, in fact, the master takes from him the little he had entrusted to him (Matthew 25:14-30). The message is that we shouldn't be irresponsible with what God provides us, whether it is little or much.

We may have turned over and over in bed this year, but today we have the promise of a new opportunity. Just because God's grace is free doesn't mean we shouldn't value it. The Lord also gives us time, resources, and gifts. Let us discard spiritual laziness and seek to make the most of what He has given us.

Father, today I want to use my time and talents to honor You.

MH

December 27

Anger is cruel, and wrath is like a flood, but jealousy is even more dangerous.

Proverbs 27:4 (NLT)

One of my favorite childhood characters was the tiny flying fairy Tinker Bell, Peter Pan's inseparable companion. One of her characteristics is that she is constantly jealous of Peter's attention and anyone can provoke her jealousy, particularly Wendy. When that happens, the beautiful fairy uses her magic powers to turn the other into a stone or a mouse. Yes, arousing jealousy in a woman can be dangerous.

In real life, jealousy is something serious. It makes us suffer, it makes us insecure, and it makes us cry. Uncontrolled jealousy has led to physical aggression, suicide, and even homicide. We were designed with the capacity to experience different sensations, and jealousy is an emotional response that arises when a person perceives a threat. The good news is that we can control ourselves.

Let us learn from Sarah. She focused her mind and energy on doing good and did not worry about anything else. "Sarah obeyed her husband, Abraham, and called him her master. You are her daughters when you do what is right without fear of what your husbands might do" (1 Peter 3:6 NLT). Instead of throwing around darts of complaint, anger, and insecurity, let us develop a pleasing personality and occupy ourselves with being better every day.

Let us not fear any threat. Give your jealousy to God and He will fight your battles. When He gives you something, no one can take it away from you. Don't get worried, get busy!

God, deliver me from jealousy and give me Your peace.

MG

December 28

People who conceal their sins will not prosper, but if they confess and turn from them, they will receive mercy.

Proverbs 28:13 (NLT)

Mexico's Penal Code stipulates that a person who commits a crime and denies having committed it is punished with the maximum penalty once the crime is exposed. However, if a person voluntarily confesses to the crime, the sentence is reduced to less than half of the sentence. Many do not like this. They think that there is no justice for the victim when someone commits a crime with premeditation, malice, and profit, and then voluntarily turns himself in to avoid the most serious punishment. What do you think?

King Manasseh is described in the Bible as worse than all the kings before him. In addition to worshipping foreign gods, he built altars to those gods in the temple of the Lord. He also sacrificed his own children in fire; he practiced sorcery, divination, and witchcraft. He filled Jerusalem with innocent blood and caused Judah to do more wickedness than all the other nations. For that reason, God decreed to destroy Jerusalem through the Chaldeans.

Because of his wickedness, the Assyrians took Manasseh prisoner and brought him to Babylon. Once there, he prayed to the Lord, greatly humiliated. The Lord heard his prayer and restored his kingdom. Then Manasseh finally realized that the Lord is the only God. The Lord wants us to come to Him in repentance, acknowledging our sin. He already died on the cross for those sins. Justice has already been done. All we have to do is come to Him in humility and confess our wickedness, even if it is the size of Manasseh's.

Thank you, Lord, for forgiving my sins.

YF

DECEMBER 29

For wisdom will enter your heart, and knowledge will fill you with joy.

Proverbs 2:10 (NLT)

In the famous Lion King movie, Simba, sad because he blames himself for his father's death, encounters Rafiki, who tells him that his father is alive and that he will show him. Rafiki takes him to a river and asks him to look down. Simba is disappointed. It is only his reflection. But Rafiki tells him, "Look deeper ... he lives in you." Then follows a song that repeats, "He lives in you, he lives in me, he watches over everything we see ... in your reflection he lives in you." Sadly, this song is not entirely true.

Although we are the image of our parents, they do not live in us. Our ancestors do not observe everything we do, nor do they change our destiny. The Lion King's ideas come from pantheism, which conceives of the universe and nature as the theological concept of what many religions consider "god." However, pantheism, which says that everything is god, does not solve man's deepest problems.

In today's Proverb we are told that wisdom enters the heart to gladden and enlighten us. But the New Testament confirms that Jesus is the wisdom of God. Read His words: "All who love me will do what I say. My Father will love them, and we will come and make our home with each of them" (John 14:23 NLT). The Lion King, in a way, was right about one thing: someone can live in us and we can be a reflection of His person. That someone is God Himself.

The heart is empty as long as it is not filled by God. Many times we try to find a guest: money, fame, love for human beings who fail us. But only Christ can fill us with joy.

"Come into my heart, O Christ, for in it there is room for You."

KO

December 30

Lizards—they are easy to catch, but they are found even in kings' palaces.
Proverbs 30:28 (NLT)

Not just anyone can get into presidential palaces, residences, and offices. There is a list of protocols to be followed. Usually a special invitation is needed, and probably requires that the person has some major accomplishment. But today we will see a small creature who does not expect to be invited.

I dread when I find a mouse or a rat in the house, and if I see something running by with a tail I am ready to be scared — until I see that it is a lizard. If one of these little critters shows up, we don't kill it; we grab it and take it back to its natural environment. In fact, it is beneficial and eats the insects in the yard.

This verse is part of several that show how small things can show wisdom. In the same way, God can use simple people without fancy titles. I am reminded of the little Jewish maid who advised her master, the commander Naaman, to consult the "prophet in Samaria" to heal his leprosy (2 Kings 5). He heeded her and was healed! God used her mightily, for Naaman also came to believe in the one almighty God.

You and I, no doubt, feel that we lack privilege and social importance. Maybe we have higher education, maybe not. Most likely our families are not royalty. But the Lord can use us where we do not imagine. In fact, we influence our children, friends, youth, or students who could have an impact on the nation or beyond. Above all, we can bring others closer to the eternal King!

My God, no matter how insignificant I feel, I trust that You can use me!

MH

December 31

She is clothed with strength and dignity, and she laughs without fear of the future.

Proverbs 31:25 (NLT)

Have you seen the Back to the Future trilogy? Emmet "Doc" Brown and Marty McFly are transported to the past or the future trying to "fix" things. They do so aboard a DeLorean automobile, equipped with a "flux capacitor" that allows them to travel back in time. From their first trip, they realize that their intervention alters people's destinies.

In a sense, the logic of the movie is correct. What we live today is the result of our decisions of yesterday, and what we want to be tomorrow depends on what we do today. There are things we can influence, but others are only in God's hands.

The book of the prophet Daniel says: "He changes times and seasons, He removes kings and sets up kings; He gives wisdom to the wise and knowledge to those who have understanding" (Daniel 2:21 ESV). God is in control. The Proverbs 31 woman knew this. She had no fear of the future and laughed in the face of it. The joy of the Lord was her strength, so she focused on her present and acted wisely. She knew that He cares for His children and wants the best for them.

Have you ever felt distressed about the future? It is natural to be afraid of sickness, loneliness, privation, and death. We can focus on making the best decisions in the present and find strength in the Lord. Billy Graham said, "I've read the last page of the Bible. It's all going to turn out all right."

Today is the last day of the year. Smile at the future, recalling the promise in Isaiah 41:10: "Fear not for I am with you" (ESV).

Thank you, God, for being with me this year. As You have helped me in the past, I know You will help me in the future.

MG